ELITE ATTACK FORCES

ALLIED SPECIAL FORCES

Simon Dunstan
and
Ian Westwell

CHARTWELL
BOOKS, INC.

This edition published by 2007 by

CHARTWELL BOOKS, INC.
A Division of
BOOK SALES, INC.
114 Northfield Avenue
Edison, New Jersey 08837

ISBN 10: 0-7858-2326-3
ISBN 13: 978-0-7858-2326-1

© 2007 Compendium Publishing Ltd, 43 Frith
Street, London, W1D 4SA
Previously published in the Spearhead series

Cataloging-in-Publication data is available from
the Library of Congress

Printed in China through Printworks Int. Ltd

Acknowledgements
Thanks to Mark Franklin for the maps; Mike
Chappell for the colour artwork; William Y.
Carman; Chris Ellis; Will Fowler; Chris Hanaford;
Mike Kenworthy; Charles Messenger; No. 4
Commando WWII Re-enactment Group; Osprey
Publishing Ltd.; Ian Palmer and Paul Watson. The
re-enactment photography in "Commndos" is by
Simon Dunstan. The colour photography in "US
Rangers" is by Tim Hawkins. Pointe du Hoc photos
were supplied by George Forty. All other photos in
"US Ragers" are from National Archives, US Signal
Corps, Fort Benning and US Army. The following
abbreviations are used in the photo credits: IWM –
Imperial War Museum; CEC – Chris Ellis
Collection; WFC — Will Fowler Collection; CMC —
Charles Messenger Collection.

Previous page: Landing craft were an essential tool
for Britain's Commandos, particularly smaller types
such as this LCA (Landing Craft Assault). With a crew
of one officer and three ratings, the LCA was 35 feet
long and 9 feet in beam with a draught of 3 feet. It
was capable of carrying a total of 35 Commandos. *CEC*

Right: The 'Steel Hand From the Sea' and the sight
that filled a German sentry with terror. The Commando
raiders tied down hundreds of thousands of German
troops along the coastline of occupied Europe. *IWM*

CONTENTS

COMMANDOS
Churchill's 'Hand of Steel'
Simon Dunstan

ORIGINS & HISTORY

As an island nation, Great Britain has relied primarily on the Royal Navy for the defence of the realm. The British have traditionally been wary of a standing army, fearing such an institution as a means of repression by autocratic monarchs. With the reformation of the monarchy in 1660, control of the army was vested in Parliament. Forces to defend Crown and country were raised by parliamentary decree, often to fight specific campaigns, usually on the Continent against the expanding power of despotic France. On 28 October 1664, during the Second Anglo-Dutch War, a new formation was specifically raised for service as 'Land Souldjers' with the 'Navy Royall and Admiralty' under the designation of 'The Duke of York and Albany's Maritime Regiment of Foot', better known as the 'Admiral's Regiment'. Thus were born the forebears of the Royal Marines and a 300-year tradition of amphibious warfare that continues to today.

These 'Sea-Soldiers' were first referred to as Marines in 1672 after the Battle of Sole Bay. Thereafter, the Marines fought in virtually every sea battle and won immortal fame in the capture of Gibraltar in 1704 and its subsequent defence. Their prowess in amphibious warfare grew throughout the 18th century, being well displayed during the Seven Years War including in a diversionary raid during Wolfe's capture of Quebec. This expertise continued to be demonstrated through the Napoleonic Wars, when the Royal Marines numbered some 30,000 men, and into the 19th century, epitomised by the Corps' motto of *Per Mare, Per Terram* – 'By Sea, By Land'. In 1855, to take account of their expanding role on land and sea, the Royal Marines were divided into the Royal Marine Artillery or 'Blue Marines' and the Royal Marine Light Infantry or 'Red Marines'. Essentially, the Blue Marines became gunners within the Royal Navy while the Red Marines conducted amphibious assaults and raids. During the Great War, the latter were formed into a Royal Navy Brigade and fought with distinction on the Western Front and during the disastrous landings at Gallipoli in 1915.

The appalling carnage of the Western Front consumed much of the resources of the Corps, both as Marine infantry within the Royal Naval Division and as gunners of the Royal Marine Artillery, while their comrades at sea served in the gun turrets of the Royal

Below: The Mersey River ferry boats *Daffodil* and *Iris* push the modified cruiser HMS *Vindictive* alongside the mole to allow the Royal Marines of No. 4 Battalion to land and attack the extensive German defensive positions of Zeebrugge on St George's Day 1918.

Zeebrugge

Le Waterloo de la Marine

(Publié par le Zeebrugge Museum)

Navy's warships. Yet the concept of amphibious warfare was not forgotten and as the war dragged on into its fifth year, the Royal Navy devised an ambitious plan to counter the growing menace of the German U-boats that were gradually strangling the British maritime supply lines in the North Atlantic. With merchant ships being lost in record numbers, Britain was close to starvation. Under the inspired leadership of Vice-Admiral Roger Keyes, the 4th Battalion Royal Marines landed on the heavily defended mole of Zeebrugge harbour on St George's Day, 23 April, 1918. Suffering ghastly casualties as they suppressed the German defences, the Royal Marines' assault allowed three blockships to be sunk across the mouth of the canal which gave the German U-boats access to the North Sea. The Zeebrugge raid was hailed as a major success and did much to raise morale among a dispirited population at home. Furthermore, it was the prototype for the great Commando raids of World War II.

In the austerity of post-war Britain, the Treasury attempted to abolish the Royal Marines in 1922. From a wartime high of 55,000, the Corps was reduced to just 9,500 men. Its prime roles remained as manning gun turret crews at sea and preparing for amphibious operations against an enemy coastline, but little development of landing craft was undertaken during the 1920s or 1930s. Indeed, the First Sea Lord declared in 1938 that he did not expect that combined amphibious operations would be mounted in the next war. At the outbreak of war in September 1939 the Royal Marines numbered just 13,472 men and reserves. The Corps quickly expanded, with new sections such as the Royal Marine Fortress Unit and the Royal Marine Siege Regiment being formed, but the principal role of amphibious warfare had been woefully neglected, a failure that was to be cruelly exposed in the Norwegian campaign of April 1940.

Above: The Zeebrugge raid of 23 April 1918 was hailed as a great success and did much to restore civilian morale during the difficult days of early 1918 when the Germans mounted a massive offensive against the British on the Western Front. For many years, there was a magnificent memorial and museum in Zeebrugge commemorating the raid that the Belgians called the 'Waterloo of the Sea' but the Germans destroyed them in World War II.

READY FOR WAR

Although rearmament had begun as early as 1936, the British Army was fearfully ill equipped to face the might of Nazi Germany and so it proved when the Phoney War was shattered with the German invasions of Denmark and Norway on 9 April 1940. This prompted the War Office to raise a new form of unit known as Independent Companies to conduct unconventional warfare against an enemy coastline. As their name suggested, they were to operate independently from the ships on which they served or in concert should the need arise. The first ten independent companies comprising some 3,000 volunteers were formed on 20 April 1940, drawn principally from the divisions of the Territorial Army.

THE INDEPENDENT COMPANIES

No. 1 Independent Company was formed from the 52nd (Lowland) Division; No. 2 was raised in Northern Ireland from the 53rd (Welsh) Division; No. 3 at Ponteland from the 54th (East Anglian) Division; No. 4 at Sizewell in Suffolk from the 55th (West Lancashire) Division; No. 5 at Lydd from the 56th (London) Division; No. 6 at Carnoustie from the 9th (Scottish) Division; No. 7 at Hawick from the 15th (Scottish) Division; No. 8 at Mundford in Norfolk from the 18th (Eastern) Division; No. 9 at Ross-on-Wye in Herefordshire from the 36th (Welsh) Division and No. 10 from the 66th (Lancashire and Border) Division. An 11th Independent Company was later formed with 115 men drawn from Nos. 6 and 8 Independent Companies.

With little time for formal training, the first five companies were despatched to Norway as 'Scissors Force' under the command of Colonel Colin Gubbins with the task of denying the ports of Bodö, Mo and Mosjöen to the Germans. After some indecisive fighting, all five Independent Companies returned to Britain by 10 June. Meanwhile, the other five Independent Companies were undergoing training in the Glasgow area or guarding coastal towns when Hitler unleashed his long awaited Blitzkrieg in the West with the invasion of the Low Countries and France on 10 May.

Three days earlier, Admiral of the Fleet Sir Roger Keyes, the commander of the Zeebrugge raid in 1918 and a Tory Member of Parliament, entered the Houses of Parliament in full naval uniform and gave a devastating critique of the Norwegian campaign. The Prime Minister, Neville Chamberlain, was forced to resign while MPs sang *Rule Britannia* and others chanted 'Go! Go!' Winston Churchill replaced Chamberlain. A new sense of purpose soon permeated the government and clear direction was now given to the military, despite the reverses being suffered in the battle for France. By the end of May, the British Expeditionary Force had been driven back to the French port of Dunkirk. Between 27 May and 4 June, the Royal Navy retrieved 338,226 officers and men,

Above: The use of live ammunition during field training exercises was standard for the Commandos, with many exercises conducted at night. *IWM – H19376*

including 139,097 Frenchmen, from the evacuation beaches where the last of the army's heavy weapons and equipment lay abandoned. Britain now stood alone against Nazi Germany whose conquests stretched from Northern Norway to the Pyrenees and eastwards to the borders of the Soviet Union. The awful prospect of invasion loomed large.

On that momentous day of 4 June, Winston Churchill addressed the House of Commons on the 'Miracle of Dunkirk' but he went on to say that wars were not won by evacuations. To this end, he had written to the Chiefs of Staff on the day before to demand:

> 'If it is so easy for the German to invade us… why should it be impossible for us to do anything of the same kind to him… The completely defensive habit of mind, which has ruined the French, must not be allowed to ruin all our initiatives. It is of the highest consequence to keep the largest numbers of German forces all along the coasts of the countries he has conquered, and we should immediately set to work to organise raiding forces on these coasts where the populations are friendly. Such forces might be composed by self-contained, thoroughly equipped units of say 1,000 up to not less than 10,000 when combined.'

Subsequently, the Prime Minister elaborated:

> 'Enterprises must be prepared with specially trained troops of the hunter class, who can develop a reign of terror first of all on the "butcher and bolt" policy. I look to the Chiefs of Staff to propose me measures for a vigorous enterprising and ceaseless offensive against the whole German occupied coastline, leaving a trail of German corpses behind.'

The Chiefs of Staff considered the Prime Minister's ideas at a meeting on 6 June and they drew up plans for the organisation of 'striking companies' of approximately 5,000 men as well as a covert force for intelligence gathering and sabotage across occupied Europe.

The latter emerged as the Special Operations Executive (SOE) on 22 July 1940 following Churchill's demand that it 'co-ordinate all action by way of subversion and sabotage against the enemy overseas.' In one of his many trenchant phrases, Churchill gave the new unit, which he dubbed the 'Ministry of Ungentlemanly Warfare', a simple directive: 'Set Europe ablaze'. The Chief of the Imperial General Staff, Sir John Dill, passed the proposal for the 'striking companies' to his Military Assistant, Lt-Col Dudley Clarke, Royal Artillery. Of South African birth, Clarke cast his mind back to his childhood and the stirring tales of the Boer Kommandos that had paralysed thousands of British Empire troops in the final months of the South African War of 1899–1902. As lightly armed riflemen riding fast, tough ponies, the Kommandos had taught the British Army a profound lesson in the value and economy of irregular warfare that it would never forget. Having also fought during the Arab Rebellion in Palestine during the 1930s, Clarke proposed a similar band of guerrillas to conduct 'tip-and-run raids of not more than 48 hours from bases in England against the Continent of Europe.' He further proposed that the 'striking companies' be called Commandos, a name that Churchill fully appreciated as he himself had been in South Africa while covering the war as a newspaper reporter and had been captured by the Boers before escaping.

Churchill immediately gave permission for the formation of the Commandos with the urgent proviso: 'Your Commando scheme is approved… get going at once. Try to get a raid across the Channel mounted at the earliest possible moment.' On the afternoon of 6 June 1940, four years to the day before the invasion of German-occupied Europe, Section MO 9 of the War Office was created under Maj-Gen R. Dewing, Director of

Below: At the outset, the Commandos had little equipment, as indicated by this wooden mock up of an assault landing craft. *IWM – OPS15*

Military Operations and Plans. He immediately issued a memorandum summarising the concept of the Commandos:

> 'The object of forming a Commando is to collect together a number of individuals trained to fight independently as an irregular and not as a formed military unit. For this reason a Commando will have no unit equipment and need not necessarily have a fixed establishment… The procedure proposed for raising and maintaining Commandos is as follows. One or two officers in each Command will be selected as Commando Leaders. They will each be instructed to select from their own Commands a number of Troop Leaders to serve under them. The Troop Leaders will in turn select the officers and men to form their own Troop. While no strengths have yet been decided upon I have in mind Commandos of strength like 10 troops of roughly 50 men each. Each troop will have a commander and one or possibly two other officers… The Commando organisation is really intended to provide no more than a pool of specialised soldiers from which irregular units of any size and type can be very quickly created to undertake any particular task.'

And quickly created they were. On 12 June, Lt-Gen Sir Alan Bourne, Adjutant-General of the Corps of Royal Marines, was appointed as Commander Offensive Operations in charge of raids against Belgium, France, Holland and Norway. Plans were immediately drawn up for the first Commando raid, despite the almost total lack of suitable boats or weapons. Twelve days later, motor launches landed the 115 men of No. 11 Independent Company, together with Colonel Dudley Clarke as an observer, on the coast of France near the port of Boulogne. With them were half of all the Tommy guns in the British Army's inventory, a total of just 40 – reputedly a gift from the mayor of New York of weapons confiscated from the city's gangsters. Unfamiliar with the weapon, an officer tried to engage a patrol of German cyclists in the Commando's first encounter with the enemy but the magazine of the Tommy gun promptly fell off and in the exchange of fire that followed Colonel Clarke was shot through the ear. Ironically, the man who conceived the Commandos was the first to be wounded in action with the enemy. With dawn approaching, the Commandos re-embarked 'grimy, dishevelled and triumphant' and returned to Dover where 'they were cheered by every ship in the harbour'. An official communiqué stated:

> 'In co-operation with the RAF, naval and military raiders carried out a reconnaissance of the enemy coast. Landings were effected, contact made with German troops and casualties inflicted before our troops withdrew without loss.'

The Times thundered: 'BRITISH RAIDERS LAND ON ENEMY COAST! SUCCESSFUL RECONNAISSANCE'. Despite the banner headlines, Operation Collar had not achieved a great deal and a second raid conducted on 14 July fared little better. Codenamed Operation Ambassador, 139 men of No. 11 Independent Company and the newly formed No. 3 Commando were intended to destroy German aircraft on an airfield situated on the island of Guernsey. Churchill was incensed that the Germans had captured the Channel Islands – the only part of the British Isles to be occupied during the war – and he personally ordered the raid, demanding: 'Plans should be studied to land secretly by night on the Islands and kill or capture the invaders. This is exactly one of the exploits for which the Commandos would be suited.' Due to navigational problems and poor weather, only 40 men of No. 3 Commando under the command of Major John Durnford-Slater

Above: Commandos practise abseiling down the front of the Achnacarry Commando Basic Training Centre in Scotland. *CMC*

were able to land and little damage was inflicted on the enemy. With 'no trail of corpses' to be had, Churchill was not best pleased: 'It would be most unwise to disturb the coasts of these countries by the kind of silly fiascos which were perpetrated at Boulogne and Guernsey – the idea of working up all these coasts against us by pin-prick raids and fulsome communiqués is one to be strictly avoided.' The Churchillian pen promptly issued a new string of directives that emerged just three days later.

On 17 July the redoubtable Admiral Roger Keyes was appointed as head of Combined Operations to oversee all raiding operations in conjunction with the Royal Navy and Royal Air Force; this was the first tri-service organisation to be created. This was subsequently reflected in its formation badge of a naval anchor, RAF eagle and a Tommy gun – the weapon that became the hallmark of the Commandos. Keyes' task was formidable. With the threat of invasion growing by the day, the War Office was disinclined to divert scarce resources and manpower to the fledgling organisation. Only the day before, Hitler had promulgated his 'Directive 16' for the conquest of Britain under the codename of Operation Sealion. Nevertheless, following a circular despatched on 20 June to each of the Home Commands requesting 'volunteers for special service of an undefined hazardous nature', many soldiers across the length and breadth of the country had come forward as only too willing to join such an elite fighting unit in the nation's hour of need.

The initial plan was to raise eleven Commando units, each with ten troops of 50 men. No. 1 Commando was to be created from personnel of the Independent Companies but for the time being they remained in being as a counter-invasion force. No. 2 Commando was intended as a dedicated parachute unit but at this stage there were neither the equipment nor aircraft for such a scheme. No. 3 and No. 4 Commandos were to come from Southern Command; No. 5 and No. 6 Commandos from Western Command; No. 7 and No. 8 Commandos from Eastern Command but No. 8 Commando was actually raised from London District and the Household Division; No. 9 and No. 11 Commando from Scottish Command and No. 10 Commando from Northern Command. In the chaotic summer months of 1940 as the Royal Air Force struggled with the marauding Luftwaffe in the skies above Britain, intentions could not always be realised and War Office opposition remained

---

SPECIAL SERVICE BRIGADE
Formed 11 November 1940 – superseded March 1941
Commander: Brigadier J.C. Haydon

1st Special Service Battalion, based in Devon
A Special Service Company, formed from Nos. 1, 2, 3 & 4 Independent Companies
B Special Service Company, formed from Nos. 5, 8 & 9 Independent Companies
(later to become Nos. 1 & 2 Commandos)

2nd Special Service Battalion, based in Scotland
A Special Service Company, formed from Nos. 6 & 7 Independent Companies and No. 9 Commando
B Special Service Company, formed from No. 11 Commando
(later to become Nos. 9 & 11 Commandos)

3rd Special Service Battalion, based in Scotland
A Special Service Company, formed from No. 4 Commando
B Special Service Company, formed from No. 7 Commando
(later Nos. 4 & 7 Commandos)

4th Special Service Battalion, based in Scotland
A Special Service Company, formed from No. 3 Commando
B Special Service Company formed from No. 8 Commando
(later Nos. 3 & 8 Commandos)

5th Special Service Battalion, based in Scotland
A Special Service Company, formed from No. 5 Commando
B Special Service Company, formed from No. 6 Commando
(later Nos. 5 & 6 Commandos)

No. 2 Commando became 11 Special Air Service Battalion, subsequently the 1st Parachute Battalion and then the Parachute Regiment.

No. 10 Commando disbanded December 1940, later to be resurrected as No. 10 Inter-Allied Commando.

No. 12 Commando remained outside the Special Service Brigade for special duties in Ireland.

obdurate. In Northern Command, there were insufficient volunteers for No. 10 Commando to be formed and in August 1940 an under-strength No. 12 Commando was raised from units stationed in Northern Ireland. On 25 August, Churchill wrote:

'I hear that the whole position of the Commandos is being questioned. They have been told "no more recruiting" and their future is in the melting pot… There will certainly be many opportunities for minor operations, all of which will depend on surprise landings of lightly equipped, nimble forces accustomed to work like packs of hounds instead of being moved about in the ponderous manner which is appropriate to the regular formations… For every reason therefore we must develop the storm troop or Commando idea. I have asked for 5,000 parachutists, and we must also have 10,000 of these small "bands of brothers" who will be capable of lightning action.'

In the late summer of 1940 the military situation facing Britain was critical. With Commando units dotted around the country undergoing training, the War Office transferred the operational control of all such troops from Combined Operations Command to Home Forces. By the autumn, with the threat of invasion receding, they reverted to Combined Operations but the War Office imposed yet another reorganisation that dispensed with the title of Commandos as it was deemed inappropriate. Henceforth they were to be referred to as 'Special Service Troops'. If the term Commando was considered inappropriate, it begs the question how the War Office believed that a formation with the same initials as Hitler's sinister SS was more seemly. On Remembrance Day 1940, the Special Service Brigade was formed with five Special Service battalions each with two Special Service companies.

The change of designation to Special Service was widely unpopular with the troops and some officers refused to recognise the new title at all. Maj John Durnford-Slater of No. 3 Commando directed his adjutant, Capt Charlie Head: 'Never let the term "Special Service Battalion" appear on our Orders.' Nevertheless, the priority was training and the procurement of modern weapons. At the outset, each Commando was responsible for the training of its troops, although many did attend the Irregular Warfare School in Scotland which was established in May 1940. Unit training therefore inevitably reflected the attitudes and vagaries of the individual commanding officers and their subordinates which led to marked differences in the operating procedures of the various units – see the box 'The Commando Catechism' (overleaf) for one version. In February 1942, however, the Commando Depot, later the Commando Basic Training Centre, was established at Achnacarry Castle, near Fort William, in the Highlands of Scotland to implement standard methods of training. The depot was commanded by the formidable Lt-Col. Charles Vaughan. Formerly a drill sergeant in the Coldstream Guards, Vaughan then joined the Buffs before serving as 2i/c of No. 4 Commando. His requirements were strict and his demands legendary. Every officer, NCO and man alike went through the same course. The first intake arrived at Achnacarry on 17 March 1942. Donald Gilchrist, a lieutenant with No. 4 Commando at Dieppe, recalled Vaughan with admiration and respect:

> 'He came through the First World War... and remembered that many men had been sent to the Western Front without sufficient training. Many had no idea of the conditions of war, especially in the winter months... Training was never stopped because of the weather or on Sunday. He said, "Hitler didn't stop the war because it was Sunday".'

Besides the basic skills of an infantryman, a fully fledged Commando was expected to have a high level of self-motivation and self-reliance to enable him to undertake a range of tasks within his unit, such as the ability to map read and use a compass should the officer or NCO be incapacitated. A high proficiency in weapons' handling was essential, using anything from the Lee-Enfield to the 3-inch mortar and from the Tommy gun to the Boys anti-tank rifle. In addition, a Commando had to have particular skills in seamanship to operate in all sorts of

Below: Commando training was rigorous and arduous with much time devoted to physical fitness, as shown by these recruits on a windswept Scottish beach. Failure to meet the high standards of the Commandos led to the shame of being RTU'd or Returned To Unit. *IWM – OPS27*

boats and landing craft. The ability to swim was desirable, no more so than when disembarking from a landing craft in full equipment order, but it was not mandatory.

Accordingly, the physical training for an aspiring Commando was strenuous in the extreme and those that could not make the grade were unceremoniously 'RTU'd' or 'Returned To Unit' – the ultimate ignominy. The work started from the first moment a recruit arrived at Spean Bridge railway station, when he was immediately required to march the ten miles to Achnacarry Castle with all his kit. On arrival, he was shown the 'graves' of other recruits who had failed. Each headstone was inscribed with a dire warning: 'This man did not clean his rifle'; 'This man stood on the skyline'; 'This man looked over cover and not around it'. A typical day began at 0630 hours with a training run and PT before breakfast at

THE COMMANDO CATECHISM
by Lt-Col Charles Newman, CO No. 2 Commando, 1940

1. The object of Special Service is to have available a fully trained body of first class soldiers, ready for active offensive operations against an enemy in any part of the world.
2. Irregular warfare demands the highest standards of initiative, mental alertness and physical fitness, together with the maximum skill at arms. No Commando can feel confident of success unless all ranks are capable of thinking for themselves; of thinking quickly and of acting independently, and with sound tactical sense, when faced by circumstances which may be entirely different to those which were anticipated.
3. Mentally. The offensive spirit must be the outlook of all ranks of a Commando at all times.
4. Physically. The highest state of physical fitness must at all times be maintained. All ranks are trained to cover at great speed any type of ground for distances of five to seven miles in fighting order.
5. Cliff and mountain climbing and really difficult slopes climbed quickly form a part of Commando training.
6. A high degree of skill in all branches of unarmed combat will be attained.
7. Seamanship and Boatwork. All ranks must be skilled in all forms of boatwork and landing craft whether by day or by night, as a result of which training the sea comes to be regarded as a natural working ground for a Commando.
8. Night sense and night confidence are essential. All ranks will be highly trained in the use of the compass.
9. Map reading and route memorising form an important part of Commando training.
10. All ranks of a Commando will be trained in semaphore, Morse and the use of W/T.
11. All ranks will have elementary knowledge of demolitions and sabotage. All ranks will be confident in the handling of all types of high explosive, Bangalore torpedoes, and be able to set up all types of booby traps.
12. A high standard of training will be maintained in all forms of street fighting, occupation of towns, putting towns into a state of defence and the overcoming of all types of obstacles – wire, rivers, high walls, etc.
13. All ranks in a Commando should be able to drive motorcycles, cars, lorries, tracked vehicles, trains and motorboats.
14. A high degree of efficiency in all forms of fieldcraft will be attained. Any man in a Commando must be able to forage for himself, cook and live under a bivouac for a considerable period.
15. All ranks are trained in first aid and will be capable of dealing with the dressing of gunshot wounds and the carrying of the wounded.
16. These are a few among the many standards of training that must be attained during service in a Commando. At all times a high standard of discipline is essential, and the constant desire by all ranks to be fitter and better trained than anyone else.
17. The normal mode of living is that the Special Service soldier will live in a billet found by himself and fed by the billet for which he will receive 6s. 8d. per day to pay all his expenses.
18. Any falling short of the standards of training and behaviour on the part of a Special Service soldier will render him liable to be returned to his unit.

TRAINING ROUTINE

Weapons training	19%
Fieldcraft, movement and tactics	13%
Firing of weapons and field firing	11%
PT including swimming, ropework and unarmed combat	10%
Boatwork	9%
Map reading	8%
Speed marches	6%
Night training	5%
Mines and demolitions	4%
Drill	4%
Climbing	3%
Set piece exercises	3%
Training films	3%
Medical lectures and first aid	3%

0800 followed by a parade and full inspection at 0900. A route march of varying distances was completed before lunch at 1300. After the meal, there was more physical training including swimming. Tea was at 1630 followed by a 45-minute lecture at 1700. The evening after 1800 was free or for company duties. The course lasted for three months, later reduced to five weeks and was divided up as shown in the table at left.

At the end of the course, there was a final 36-hour live firing exercise involving a night attack to simulate a Commando raid. During World War II, 25,000 men passed through Achnacarry Castle to become Commandos and entitled to wear the Green Beret. They came from many nations and included Belgians, French, Dutch, Norwegians, Poles and US Rangers, the American equivalent of the Commandos. After their time at the Commando Basic Training Centre, the proud owners of the Green Berets transferred to the holding operational Commando where they underwent further training in specialised tasks and occupations. When fully qualified, they then joined their own Commando units, most of which were stationed around the coast where nautical training could continue. The Commandos preferred to live in civilian billets rather than barracks where ordinary soldiers had to undertake many irksome chores such as guard duties and cookhouse fatigues. To this end, each individual Commando was given a daily allowance for his food and lodgings. An officer received 13s. 4d. (£0.67) while the other ranks got 6s. 8d. (£0.33) which was generous by the standards of the day.

Stan Weatherall joined No. 6 Commando in 1940:

'I was in No. 1 Troop. The Commando was in civilian billets with civvy ration cards and we were paid 6s 8d [33 pence] a day billeting allowance. The landladies in Scarborough asked £1. 10s [£1.50] a week, so the lads benefited by 16s 8d [83 pence] a week, which was not to be sneezed at when a pint of beer was just 6d [2.5 pence] and the better brands of fags 6d for twenty.'

By 1941 the Special Service Brigade comprised 11 Commandos. In February Nos. 1 and 2 Commandos left the brigade to become paratroopers. Each Commando unit now

Below: Landing craft were the essential tool for the Commandos, particularly smaller types such as this LCA or Landing Craft Assault. With a crew of one officer and three ratings, the LCA was 35 feet long and 9 feet in beam with a draught of 3 feet. It was capable of carrying a maximum of 35 Commandos. *CEC*

consisted of six troops rather than the original ten, with three officers and 62 other ranks in each troop. This allowed a troop to be carried in a pair of the new Assault Landing Craft or ALC then entering service. The chronic shortage of landing craft and assault ships to carry the Commandos had hitherto constrained Admiral Keyes and the staff of Combined Operations from planning large-scale raids as envisaged by Prime Minister Winston Churchill.

Above: With the Combined Operations badge on his arm, a Royal Navy rating oversees the disembarkation of Commandos from an LCA during a demonstration before King George VI. *CEC*

After contemplating operations in the Mediterranean, Keyes turned his eyes northwards to Norway, but not before three Commandos, Nos 7, 8 and 11 (Scottish), were despatched to the Middle East where they joined two locally recruited Commando units, Nos. 50 and 52 (ME). Together they became known as Layforce, of which more later. Layforce was named after its commander, Col Robert Laycock who was to become a legendary Commando leader during World War II.

From the moment he took over command of Combined Operations, Keyes had been obstructed by the higher echelons of the War Office. To them, the Commandos were an unacceptable drain of capable men and scant resources from the conventional forces which were desperately needed for home defence and the North African campaign. But, with Churchill's backing, the Commandos were not to be stifled at birth by Whitehall bureaucrats. The Prime Minister continued to badger for direct action against Nazi-occupied Europe through Commando raids that in his words:

'There comes out from the sea from time to time a hand of steel which plucks the German sentries from their posts with growing efficiency.'

IN ACTION

THE STEEL HAND FROM THE SEA

The target for the first major Commando raid was the Norwegian Lofoten Islands lying just inside the Arctic Circle some 900 miles from Britain. The sparsely populated islands were home to generations of hardy fishermen with factories producing cod liver oil for medicinal purposes and glycerine that was a vital constituent in the manufacture of high explosives for the German war machine. These factories were located at four different ports: Brettesnes, Henningsvær, Stamsund and Svolvær. They were the targets for Operation Claymore. The raiding force embarked aboard a pair of converted cross-Channel ferries, the *Princess Beatrix* and *Princess Emma*, at Scapa Flow on 21 February 1941. Escorted by five destroyers of the Royal Navy, the raiders of Nos. 3 and 4 Special Service Battalions stopped off at the Faroe Islands for final training in assault landings. Once there they were given the instruction that the SS Battalions were to revert to the original Commando designation, with No. 3 SS Battalion becoming No. 4 Commando and No. 4 SS Battalion becoming No. 3 Commando. The force of Commandos comprised some 500 men supported by 52 Royal Engineers to undertake demolition tasks and 52 volunteers drawn from the Free Norwegian Forces to act as guides and interpreters. The task force set sail for Norway on 1 March 1941.

Designed as ferries for the relatively sheltered waters of the English Channel, the newly converted infantry landing ships wallowed and plunged their way across the turbulent North Sea and virtually every man aboard was seasick, but the flotilla arrived off the Lofoten Islands on schedule in the early hours of 4 March. In the intense cold, the Commandos clambered into their landing craft, huddling under their gas capes against the freezing sea spray, and made for the shoreline that was illuminated with no thought of blackouts in these northern climes. One Commando recalled: 'I was wearing two vests, two pullovers, a shirt, a Gieves waistcoat, a wool-lined mackintosh, and a pair of fur-lined boots and I was still cold.' The raiders achieved total surprise as they scrabbled over the icy quays and piles of frozen fish. At first, the Norwegian inhabitants thought it was a German landing exercise and gave the Commandos a half-hearted Nazi salute, but once the interlopers were recognised, jubilation erupted. However, there was no German garrison and so, to the Commandos' dismay, no fighting to be had, although several German soldiers were rounded up during the day. Lord Lovat of No. 4 Commando was not to be denied some action so he commandeered a motorbus and drove to a nearby seaplane base where he captured any German he could find. Meanwhile, the Sappers began the demolition of the various fish processing factories and the storage tanks of fish oil. In addition, 800,000 gallons of petrol and heating oil was destroyed as well as 18,000 tons of shipping. Among this total was a German gunboat, the *Krebs*, that gallantly engaged the destroyer HMS *Somali*, which promptly set it on fire.

Right: Map of the main actions on the Continent by Commandos from British bases.

Below: Buildings and stores burn fiercely during the raid on Vaagsø as the troops of No. 3 Commando advance into the town against fierce German resistance. *IWM – N459*

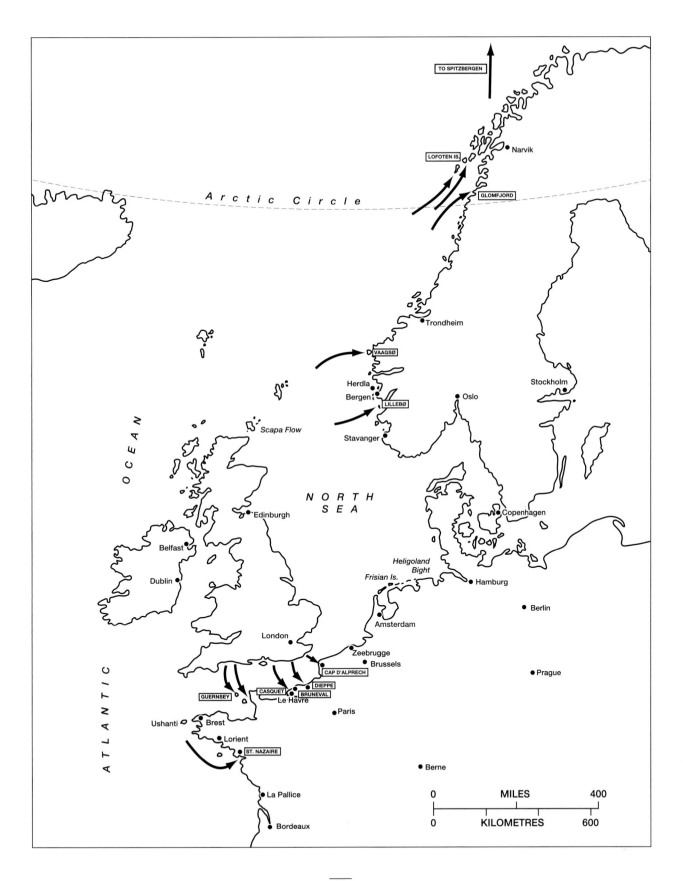

TO SPITZBERGEN

Narvik

A r c t i c   C i r c l e

LOFOTEN IS.

GLOMFJORD

Trondheim

VAAGSØ

Herdla

Bergen

LILLEBØ

Oslo

Stockholm

Stavanger

Scapa Flow

O C E A N

N O R T H
S E A

Edinburgh

Copenhagen

Belfast

Heligoland
Bight

Dublin

Frisian Is.

Hamburg

Amsterdam

Berlin

London

Zeebrugge

Brussels

Prague

CAP D'ALPRECH

DIEPPE

CASQUET

BRUNEVAL

GUERNSEY

Le Havre

Paris

Ushanti

Brest

Berne

Lorient

ST. NAZAIRE

La Pallice

A T L A N T I C

Bordeaux

0	MILES	400

0	KILOMETRES	600

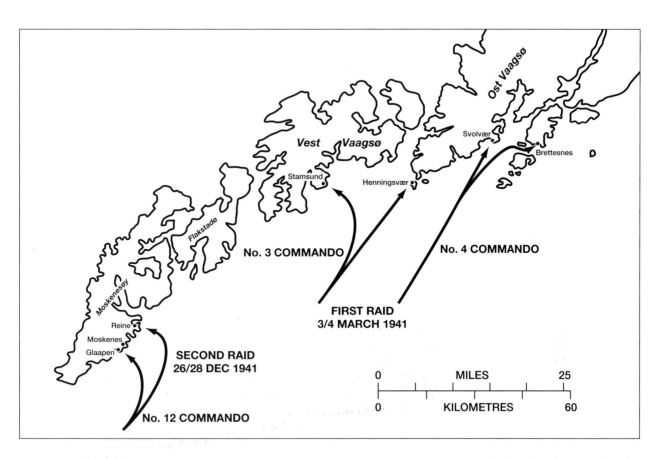

Vest *Vaagsø*

Ost Vaagsø

Svolvær

Brettesnes

Stamsund

Henningsvær

Flakstadø

No. 3 COMMANDO

No. 4 COMMANDO

FIRST RAID
3/4 MARCH 1941

Moskenesøy

Reine

Moskenes

Glaapen

SECOND RAID
26/28 DEC 1941

No. 12 COMMANDO

| 0 | | MILES | | 25 |
| 0 | | KILOMETRES | | 60 |

After some six hours ashore, the raiders withdrew, taking with them some 225 Germans, mostly merchant seamen, as prisoners of war, ten Quislings (Nazi collaborators) rounded up by the Norwegian detachment and 314 men and women who wished to join the Free Norwegian Forces in the war against Nazi Germany. Among the spoils of war was an incomplete set of wheels from a German Enigma encoding machine that proved to be of particular significance to the code breakers of Bletchley Park. Having suffered no serious casualties beyond an officer who shot himself in the thigh, the Commandos declared Operation Claymore a great success and they returned to a rapturous reception at Scapa Flow. The CO of No. 3 Commando, Lt-Col Durnford-Slater wrote: 'Altogether it had been a highly successful operation with no casualties and a good start to large-scale raids.'

But this was not to be. Much-needed landing craft were transferred to the Middle East and a task force, Force 110, was assembled for an assault on the Canary Islands but Operation Puma was cancelled, although elements of Force 110 were subsequently despatched to West Africa where they languished until February 1942. In August a successful attack by regular Canadian troops against the coalmines on the Norwegian Island of Spitzbergen did much to devalue the concept of Commandos as elite raiders in the eyes of the War Office. The Commandos were still seen as 'Churchill's Private Army' and few in the military hierarchy had any time for private armies. Their answer to the problem was to deny the Commandos the resources they needed, such as training areas or intelligence reports to allow them to mount raids. Further obstructionism was typified by the refusal of the War Office to allow the Commandos their own distinctive headgear, such as the 'red beret' that had recently been authorised for the Parachute Regiment, a younger formation than the Commandos.

Above: Attack on the Lofoten Islands, December 1941.

Left: With a Fairbairn-Sykes fighting knife between his teeth, a sergeant and his men of No. 6 Commando fit fuses into their No. 36 grenades as their ship approaches the Norwegian coast prior to the raid on Vaagsø. *IWM – N503*

Right: Using ships' lifeboats as landing craft, members of No. 50 Middle East Commando come ashore at Kabrit on the shores of the Great Bitter Lake in August 1940. *CMC*

It was too much for Admiral Keyes. On 27 October, he stepped down as the Chief of Combined Operations and took his grievance to Parliament where he announced: 'After fifteen months as Chief of Combined Operations and having been frustrated at every turn in every worthwhile offensive action I have tried to undertake, I must fully endorse the Prime Minister's comments on the negative power of those who control the war machine in Whitehall.' The War Office's response was to send him a copy of the Official Secrets Act to ensure his silence. This was but naught to the tragedy to come. Just three weeks later, Admiral Keyes' son Geoffrey was killed leading a raid on Rommel's headquarters in North Africa. It could be of little consolation that Lt-Col Geoffrey Keyes was posthumously awarded the first Victoria Cross to be won by a Commando.

LAYFORCE AND THE MIDDLE EAST COMMANDOS

Concurrently with the formation of the first Commandos in Britain, GHQ Middle East Land Forces was instructed to raise similar units from soldiers serving in Egypt and Palestine. The task was entrusted to Lt-Col George Young, Royal Engineers. The first to be formed was No. 50 Commando (Middle East) in July 1940 followed by Nos. 51 and 52 (ME) in October and November respectively. Once again, there were plenty of volunteers, including 70 Spaniards, veterans of the Spanish Civil War, who wished to serve in the British Army and gain British citizenship. No. 51 was unusual in that it was raised in Palestine and included both Arabs and Jews in an integrated unit under the command of a dynamic officer, Lt-Col Henry Cator.

Again, there were numerous objections heard from the commanding officers of line infantry units who were losing many of their best men. Some of these even took the opportunity to encourage their 'bad eggs' or more difficult soldiers to 'volunteer' for the Commandos and many of these ended up in No. 52 (ME). As is so often the case, many

Below: Commando operations in the Mediterranean theatre.

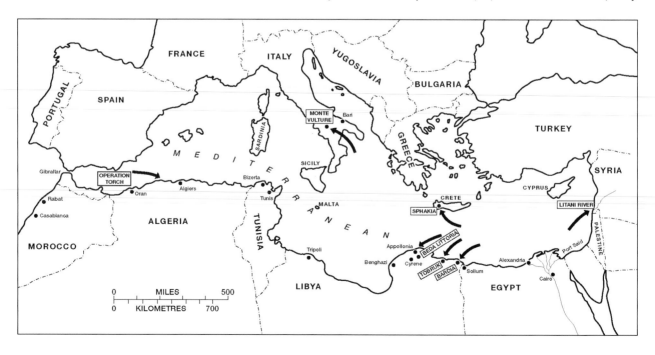

of these 'bad eggs' made excellent fighting men when allowed to escape the stifling discipline of normal units and follow the Commando credo of self-reliance although in No. 52 (ME), it did go too far as David Smiley, a company commander, recalled:

> 'Men were termed as "raiders." There was no saluting, no saying "Sir", no calling to attention on parades, and no marching in step. Some of the worst disciplined took advantage of this with disastrous results. When discipline had almost ceased to exist, normal army discipline was reintroduced with resulting improvements.'

All three units endured a similar regime of rigorous training with much emphasis on physical toughness including endurance marches across the desert and broken terrain of the 'jebels' with only limited water supplies. At the outset, the Commandos were based at Geneifa on the Great Bitter Lakes where amphibious training was undertaken. Due to a lack of landing craft, much of this was done using lifeboats borrowed from the ships at anchor in the lakes. Besides adopting the bush hat as their own particular headgear, the Middle East Commandos acquired their own type of fighting knife rather than the Fairbairn-Sykes dagger. Known as the 'fanny', it was a combination of a knuckleduster with a 7-inch blade; the fanny also became the design for the Middle East Commandos' own cap badge.

The first Commando raid by No. 50 (ME) was scheduled to occur on the night of 27/28 October 1940 with an attack on the Italian seaplane base at Bomba but, like so many other raids, it was cancelled at the last moment, on this occasion because of the Italian invasion of Greece. This action prompted the deployment of No. 50 Commando (ME) to Crete aboard the battleships HMS *Warspite* and *Valiant*. There they became part of 14 Infantry Brigade with the task of defending the island against an Axis invasion, a mission not best suited to the training and equipment of Commandos. It was made more difficult by the hospitality of the Cretans and the generous provision of wine over the Christmas period. Neither of the other two Commandos enjoyed any more success at this time with various schemes and raids cancelled or postponed although No. 52 (ME) was despatched to the Sudan where it arrived on 20 December 1940 to join the campaign against the Italians over the next months, as did No. 51 (ME) towards the end of January. Both Commandos fought with distinction and played a significant part in the defeat of the Italians in Ethiopia and Eritrea over the coming year.

As recounted above, Nos. 7, 8 and 11 (Scottish) Commandos were despatched to the Middle East as Force Z on 31 January 1941 aboard the new infantry assault ships HMS

REORGANISATION OF SS COMPANIES INTO COMMANDOS

Special Service Brigade
(Brig R.E. Laycock)

No. 1 Cdo
No. 2 Cdo
No. 3 Cdo
No. 4 Cdo
No. 5 Cdo
No. 6 Cdo
No. 9 Cdo
No. 10 (Inter-Allied) Cdo
No. 12 Cdo
No. 14 Cdo
No. 30 Cdo
No. 40 (RM) Cdo
No. 41 (RM) Cdo
No. 62 Cdo
Special Boat Section
(and combined operations
assault pilotage parties)
Depot Section
(and snow warfare camp)

Right: The Chief of Combined Operations, Lord Louis Mountbatten, addresses the men of No. 6 Commando prior to Operation Myrmidon in April 1942 – an abortive raid on the Adour estuary in France. *IWM – H18696*

Below: The Italian garrison of Amba Alagi surrenders on 17 May 1941 after the decisive attack by No. 51 Middle East Commando on a feature later called Commando Hill. After a successful campaign in Eritrea and Ethiopia, No. 51 ME Commando returned to Geneifa in Egypt and was disbanded. *CMC*

Glenearn, *Glengyle* and *Glenroy*. These were ships of the Glen Line that had been converted for Commando use with the lifeboat davits adapted to take assault landing craft and motor launches. Finally, the Commandos were procuring the naval assistance that was vital to their purpose. Under the command of Lt-Col Robert Laycock, Force Z sailed via South Africa and arrived at Geneifa on 10 March when it was renamed 'Layforce' for security reasons to disguise the fact that Commandos were in the Middle East theatre of operations. There they met up with Nos. 50 and 52 Commandos (ME) which had recently returned from Crete and the Sudan respectively. The two units were now amalgamated and placed under command of Layforce, which now had a strength of some 2,000 Commandos. This represented a formidable raiding force, but to avoid any reference to their Commando role, they were redesignated with No. 7 Commando becoming A Battalion; No. 8 – B Battalion; No. 11 (Scottish) – C Battalion, and the amalgamated Nos. 50 and 52 (ME) became D Battalion.

In the following months, various raids were proposed, planned and then cancelled, usually at the last minute, although A Battalion conducted a raid on the port of Bardia on the night of 19/20 April. Unfortunately this inflicted only minor damage at the high cost of 67 prisoners of war and several dead and injured. With the deteriorating military situation in Greece, Layforce was now stripped of its assault ships. When A Battalion disembarked from HMS *Glengyle* for the last time at the beginning of May it left a heartfelt message in one of the troop decks: 'Never in the whole history of human endeavour have so few been buggered about by so many.' By the end of the month, Layforce was broken up, with C Battalion being deployed to Cyprus and the remaining battalions to Crete where they arrived on 27 May to counter the German airborne

invasion that had been underway for a week. Under the command of Col Laycock, the 800-man force landed at Suda Bay just as survivors from the sunken destroyers HMS *Kashmir* and *Kelly* were being rescued. The captain of the stricken HMS *Kelly* was soon to figure highly in the story of the Commandos. As the military situation in Crete fell apart, Layforce fought a series of rearguard actions across the rugged island to the south coast where the Royal Navy evacuated the British Commonwealth forces from Sphakia. All the while, German Stukas subjected them to repeated dive-bombing raids. Among the Commandos was the famous writer, Evelyn Waugh, who summed up the general opinion of the dive-bombing by commenting 'that like all things German it was very efficient and went on much too long.' Tragically, just 200 Commandos escaped from the Crete debacle, a casualty rate of 75 per cent.

In June and July Commando operations continued, with C Battalion fighting on the Litani River in Vichy French Syria and B Battalion conducting a successful raid on Tobruk, but the number of casualties suffered was far too high to be sustained and in August Layforce was disbanded by order of GHQ Middle East Land Forces. In London, Churchill was furious and he immediately demanded that a new Commando force be created but this time under the command of the Royal Navy because, in his words: 'Middle East Command has indeed maltreated and thrown away this valuable force.' With Brigadier Laycock as the local Director of Combined Operations, the much-depleted Middle East Commando comprised various elements of the Special Forces in the region with L Detachment of the Special Air Service (SAS) as No. 2 Troop; the remnants of C Battalion or No. 11 Commando (Scottish) as No. 3 Troop under the command of Lt-Col Geoffrey Keyes; No. 51 Commando (ME) as Nos. 4 and 5 Troops and the Special Boat Service as No. 6 Troop. There was also an HQ and Depot Troop based at Geneifa.

As indicated above, No. 3 Troop was formed from men of C Battalion but they had always referred to themselves as No. 11 Commando (Scottish) throughout all the various redesignations of the previous year. They were now to embark on one of the most dramatic Commando raids of the war – the attempted assassination of the 'Desert Fox', General Erwin Rommel, the commander of the German Afrika Korps. The attack was to coincide with the launching of a major offensive by the British Commonwealth Eighth Army to relieve the entrapped garrison at Tobruk under the codename of Operation Crusader. The object of the raid was to disrupt the Axis High Command before battle was joined. The raid was known as Operation Flipper and the six officers and 53 men of the 'Scottish Commando', under the command of Brigadier Laycock, embarked aboard two submarines on the evening of 10 November with four specific targets, including Rommel's house at Beda Littoria and Italian HQ buildings.

Due to heavy seas, only two detachments were able to land, including Lt-Col Keyes and 17 Commandos from HMS *Torbay*. On the stormy night of 17/18 November 1941, friendly Arabs guided Keyes and his men to a building at Sidi Rafa, and not Beda Littoria, that was supposedly Rommel's resting place for the night. At the stroke of midnight, they attacked and in the ensuing firefight Keyes was mortally wounded. Unfortunately Rommel was absent at the time, but three colonels on his staff and a number of other soldiers were killed and wounded. The rest of the raiders withdrew to the beaches, a distance of some 18 miles over difficult terrain, where they found the seas too rough for them to be picked up by the Royal Navy so they were forced to go into hiding. Over the coming days, the Germans and hostile Arabs tracked down the dwindling band of Commandos and they were either killed or captured. Only Brig Laycock and Sgt Jack Terry, who had fought side by side with Col Keyes, escaped in an epic 41-day march across the desert to reach friendly lines on Christmas Day 1941. Although Operation Flipper failed in its intention, the Commandos gained their first Victoria Cross, which was awarded posthumously to Keyes.

In mid-1942, Sgt P. King of the Army Dental Corps wrote a letter to Winston Churchill stating his dismay at not being allowed to transfer to a combat unit and explaining that he had decided that he and another soldier, Pte L. Cuthbertson, would conduct their own Commando raid on France and kill at least 50 Germans. The two went AWOL after taking two pistols and 41 rounds of ammunition. On 2 May, they hired a motorboat with seven gallons of fuel and set off for France, landing near the port of Cherbourg. After failing to engage the enemy, they returned to their boat but ran out of fuel and they drifted in the Channel for 15 days before being picked up by a destroyer. After a spell in hospital, the two were court-martialled but both subsequently got their wish, with Cuthbertson joining the Durham Light Infantry and the now Private King being posted to the Commandos. King regained his sergeant's stripes and won a battlefield commission with No. 4 Commando in Normandy. He finished the war as a lieutenant with a Military Cross. *CMC*

Right: Lt-Col Charles Vaughan was the dynamic and forceful commandant at Achnacarry and insured the high level of training that was characteristic of all Commandos. *CMC*

Below: A sergeant of No. 2 (Dutch) Troop of No. 10 (Inter-Allied) Commando demonstrates the use of Commando toggle ropes in making a makeshift bridge during training at Portmadoc harbour in Wales. *CMC*

Far right: With a toggle rope around his neck Sgt Joseph Peirlot of No. 4 (Belgian) Troop of No. 10 (Inter-Allied) Commando displays his Belgian Royal Lion cap badge on his green beret. *CMC*

Right: The attack on Vaagsø.

As the fateful year of 1942 dawned, the Middle East Commando was allowed to wither on the vine, despite Churchill's demands, and its personnel were gradually absorbed into the plethora of Special Forces now operating in the vast sand seas of North Africa including the SAS, the Long Range Desert Group, Popski's Private Army and the Special Interrogation Group.

1942 – THE YEAR OF THE GREAT RAIDS

After his eventful time during Operation Flipper, Brig Laycock returned to Britain to succeed Brig Charles Haydon as Commander, Special Service Brigade. Haydon was promoted to major-general and became the deputy to the new Chief of Combined Operations, Lord Louis Mountbatten, the erstwhile captain of HMS *Kelly* that had been sunk in the battle for Crete. Now promoted to Commodore and shortly to become Vice-Admiral, Mountbatten succeeded Admiral Keyes on 27 October 1941. As a cousin of the King and a consummate establishment figure, he had far more influence within the military hierarchy than his predecessor and he put it to good effect to promote the Commandos. Mountbatten was determined to conduct the large-scale raids as originally envisaged by Churchill and Keyes. With his naval background, he was able to command greater resources from the Senior Service, particularly in the construction of more landing craft.

With the Soviet Union now an ally under dire threat from the advancing German Panzers, planning went ahead for another raid on Norway to relieve some pressure on the Russians. Codenamed Operation Archery, the objective was to attack the German garrison in the town of Vaagsø in southwest Norway. The troops chosen for the raid were Lt-Col Durnford-Slater's No. 3 Commando supported by two troops from No. 2 Commando and a medical detachment from No. 4 Commando as well as a party of demolition specialists from 101 Troop and some soldiers of the Free Norwegian Forces. As a diversion, 300 men of No. 12 Commando were to mount another raid on the Lofoten Islands under the codename Operation Anklet. The naval task force set sail from Scapa Flow on Christmas Eve 1941, with the Commandos aboard the infantry assault ships *Prince Charles* and *Prince Leopold*. On the following day, the Commandos made five separate landings in and around the port of Vaagsø and the neighbouring island of Maaloy where the coastal artillery batteries were situated. The German garrison in Vaagsø was taken completely by surprise when the 600 Commandos stormed ashore but they soon began a stiff resistance. Lt-Col Durnford-Slater led the main assault party of No. 3 Commando against the town of Vaagsø while his second-in-command, Maj Jack Churchill, attacked the nearby small island of Maaloy. Another of the great wartime Commandos, 'Mad Jack' Churchill, entered battle playing the bagpipes before drawing his Claymore. With him was another legendary Commando, Capt Peter Young, the commander of 6 Troop, and together these attackers soon overran the gun batteries on Maaloy.

However, the fighting in Vaagsø was now fierce, with the Germans resisting house by house. Capt Young and his troop were despatched from Maaloy to the town as reinforcements. They were soon in the thick of the fighting, as one of his men recalled:

> 'Our Captain led the attack here, and although it was slow as we had to go from house to house, we were able to spot and shoot the snipers who were doing the damage… One of our sergeants received three shots in the back from a sniper who had let us pass. We opened fire on this sniper's window and settled him. We dashed to the next house… we threw in petrol, set fire to it and went on our way…'

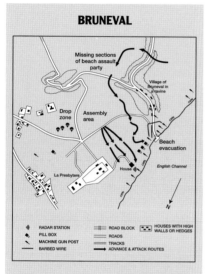

BRUNEVAL

Missing sections of beach assault party

Village of Bruneval in a ravine

Drop zone

Assembly area

Beach evacuation

English Channel

La Presbytère

House

N

- ⚑ RADAR STATION
- ▲ PILL BOX
- ◆ MACHINE GUN POST
- — BARBED WIRE
- ⊞ ROAD BLOCK
- ═ ROADS
- ⋯ TRACKS
- ➤ ADVANCE & ATTACK ROUTES
- ▦ HOUSES WITH HIGH WALLS OR HEDGES

The Parachute Regiment began life as a commando unit before becoming a separate entity with the famous 'red beret'. Its first major success was the airborne raid on a German radar station at Bruneval near the port of Le Havre on the night of 27/28 February 1942. Under the command of Maj John Frost, 120 men of the 2nd Parachute Battalion dropped near to the Würzburg radar site together with Royal Engineers and a radar specialist to learn its secrets and remove critical parts for analysis. Meanwhile, Commandos had landed to attack the beach pillboxes defending the radar site from a seaborne assault and cover the withdrawal of the raiders to the waiting landing craft for their return to England. At a cost of just two dead and four wounded, the secrets of the Würzburg were revealed and Operation Biting was a classic example of Combined Operations with various different formations working in concert.

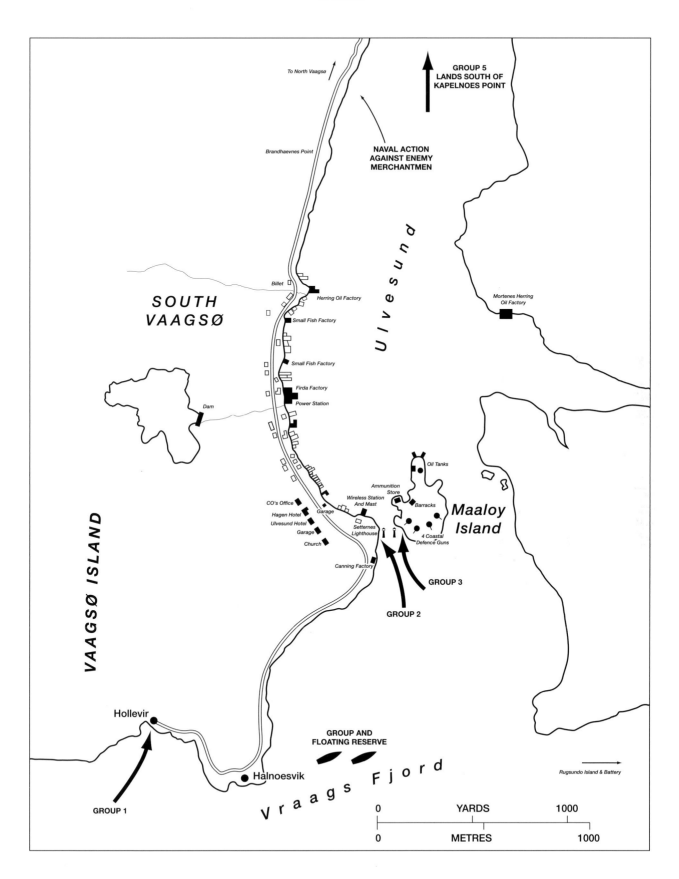

To North Vaagsø

GROUP 5
LANDS SOUTH OF
KAPELNOES POINT

Brandhaevnes Point

NAVAL ACTION
AGAINST ENEMY
MERCHANTMEN

U l v e s u n d

Mortenes Herring
Oil Factory

SOUTH
VAAGSØ

Billet

Herring Oil Factory

Small Fish Factory

Small Fish Factory

Firda Factory

Power Station

Dam

Oil Tanks

Ammunition
Store

Wireless Station
And Mast

Barracks

Maaloy
Island

CO's Office

Garage

Hagen Hotel

Ulvesund Hotel

Garage

Church

Setternes
Lighthouse

4 Coastal
Defence Guns

GROUP 3

Canning Factory

GROUP 2

V A A G S Ø   I S L A N D

Hollevir

GROUP AND
FLOATING RESERVE

Halnoesvik

V r a a g s   F j o r d

Rugsundo Island & Battery

GROUP 1

0	YARDS	1000
0	METRES	1000

Right: Map of the St Nazaire action.

Peter Young and his sergeant, George Herbert, were observed by Lt-Col Durnford-Slater who reported: 'They appeared to be enjoying themselves.' For his actions, Capt Young was awarded the first of his three Military Crosses. By the early afternoon the town was cleared with some 150 Germans killed. The raiders then withdrew to their ships and were re-embarked by 1445 hours.

Operation Archery had been a success but not without cost. Commando casualties were 19 dead and 57 wounded, but they left behind widespread destruction; the fish processing factories had been razed to the ground and 15,000 tons of shipping sunk by the supporting Royal Navy warships. In addition, 98 Germans were taken as prisoners of war together with four Quislings, but these were greatly outnumbered by the 70 loyal Norwegians who wished to join the Free Norwegian Forces. Tragically, the Germans exacted a terrible revenge and many Norwegians were either executed or deported to concentration camps as reprisals for the raids. Accordingly, at the behest of King Haakon of Norway, no further Commando raids were conducted against his country, but the Vaagsø and Lofoten raids convinced Hitler that Norway remained 'the zone of destiny' and a probable invasion route for the Allies. German reinforcements of men and capital ships poured into the country, and by the end of the war almost 400,000 troops and all their equipment were stationed there at the expense of the fighting fronts – which was a remarkably cost-effective return for a few daring raids conducted by less than a thousand Commandos supported by the long reach of the Royal Navy. The steel hand had certainly struck from the sea.

ST NAZAIRE

With the *Tirpitz* now stationed in Norwegian waters and lurking deep inside various fjords, the mighty battleship posed a serious threat to Britain's supply convoys plying through the inhospitable Arctic Sea to the Soviet Union. Equally, if the *Tirpitz* were to break out into the North Atlantic, as its sister ship the *Bismarck* had done the year before, Britain's own maritime supply lines would lie at the mercy of the massive surface raider and her cohorts, the battlecruisers *Scharnhorst* and *Gneisenau*. The *Tirpitz* became an obsession with Churchill and he wrote: 'The whole strategy of the war turns at this period on this ship.' At his direction, all measures were to be taken to deny it the opportunity of operating in the Atlantic Ocean. Various studies were undertaken to this end. To be viable as a surface raider, the *Tirpitz* needed a base on the Atlantic seaboard where it could be replenished and, if necessary, repaired. There was only one port in France with a dry dock large enough to accommodate the 42,000-ton battleship – St Nazaire and its huge Forme Ecluse, which was the largest dry dock in Europe, capable of taking ships up to 85,000 tons. It was the birthplace of the pre-war French luxury liner *Normandie* and it was by this name that the dock was normally known. If the Normandie Dock was denied to the Germans, it was unlikely that the Kriegsmarine would risk its only remaining modern battleship in the open seas of the Atlantic.

The idea of destroying the dock was first mooted by Admiral Keyes in July 1941 and preliminary planning was undertaken. Bombing by the RAF was considered but it was soon discounted, as any attack from the air would have inflicted unacceptable casualties among the French population of St Nazaire. Furthermore, the massive concrete structure was largely impervious to high explosives. The key elements of the Normandie Dock were the caissons or dock gates that held back the waters when a ship was in dry dock; the pumping house that drained the waters from inside the dock and the winding mechanism that moved the caissons across the entrances to the dock itself. Together, they presented a formidable target; each caisson was a massive steel structure weighing hundreds of tons.

The task of destroying the dock was given to Combined Operations and specifically to No. 2 Commando under Lt-Col Charles Newman. The main assault force comprised some

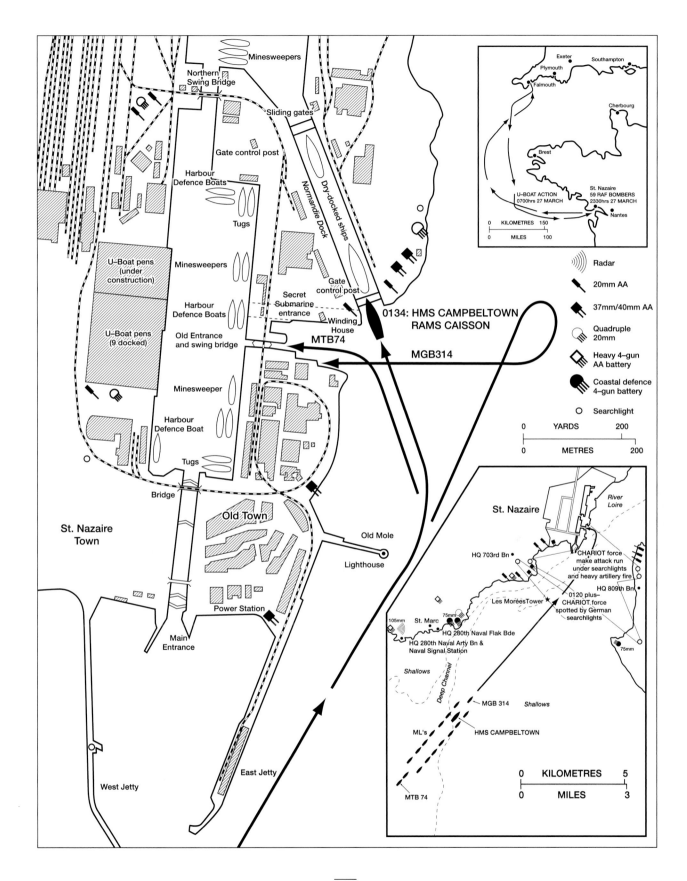

FAIRBAIRN AND SYKES

The Fairbairn-Sykes fighting knife became the symbol of the Commandos during World War 2 and remains one of the most famous military edged weapons of all time. Capt William Ewart Fairbairn was formally an Assistant Commissioner of the Shanghai Municipal Police during the 1930s when the Chinese port had a widespread reputation as a decadent but lawless city. Fairbairn was in charge of the crack Reserve Unit (the equivalent of a modern SWAT team) that fought a continuous campaign against the drug and prostitution rackets of the fearsome Triads. As part of the Reserve Unit there was a special Sniper Unit commanded by Capt Eric Antony Sykes. During their time in Shanghai, the two policemen encountered all the multifarious edged weapons of the Chinese underworld and gained extensive knowledge and expertise in knife fighting. Their skills were readily employed by the Commandos when Fairbairn and Sykes became the principal instructors in close combat training at the Commando Basic Training Centre at Achnacarry. The two officers sought and received approval from the War Office to design a fighting knife specifically for the Commandos, which could be attached wherever on the uniform or webbing for immediate accessibility. Fairbairn's philosophy was simple – 'In war you can't afford the luxury of squeamishness. Either you kill or capture or you will be captured or killed. We've got to be tough and we've got to be ruthless – tougher and more ruthless than our enemies'. Fairbairn especially favoured attacks on the brachial, radial, carotid and subclavian arteries. The thrust to the carotid was preferred for the rapid elimination of a sentry, since loss of consciousness usually occurred within five seconds and death soon thereafter. Harry Pexton of No.2 Commando recalled the two close combat instructors – 'They were lethal. They had loops inside their coats with knuckle-dusters and knives and hand grenades and sawn-off revolvers. They were a terrible pair of men, but very nice men. They could teach you all sorts of very nasty ways to kill people. Fortunately, I suppose we never had need to practise them properly, but they were there just in case'.

150 men from No. 2 and demolition parties from Nos. 1, 3, 4, 5, 9 and 12 Commandos making up another 80. But any amount of explosives carried by these men would make little impression on the steel caisson. Accordingly, Capt John Hughes-Hallett, RN, one of the most brilliant minds in Combined Operations during World War II, came up with the idea of ramming the outer caisson at high speed with a destroyer whose bows were to be packed with four tons of explosives. These were to be detonated by time delay once the raiders had withdrawn. The vessel chosen for the task was the elderly American 'four stacker' USS *Buchanan* that had been transferred to the Royal Navy and renamed HMS *Campbeltown*. Her captain was Lt-Cdr Sam Beattie, RN.

However, the port of St Nazaire lay six miles up the Loire River and its approaches were protected by heavy coastal defences with numerous weapons ranging from 20mm to 170mm guns as well as a 240mm rail-mounted gun for engaging warships closing with the coastline. Most of these guns were sited to cover the deep water channel from the estuary to the port so the British decided to approach over the mudflats, though these were only navigable at a high spring tide. This determined the date of the raid but even so the Commandos were obliged to use vulnerable shallow-draught wooden motor launches rather than their armoured assault landing craft. HMS *Campbeltown* had to be stripped of excess weight to reduce its draught so that she could negotiate the mudflats. She was also modified by removing two of the four funnels to resemble the *Möwe* Class German frigates that were based at St Nazaire. By this subterfuge, and by flying Kriegsmarine battle flags, it was hoped that the naval force and the accompanying Commandos in their motor launches would be able to negotiate much of the Loire estuary and reach St Nazaire before the German defenders engaged them. Once they gained the port and HMS *Campbeltown* had rammed the caisson, the Commandos were to destroy the pump house and the winding mechanism and, if the opportunity arose, inflict as much damage as possible on the nearby U-boat pens. It was a high-risk venture by any stretch of the imagination and one senior officer was heard to say: 'There's certainly a VC in it.' In the event there were to be five.

The Chiefs of Staff approved the plans for Operation Chariot on 3 March. A full-scale rehearsal was conducted against Devonport dockyard as it bore some resemblance to St Nazaire. The raiders were routed by the elderly Home Guard defenders of the dockyard. Corporal Arthur Woodwiss of No. 2 Commando recalled the occasion:

'We had plans of the dock area [St Nazaire] which we had to draw and redraw and a wonderful scale model which we could study in different light to help us identify our targets. As an assault group commander I rehearsed street fighting to the gun positions I had to demolish. Our full dress rehearsal at Devonport against the Home Guard was an absolute disaster and the Home Guard were delighted but we knew it would be all right on the night. If you have to make mistakes it is best to make them in training.'

The demolition parties also practised at the King George V Dock at Southampton which had similar pumping and winding machinery buildings to those of the Normandie Dock. The teams were soon able to undertake their demolition tasks in complete darkness. The plan was now set and it only waited on the spring tides for the maximum depth of water over the mudflats of the Loire estuary. The tides were high when Admiral Karl Dönitz, the Commander-in-Chief of the Kriegsmarine's U-boat forces, visited St Nazaire on 27 March 1942. He asked the garrison commander what preparations had been made in case of a seaborne assault to which he was told that plans were in place but nobody actually believed that such a raid was feasible. Dönitz replied tersely: 'I shouldn't be too sure of that.' He was absolutely right; the raiders were already on the high seas.

Operation Chariot got underway on 26 March 1942 when the naval force, under the command of Capt Robert Ryder, RN, set sail from Falmouth accompanied by 16 Fairmile motor launches carrying most of the 277 Commandos; a total force of 630 sailors and soldiers. After several scares en route that might have compromised the security of the operation, the 19-strong flotilla entered the Loire estuary at 2300 hours on 27 March and, with HMS *Campbeltown* in the van, it sailed up the river over the mudflats. Twice the ancient destroyer shuddered as it touched ground but it wrenched herself free each time. At 2330 hours, the RAF began a diversionary air raid but it only alerted the defenders and they began to signal *Campbeltown* as to its identity despite the Kriegsmarine battle flag. A fluent German speaking Royal Navy signaller, Leading Signaller Pike, wearing the uniform of a German petty officer, countered the challenge by using responses gleaned from German naval code books captured during the Vaagsø raid. The German gunners held their fire for several vital minutes as *Campbeltown* surged on towards the target. Searchlights now played on the flotilla from the shoreline and the Germans opened fire at 0122. Captain Ryder in *Motor Gun Boat 314* sent the international signal: 'Am being fired on by friendly forces.' The fire slackened and by now the flotilla had passed the heaviest batteries. At 0127 *Campbeltown* came under heavy fire. The crew hauled down the false colours and the White Ensign broke out at the masthead.

Capt Ryder later wrote: 'For about five minutes the sight was staggering, both sides loosing off with everything they had. The air was full of tracer, flying horizontally and at close range.' Casualties began to mount aboard the vulnerable motor launches and on the decks of HMS *Campbeltown*, despite the armoured shields for the Commando demolition teams. The bridge was hit and the coxswain killed. *Campbeltown* veered off course as a Commando wrestled with the wheel before a naval officer regained control and steered the ship at high speed towards the target. *Campbeltown* rammed the caisson at 0134 hours, just four minutes behind schedule. The first 36 feet of the bows were

Above: With the prow of HMS *Campbeltown* deeply embedded in the caisson of the Normandie Dock, the Commando demolition parties use assault ladders to disembark before they destroy the dock's pumping and winching equipment. At 1130 hours on 28 March 1942, the four tons of explosives packed inside the destroyer exploded killing at least 380 Germans and disabling the dock. Without the use of the Normandie Dock, the mighty battleship *Tirpitz* did not dare to venture into the Atlantic and never sank a single ton of Allied shipping. It remained lurking in Norwegian fjords until sunk on 12 November 1944 by Tallboy bombs dropped by the Lancasters of Nos. 9 and 617 Squadrons RAF. Operation Chariot was recognised as the 'greatest Commando raid of all' and the Normandie Dock was not fully repaired until 1948. *Reproduction courtesy of the artist David Rowlands*

compressed by the force of the impact and the ship was well and truly lodged. In any case the crew next scuttled the ship to prevent the Germans from ever possibly pulling it free before the hidden explosives in the hull were detonated. The demolition teams scrambled over the sides and onto the docks. They were met with fierce firing as they sprinted to their targets. Most of the motor launches had been shot to pieces during the approach and fewer than 100 Commandos ever got ashore. They faced some 5,000 German defenders in the local area, many armed with heavy weapons.

While the assault parties attacked the numerous gun emplacements, the demolition teams rushed to the buildings housing the vital machinery of the Normandie Dock. With great skill and determination, they placed their charges with precision and set the fuses for detonation. After this had been successfully achieved, the Commandos withdrew to the rendezvous point on the Old Mole where Lt-Col Newman had established his command post. There they awaited the motor launches for re-embarkation. Tragically, few of these had survived the battle; most had been blown apart by shellfire or were now burning fiercely with their crews incinerated. Nevertheless, Ryder's *MGB 314* and the few remaining launches limped back to sea with as many Commandos as they could carry. Those left stranded ashore decided to break out of the town and there followed what the Commandos called 'The St Nazaire Steeplechase' as they jumped over innumerable garden fences and other obstacles in their efforts to escape. Most fell into enemy hands but five Commandos did evade capture and made it home via Spain and Gibraltar.

Out at sea, the surviving vessels headed for home, but they were not out of danger yet. Five *Möwe* Class frigates of the type that HMS *Campbeltown* had been modified to resemble were at sea that night. As dawn was breaking, one of them, the *Jaguar*, encountered *ML 306*, commanded by Lt I.B. Henderson. With him were 13 sailors and 14 Commandos including Sgt Tom Durrant of No. 1 Commando. The *Jaguar* opened fire on the hapless motor launch but the Commandos promptly returned fire with their personal weapons against the powerful adversary. Within a short time 20 of the British were dead or wounded. The German frigate stopped firing and demanded Lt Henderson that he surrender his command. Henderson declined and firing resumed with Sgt Durrant manning a twin Lewis gun mounting at the stern of the craft. Although repeatedly wounded, he continued to engage the enemy until he was killed. The unequal contest had lasted for an hour when the *Jaguar* once more came alongside the sinking launch. Only one man, Lt Swayne of No. 1 Commando, remained unwounded on board *ML 306*. He rose unsteadily to his feet and called out, apologetically, 'I'm afraid we can't go on.' The captain of the *Jaguar* was so impressed by the action of the Commandos, particularly by Sgt Durrant manning the twin Lewis machine guns, that he later sought out Lt-Col Newman in a prison camp and told him: 'You may wish to recommend this man for a high decoration.' Sgt Tom Durrant was subsequently posthumously awarded the Victoria

Cross, the first time that a VC had been awarded to a soldier for a naval action on the recommendation of an enemy officer.

A further four VCs were awarded for exceptional acts of valour in the raid on St Nazaire: to the captain of HMS *Campbeltown*, Lt-Cdr Samuel Beattie, RN; to the naval commander, Capt Robert Ryder, RN; posthumously to Able Seaman William Savage; and the other Commando VC to Lt-Col Charles Newman. Of the 19 naval craft that entered the Loire estuary, only four returned. Some 169 men were killed and another 200 were taken prisoner. Only 270 of the 630 men who set out on the raid returned home safely. On the following day, 29 March 1942, the delayed action charges on board HMS Campbeltown exploded, killing a great number of Germans and incapacitating the dry dock for the remainder of the war. For the Commandos St Nazaire was and remains 'the greatest raid of all'.

MADAGASCAR AND THE STORMING OF DIEGO SUAREZ

Despite the heavy losses, Operation Chariot was deemed a great success and a full vindication of the Commando concept. Both Churchill and Mountbatten were anxious to extend Commando operations far and wide. After the disastrous fall of Singapore and the sinking of the battleship HMS *Prince of Wales* and the battlecruiser HMS *Repulse*, the Prime Minister was keen to find an alternative naval base in the Indian Ocean and suggested seizing the island of Madagascar from the Vichy French. This would also serve to protect the extended sea-lanes from Britain to the Middle East. After several months of planning, a task force set sail on the 9,000-mile journey on 23 March 1942. Operation

Below: The storming of Diego Suarez.

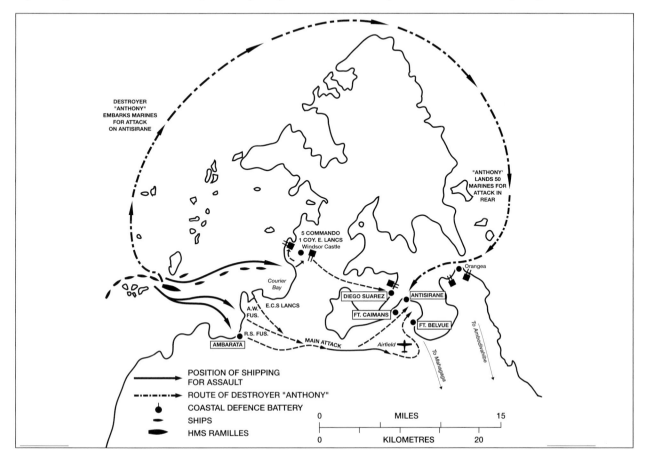

Ironclad was mounted against the port of Diego Suarez on the northern tip of the island on 5 May with No. 5 Commando leading the assault in conjunction with 29 Infantry Brigade. The Commandos' task was to eliminate two coastal artillery batteries which dominated the landing beaches. At 0430 hours, the 365 men of No. 5 Commando and a company of the East Lancashire Regiment landed from LCAs at Courrier Bay some 11 miles north of Diego Suarez. The raiders climbed the cliffs and caught the Vichy gunners fast asleep. However, at first light, French colonial troops mounted a counter-attack. The Commandos responded with a bayonet charge that killed the French NCOs and the rest promptly surrendered.

The Commandos then began the long march in sweltering heat towards Diego Suarez. En route they encountered a force of French Foreign Legionnaires and, in the words of Geoffrey Riley of No. 5 Commando: 'We shot them up a bit before they surrendered and there were about 50 wounded. We carried out mopping-up operations against colonial troops while the two infantry brigades took the town of Antsirane with heavy casualties.' The attack on the town, which lies across the water from Diego Suarez, had faltered. In the words of the Land Force commander, Maj-Gen Robert Sturges: 'Every Frenchman who can hold a rifle appears to be defending the neck of land on the Antsirane peninsula.' He called for a diversionary attack by a Royal Marine landing party from the battleship

Right: Another view of members of No. 50 Middle East Commando at Kabrit on the shores of the Great Bitter Lake in August 1940 — a graphic example of the pitiful state of equipment for the Commandos in the early months of their existence. *CMC*

No. 10 (INTER-ALLIED) COMMANDO

As it name implied, No. 10 (Inter-Allied) Commando was composed of volunteers from many countries of occupied Europe. It was formed on 11 July 1942. All its personnel were highly motivated and it fought in every theatre of war with considerable success. Under British command, each troop had an authorised strength of four officers and 83 other ranks.

British Headquarters
No. 1 (French) Troop
No. 2 (Dutch) Troop
No. 3 or X Troop — this troop was made up of personnel from Eastern Europe including some Germans.
The Belgian Troop HQ
No. 4 (Belgian) Troop
No. 5 (Norwegian) Troop
No. 6 (Polish) Troop
No. 7 (Yugoslav) Troop
No. 8 (French) Troop
No. 9 (Belgian) Troop
No. 10 (Belgian) Troop

HMS *Ramillies* on the night of 6 May. Under the command of Capt Martin Price, the 50 Marines boarded the destroyer HMS *Antony* and sailed round the northern tip of Madagascar (see map on page 35) and approached the quayside at Antsirane in pitch darkness under heavy fire from shore batteries. The Marines leapt ashore under heavy machine-gun fire. Their task was to cause disruption in the dockyard but not to attack the barracks or the main magazine, which were believed to be heavily defended by Vichy French troops. In the event, the Royal Marines overran the whole town in short order at the cost of just one casualty. In the words of the official after-action report: 'These fifty Royal Marines created a disturbance out of all proportion to their numbers.' It was a classic 'cutting-out' operation in the long tradition of the Royal Marines in their assaults from the sea.

To many, the Royal Marines had been undertaking the actual role of the Commandos for hundreds of years. However, there was considerable opposition from the Corps of Royal Marines to the notion of fighting on land. The higher echelons of the Corps maintained that naval gunnery was the prime purpose of the Royal Marines and not amphibious operations. However, it was recognised that such a role was necessary in the current war and a Royal Marine Brigade had been formed in January 1940. It was too late to see action in the Norwegian campaign but it was despatched on the abortive

NO. 62 COMMANDO – SMALL SCALE RAIDING FORCE

At the personal instigation of the commander of Combined Operations, Vice-Admiral Mountbatten, the Small Scale Raiding Force was formed early in 1942 for clandestine operations along the coastline of occupied Europe in co-operation with the Special Operations Executive (SOE). It was given the cover name of No. 62 Commando. Originally formed by Capt Gus March-Phillipps and Lt Geoffrey Appleyard from members of B Troop of No. 7 Commando, this unit was also known as the Maid Honor Force from the name of the fishing trawler it used for raiding. It gained notoriety for attacking Italian and German shipping in the neutral Portuguese colonial port of Fernando Po in the Gulf of Guinea during Operation Postmaster in January 1942. On its return to England, the SSRF conducted cross-Channel raids using a specially modified motor torpedo boat, *MTB 344*, which was known as 'The Little Pisser'. In September 1942 the SSRF conducted three raids. A typical one was Operation Dryad on 2/3 September when *MTB 344* landed troops that attacked the lighthouse on Les Casquets north of the Channel Islands. Radios, code books and prisoners were captured and the raiders returned without any casualties.

The SSRF and men of No. 12 Commando mounted a subsequent raid against the Channel Island of Sark on the night of 3/4 October as Operation Basalt. The force included some fabled Commando raiders such as Capt Philip Pinckney and the 'Fighting Dane', Lt Anders Lassen. In the attack on Dixcart Hotel, several prisoners were taken and tied up with Commando toggle ropes. As the raiders withdrew, four prisoners were shot dead and the Germans subsequently found their bound bodies. This incident led to Hitler's order that all Commando raiders be executed on capture. In the spring of 1943, the SSRF was disbanded and its personnel transferred either to No. 12 Commando or the Combined Operations Pilotage Parties (COPP). The role of the COPP was beach reconnaissance prior to a raid or assault landing using two-man canoes. With the canoe or 'cockle' standing offshore, one of the crewmen swam to the beach to determine essential data such as gradients and ground composition. COPPs were first employed during Operation Torch and were a part of virtually every subsequent assault and major river crossing of the war.

expedition to Dakar in West Africa in August 1940. In the same month, it was decided to expand the formation into a Royal Marine Division. This was achieved by 1941 but it spent most of the year languishing in Scotland and Wales waiting for an operational role. When the War Office blocked the formation of any more Army Commando units, Mountbatten cast his eyes around for more men to enlarge his Combined Operations command. They fell on the Royal Marines. The Admiralty agreed to the raising of a Royal Marine Commando with volunteers from the RM Division. Under the command of Lt-Col Joseph Picton Phillipps, the Royal Marine Commando was formed at Deal in Kent on 14 February 1942. It was soon to see action in the largest Combined Operations amphibious assault of the war so far.

OPERATION JUBILEE – THE DISASTER AT DIEPPE

By the summer of 1942 the Nazis were at the height of their conquests. The Third Reich stretched from the Pyrenees in the west to the Urals in the east and still the Panzers plunged deeper into the Soviet Union towards the oilfields of the Black and Caspian Seas. From Norway in the Arctic to the Egyptian desert on the Mediterranean, Hitler's armies occupied most of Europe and much territory beyond. To the British, the last six months of the war had brought a string of crushing defeats culminating in the largest surrender of British forces in the history of the British Empire at Singapore. For Winston Churchill, it was one of the darkest times of the war. He came under intense pressure from Stalin to mount a diversionary attack in Western Europe to divert German manpower away from the Eastern Front. President Roosevelt was also keen to open a 'Second Front' as soon as possible under the codename Operation Sledgehammer.

Anxious to build on the earlier Commando successes, Admiral Mountbatten and other Allied leaders decided to mount a much larger raid against another French port with the aim of capturing the town for some 12 hours as a rehearsal for the invasion of mainland Europe at a later date. It was a risky enterprise against an entrenched enemy in strongly fortified positions. The port chosen for the raid was Dieppe as it was within range of RAF fighters which would need to provide air cover. Neither the Royal Navy nor the RAF was willing to provide major warships or heavy bombers to support the landings or destroy the gun emplacements on the headlands that covered every approach to Dieppe. It was

Below: The disaster at Dieppe – lessons learned from this action delayed D-Day by at least a year because it made obvious the fact that landings would have to be made on beaches rather than a defended port. Dieppe also made the German defenders overconfident in the strength of their Atlantic Wall.

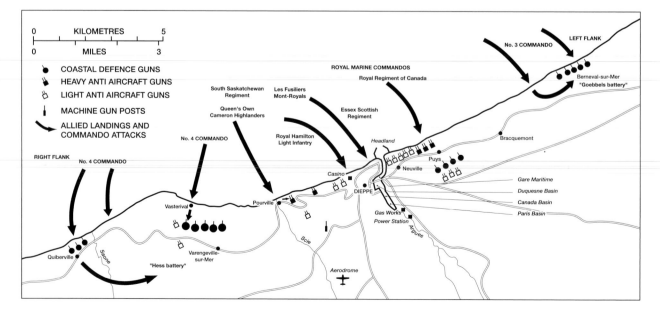

a task well suited to airborne assault by paratroopers or gliders, as the Germans had proved so effectively in the capture of the massive Belgian fortress of Eben Emael in 1940. But Mountbatten vetoed any airborne attack and substituted a Commando seaborne assault to go in some 30 minutes before the main landings by conventional Army troops. The mission was passed to detachments from Nos. 3 and 4 Commandos together with No. 10 (Inter-Allied) Commando and a small party of United States Rangers. The newly formed Royal Marine Commando was given the task of seizing any coastal craft and barges inside Dieppe harbour and sailing them back to England. (The RM Commando subsequently became A Battalion when the formation doubled in size in October 1942 before it became No. 40 RM Commando; a title it retains to this day. Sixty years on, No. 40 RM Commando led the British assault by 3 Commando Brigade against the Al Faw peninsula during Operation Telic/Iraqi Freedom in March 2003.)

While British Empire troops from Australia, India, New Zealand and Africa were fighting side by side with the British in the Western Desert, over 200,000 Canadian soldiers were now present in Britain undergoing military training. Although keen volunteers, the Canadians were woefully inexperienced and had rarely trained at any unit size greater than battalion strength. However, the Canadian 2nd Division of some 6,000 men was chosen for the raid, together with the more experienced British troops of Nos. 3 and 4 Commandos. Originally codenamed Operation Rutter, the raid was repeatedly postponed and some troops did trial landings along the south coast as many as half a dozen times, which did little to maintain security. It was further compromised as the Canadian troops were being embarked onto landing craft when three hit-and-run Focke-Wulf FW190 fighter-bombers swept down and strafed some ships causing several casualties. The decision was taken to cancel the operation and many in the High Command breathed a sigh of relief.

On 19 June Britain suffered a further defeat when the isolated town of Tobruk surrendered to the Afrika Korps after a short siege. Having resisted Rommel's Panzers in the previous year, Churchill had great hopes that the garrison would repeat the feat of arms but to no avail and he was plunged into deep depression. Under further pressure from Roosevelt and Stalin to create a Second Front in Europe, Churchill reluctantly agreed to resurrect the Dieppe raid. Now codenamed Operation Jubilee, the plan was brutally simple, with Canadian infantry, supported by 28 new Churchill infantry tanks, attacking frontally across the beach. Further landings on the headlands overlooking the town were to be mounted to guard the flanks, while the two Commando forces were to destroy enemy gun emplacements further up the coastline codenamed 'Goebbels' and 'Hess'. In total the raiding force numbered some 6,100 men including 50 US Rangers; the first Americans to see action in the European Theatre of Operations.

In the early morning darkness of 19 August 1942, the 250-strong fleet of landing craft and warships congregated near the Isle of Wight and steamed towards occupied France. At 0347 hours, it was spotted by a German convoy and one of the German escorts fired starshells that exposed the amphibious force and alerted the

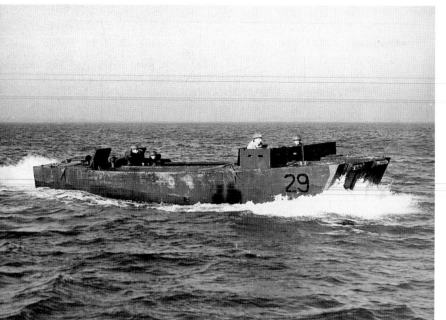

Below: The first Royal Marine Commando unit was formed in February 1942 and it fought at Dieppe during Operation Jubilee. Here, Royal Marines undergo training in their LCA. *CEC*

coastal batteries. In the ensuing mêlée, the two German escorts were sunk but the landing craft were scattered and many failed to regain formation, including some belonging to No. 3 Commando. As the remainder approached the shoreline, they were illuminated by searchlights and engaged by gunfire. The situation was already hopeless but the Canadians pressed on regardless. As their landing craft grounded on the pebble beach, the German machine guns cut loose with awful precision. The initial casualties were so terrible that the open ramps became clogged with the dead and injured and the following troops had to climb over their fallen comrades into the surf to reach the beach.

The infantry of proud Canadian regiments which had won many battle honours in the Great War were now cut down by the score; German snipers eliminated their officers, senior NCOs and signallers one by one until virtually all had been killed. At the headland of Pourville to the west of Dieppe, the Queen's Own Cameron Highlanders of Canada and the South Saskatchewans landed on the wrong side of a river from the village and guns which were their target. Every attempt to cross was met with murderous fire and within a few hours both regiments were rendered ineffective with less than 350 men being evacuated; 144 were killed and 541 captured.

On the other headland to the east of Dieppe at the village of Puys, the situation was equally dire. At 0500, the Royal Regiment of Canada had scrambled ashore into the teeth of murderous fire with its task made more difficult by the steepness of the pebble beach and the density of barbed wire entanglements. Few were able to get clear of the beach and those caught along its length were fired on from the nearby cliff tops, which remained in German hands throughout. By 0830 the regiment had suffered over 300 casualties and the survivors surrendered. In all, the Royals lost 209 men dead and 100 wounded, of whom 20 died subsequently in captivity, plus 262 prisoners of war.

With both headlands still held by the enemy, the troops on the Dieppe beaches were caught on three sides under German guns. Despite this, the main assault force of the Essex, Scottish and the Royal Hamilton Light infantry splashed ashore with remarkably few casualties following a fierce naval bombardment of the shoreline and repeated

Above: Due to a chance naval encounter with German warships in the Channel, only five of the 20 landing craft carrying No. 3 Commando to Dieppe reached their designated beaches. Eighteen men of No. 6 Troop under the command of Maj Peter Young were able to land at Yellow Beach 2 below the cliffs of Berneval and neutralise the Goebbels battery on the left flank of the Dieppe landings. Here, LCAs circle offshore as the Commando raid takes place against the gun batteries dominating the beaches of Dieppe. Accompanying the raid were 50 US Rangers in their first ever action and the French Troop of No. 10 (Inter-Allied) Commando. *WFC*

strafing by Hurricane fighters. As they reached the seawall their progress was checked. Before them was an open grass esplanade and all attempting to cross it were cut down time and again. Following the infantry came the heavy Churchill tanks of the Calgary Regiment; 27 out of a total of 29 committed landed safely but they were met by the concentrated fire of German large calibre weapons. Others were unable to negotiate the steep sloping beach as their tracks thrashed helplessly in the shingle. Even so 15 tanks managed to mount the seawall onto the esplanade but anti-tank obstacles blocking every street into the town halted any further progress. Trapped on the promenade, they fought on, their tracks dripping with blood from the dead and injured that were crushed as they manoeuvred about, until their ammunition was exhausted, whereupon the crews were forced to surrender. Only one crewman from the tanks landed at Dieppe returned to England.

For the infantry, there was no respite and the slaughter continued unabated. Some Canadians managed to break into the fortified buildings, mostly hotels, that overlooked the beaches, but the Germans remained firmly in control. Their machine guns and mortars continued to dominate every approach. By now, even the gallant Canadians were becoming disheartened. More and more began surrendering to the Germans. At sea, the force commander, Major-General J.H. Roberts, had little idea of events on the beaches as most signallers were dead and the shoreline was obscured by smoke. At 0700 he committed his reserves including the French-Canadian Mont-Royal Fusiliers and the Royal Marine Commando. Few of the Fusiliers ever made it ashore as their landing craft were blown apart by accurate gunfire; the majority were massacred. Colonel Phillipps did not demur when his Royal Marines were ordered into the attack and, as the official after-action report stated: 'With a courage terrible to see, the Marines went in to land determined, if fortune so wished, to repeat at Dieppe what their fathers had accomplished at Zeebrugge.' But as they approached the shore, Phillipps realised the hopelessness of the situation. Wearing his characteristic white gloves so that his Marines could recognise him in battle, he leapt onto the raised decking of his landing craft and signalled for the others to turn about. One by one they acknowledged his hand

Left: At Dieppe both Nos. 3 and 4 Commandos had to attack up the steep chalk cliffs through narrow defiles choked with barbed wire to reach their objectives. Nevertheless, both attacks were successful against the Goebbels and Hess gun batteries. *WFC*

Opposite, Above: During Operation Cauldron, Capt (acting Maj) Pat Porteus displayed great gallantry and was subsequently awarded the Victoria Cross for which the citation stated: 'Maj Porteus was shot at close range through the hand, the bullet passing through his palm and entering his upper arm. Undaunted, Major Porteus closed with his assailant, succeeded in disarming him and killed him with his own bayonet thereby saving the life of a British Sergeant on whom the German had turned his aim.' As the final attack of No. 4 Commando went in, Maj Porteus was in the van, as the citation described: '… the larger detachment was held up, and the officer leading this detachment was killed. Major Porteus, without hesitation and in the face of a withering fire, dashed across the open ground to take over command of this detachment. Rallying them, he led them in a charge which carried the German position at the point of a bayonet, and was seriously wounded a second time. Though shot through the thigh he continued to the final objective where he eventually collapsed from loss of blood after the last of the guns had been destroyed.' After recovering from his wounds, Porteus fought with the Small Scale Raiding Force. *IWM – HU2018*

Opposite, Below: The attack by No. 4 Commando against the Hess gun battery was codenamed Operation Cauldron. The Commandos were divided into two teams with 88 men in Group 1 under Lt-Col the Lord Lovat and 164 in Group 2 under Maj Derek Mills-Roberts. While the latter engaged the battery with fire, Group 1 outflanked the position and took it from the rear in a well co-ordinated manoeuvre. The six 155mm howitzers of Hess battery were destroyed by demolition charges. *WFC*

signals, but the German gunners had also seen them. Phillipps fell mortally wounded when hit by machine-gun fire but he had saved most his men from almost certain death. Despite his sacrifice some others continued onwards to the carnage of White Beach.

The German Commander-in-Chief in France, Field Marshal Gerd von Rundstedt, had also decided to commit his reserves. He called forward two powerful divisions, the 1st SS Panzer 'Leibstandarte Adolf Hitler' and 10th Panzer, which were recuperating nearby after service on the Eastern Front. As they advanced on the trapped Canadians in Dieppe, General Roberts and the amphibious force commander, Captain John Hughes-Hallett, RN, decided on withdrawal. The signal: 'Vanquish', meaning evacuation, was sent to the embattled troops. Under heavy fire, the Royal Navy was only able to recover some 300 survivors from the beaches of Dieppe. At Pourville and Puys, others were able to escape but the casualties were high.

Only the Commando attacks on the gun emplacements of Hess and Goebbels had been in the least successful. At Varengeville-sur-Mer, No. 4 Commando under the command of Lt-Col the Lord Lovat destroyed the Hess Battery of six 150mm guns and killed approximately 150 Germans at a cost of 12 dead and 20 wounded. On the other flank, the assault by No. 3 Commando was struck with disaster at the outset when six of its landing craft, including the one carrying its commanding officer, Lt-Col Durnford-Slater, were lost in the initial encounter with the German convoy in the Channel. A much depleted force of just 19 Commandos under the command of Major Peter Young, one of the most decorated Commando soldiers of the war, landed on a fire-swept beach and climbed the cliffs beneath the Goebbels Battery. Under constant fire, the Commandos advanced on the position killing its crew but the guns remained intact. Short of ammunition, Major Young withdrew his men to the beach from where they were evacuated.

The raid on Dieppe had been a disaster. The losses were grievous. In less than 12 hours, the Army sustained 3,367 casualties, mainly Canadian, with 1,027 dead and

Below: Under the devastating fire of German coastal artillery, the landing craft carrying Canadian troops approach the beaches of Dieppe where the attackers were cut down by the score. Whereas the overall Allied losses during the Dieppe raid were approximately 60 per cent, the Commandos suffered a casualty rate of 23 per cent and the 50 men of 1st US Ranger Battalion 26 per cent. *Canadian National Archives*

2,340 captured. Among the dead was the first American soldier to be killed in action in Europe, Lieutenant Edwin Lousalot of the 1st US Rangers. The Canadians lost more prisoners of war in one day than they did in the whole of the campaign in North-West Europe in 1944–45. The Royal Navy lost one destroyer and numerous landing craft as well as 550 casualties; the Royal Air Force lost 106 aircraft and 53 aircrew. All the tanks and equipment that had been landed were abandoned. German losses were approximately 600 men. At 1740 Field Marshal Rundstedt noted in his war diary, 'No armed Englishman remains on the Continent', ignoring the fact that the majority of the raiders had been Canadian.

Many lessons were learned on that day but the price had been awfully high. On the one hand Admiral Mountbatten claimed: 'The Duke of Wellington said the battle of Waterloo was won on the playing fields of Eton. I say that the battle of Normandy was won on the beaches of Dieppe. For every man that died at Dieppe ten would live on D-Day.' One of the Royal Marines that did land at Dieppe and saw the carnage for himself described the battle as: 'the biggest cock-up since the Somme'. His opinion is arguably nearer the truth but nothing should detract from the courage and sacrifice of the Canadian Army. Writing after the war, Churchill stated: 'Dieppe occupies a place of its own in the story of war and the grim casualty figures must not class it as a failure... honour to the brave that fell. Their sacrifice was not in vain.' Twenty-two months later, the Allies returned to France – Americans, British and Canadians as well as Commandos just like at Dieppe – but this time they attacked over the open beaches of Normandy and brought their own harbours with them – an idea conceived by Capt Hughes-Hallett as he sailed back to England from the Dieppe disaster.

Above: A graphic drawing by Cpl Brian Mullen depicts the withdrawal of No. 4 Commando after the successful attack on Hess battery. With the LCAs under fire from German fighter planes, No. 18 smoke generators create a smokescreen to mask the withdrawal. Of the 252 men of No. 4 Commando in Operation Cauldron, 12 were killed, 20 wounded and 13 missing in action. *CMC*

1943 COMMANDO ORDER OF BATTLE

Each Commando had a complement of 460 all ranks. The order of battle was:

HQ and Sig Troop
5 x Troops, each of 2 x Sections (HQ of three; 2 x subsections of 14 men)
1 x Heavy Weapon Troop (with 1 x Med MG Section and 1 x 3-inch mortar Section)

KOMMANDOBEFEHL

Despite the failure of Operation Jubilee, the Germans felt obliged to bolster their defences in Western Europe. They began the construction of massive coastal fortifications to create the 'Atlantic Wall' of *Festung Europa*. Weapons and manpower were diverted from the fighting fronts so the objective of relieving the pressure on the Russians was partially achieved thanks to the raid on Dieppe. Furthermore, the Commando raids were proving extremely irksome to the German High Command and Hitler in particular. Among the detritus the Germans discovered on the beaches of Dieppe were the Battle Orders of the 6 Brigade commander that contained the chilling phrase: 'Tie the hands of all POWs'; this was notionally to stop prisoners from destroying sensitive documents. This directive was in direct contravention of the Geneva Conventions. In addition, the Germans found the bodies of 12 of their soldiers who had been bound and trussed.

Hitler was outraged. He was further incensed following an attack by the Small Scale Raiding Force (SSRF) and men of No. 12 Commando on the night of 3/4 October against the island of Sark. A German command post in the Dixcart Hotel was ransacked and five Germans taken as POWs. Their hands were tied and they were led to the beach for transport to England but four of them were killed in unexplained circumstances and their bodies left behind. Hitler then issued his infamous *Kommandobefehl* or 'Commando Order' which went as follows.

'For some time now our enemies have been using methods in their prosecution of the war which are outside the agreements of the Geneva Convention. Especially brutal and vicious are the members of the so-called Commandos, which have been recruited, as has been ascertained to a certain extent, even from released criminals in enemy countries. Captured orders show that they have not only been instructed to tie up prisoners, but also to kill them should they become a burden to them. At last orders have been found in which the killing of prisoners is demanded.

For this reason... Germany will in future use the same methods against these sabotage groups of the British, that is they will be ruthlessly exterminated wherever German troops may find them.

I therefore order: that from now on all enemy troops who are met by German troops while on so-called Commando raids, even if they are soldiers in uniform, are to be destroyed to the last man, either in battle or while fleeing.

This order does not affect the treatment of enemy soldiers taken prisoner during normal battle actions (major attack, major seaborne or airborne landings). It also does not affect prisoners taken at sea or flyers who saved themselves by parachute and were taken prisoner.

I shall have all commanders and officers who do not comply with this order court-martialled.'

However, Gen Jodl, one of Hitler's principal staff officers, realising this order was tantamount to a war crime, appended a note saying: 'This order is intended for senior commanders only and is on no account to fall into enemy hands.' The first victims of the notorious *Kommandobefehl* were not long in coming.

Above: Commando snipers were issued with a camouflaged version of the windproof smock and trousers and a customised version of the No. 4 rifle.

Left: The Commandos had a higher complement of snipers than standard units and they were employed extensively to harass the enemy in both offensive and defensive operations. This sniper adopts a heroic pose with his head covered with a camouflage face veil. He is wearing a paratrooper's Denison smock and is armed with a Rifle No. 4 Mark 1* (T), No. 36 grenades and a Webley revolver. *CEC*

Right: Operation 'Frankton'.

SPECIAL SERVICE GROUP ORDER OF BATTLE 1944–45

1 Special Service Brigade
CO: Brig the Lord Lovat
No. 3 Cdo
No. 4 Cdo
No. 6 Cdo
No. 45 RM Cdo
(UK)

2 Special Service Brigade
CO: Brig Jack Churchill
No. 2 Cdo
No. 9 Cdo
No. 40 RM Cdo
No. 43 RM Cdo
(Italy)

3 Special Service Brigade
CO: Brig D. I. Nonweiler
No. 1 Cdo
No. 5 Cdo
No. 42 RM Cdo
No. 44 RM Cdo
(India)

4 Special Service Brigade
CO: Brig B. W. Leicester
No. 10 Cdo
No. 41 RM Cdo
No. 46 RM Cdo
No. 47 RM Cdo
(UK)

Special Boat Unit
RM Engineer Cdo

Holding Commando
Basic Training Centre
Mountain Warfare Centre
Group 2nd Echelon

OPERATION FRANKTON – THE COCKLESHELL HEROES

While the scale of Commando operations had grown during 1942, there were also several classic hit-and-run attacks undertaken by small bands of raiders; a plethora of new and ever more specialised Special Forces units were being created such as the SSRF and the COPP. One of these units, which was to win lasting fame, went under the splendid euphemistic designation of the Royal Marine Boom Patrol Detachment, soon to be known as the Cockleshell Heroes from the type of canoe they used for their sabotage missions. The most famous of these was against shipping in the French port of Bordeaux. The Germans had occupied the city in June 1940 and it had become an important conduit for raw materials from around the world that were vital to the Nazi war effort. Ships that formerly had to run the British blockade to reach ports in Germany were now unloaded in well-protected French harbours and their cargoes transported to Germany by the safer methods of road or rail. In particular, vital supplies of rubber, oil, tin and other scarce metals were arriving at ports in southwest France in such significant quantities that the British Minister for Economic Warfare, Lord Selbourne, wrote to the Prime Minister, Winston Churchill, suggesting the flow be stemmed. During the previous 12 months over 25,000 tons of rubber had been landed in France: rubber was one of the few items that German industry had been unable to create satisfactorily in ersatz form at an economical rate.

Bombing of these ports by the Royal Air Force was deemed to be too inaccurate and would have resulted in unacceptable French civilian casualties. Bombardment from the Bay of Biscay by the Royal Navy was an option. Such a means had been shown to be effective in the destruction of the French fleet at Mers el Kebir in Algeria on 3 July 1940. However, it was too risky to operate off the French coast as capital ships would be vulnerable to air attack from land-based aircraft as had been proved by the sinking of the battleship *Prince of Wales* and the battlecruiser *Repulse* by the Japanese on 10 December 1941. An assessment by the British had estimated that an amphibious force of some two divisions would be necessary to mount an attack on similar lines to the successful raid on the French port of St Nazaire. An operation on such a scale was not possible at this stage of the war as most British resources were being employed in North Africa against Rommel's Afrika Korps and for home defence. Additionally, an attack on a defended port was a dangerous and costly undertaking, as was be shown at Dieppe in August 1942.

The problem was passed to the Combined Operations staff to see if there was an unconventional means for the destruction of the German blockade-runners. Mindful of the success of Italian human-torpedo attacks against British ships in Alexandria in Egypt in December 1941, consideration was given to midget submarines but no British equivalent was as yet operational. There was, however, no shortage of ideas and a suggestion was made by Major H.G. Hasler for a raiding party to be formed using canoes, a method he had used to insert and extract agents from Norway earlier in the war. Captain T.A. Hussey, RN, pursued the idea and a unit called the Royal Marines Harbour Patrol Detachment was created to test the concept. 'Blondie' Hasler, as he was known, was placed in command and training began at Southsea with volunteers drawn from the Royal Marines' Small Arms School at Gosport. Rejecting the Folboat as used by the Special Boat Squadron, he approached the versatile marine designer Fred Goatley to build a suitable craft for his raiders. Goatley produced a two-man canoe capable of carrying 600 pounds which could be collapsed for easier stowage on board submarines. Known as the Cockle Mark 2, it had a flat bottom to allow it to be towed across beaches or land without damage. With its low profile in the water, it was undetectable by radar. It was propelled by its crew using double-bladed paddles that were readily converted into a single-bladed type for covert approaches to a target. Amongst the stores carried, the

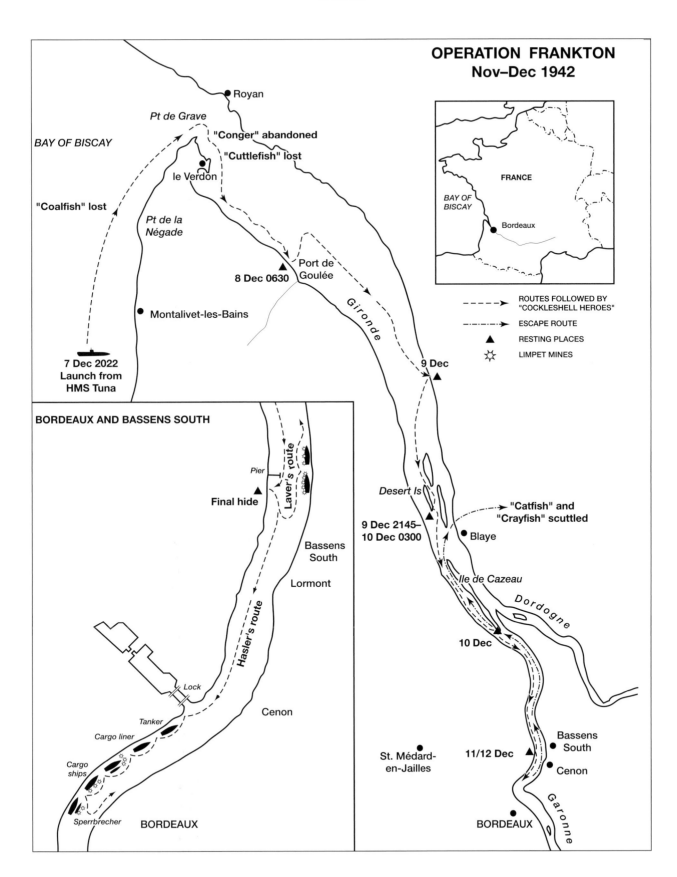

OPERATION FRANKTON
Nov–Dec 1942

Royan

Pt de Grave

BAY OF BISCAY

"Conger" abandoned

"Cuttlefish" lost

le Verdon

"Coalfish" lost

Pt de la Négade

▲ 8 Dec 0630

Port de Goulée

● Montalivet-les-Bains

Gironde

7 Dec 2022 Launch from HMS Tuna

FRANCE

BAY OF BISCAY

● Bordeaux

- - - → ROUTES FOLLOWED BY "COCKLESHELL HEROES"

-·-·-→ ESCAPE ROUTE

▲ RESTING PLACES

☆ LIMPET MINES

9 Dec ▲

Desert Is

9 Dec 2145– 10 Dec 0300 ▲

● Blaye

"Catfish" and "Crayfish" scuttled

Ile de Cazeau

10 Dec ▲

Dordogne

BORDEAUX AND BASSENS SOUTH

Pier

Final hide ▲

Laver's route

Bassens South

Lormont

Hasler's route

Lock

Tanker

Cargo liner

Cargo ships

☆
☆
☆

Sperrbrecher

BORDEAUX

Cenon

● St. Médard- en-Jailles

11/12 Dec ▲

Bassens ● South

● Cenon

BORDEAUX ●

Garonne

Above: Commandos of 101 Troop disembark from their Folboat during an exercise in Scotland in 1941. Originally part of No. 6 Commando, 101 Troop was the first independent unit of canoeists to be formed in November 1941 and subsequently became the Special Boat Section. *IWM – H14594*

most important were limpet mines to be attached by magnets to the target vessels as far below the waterline as possible by using a special rod. A timing device allowed the raiders to escape to a safe distance before they exploded.

As training proceeded, the name of the unit was changed to the Royal Marine Boom Patrol Detachment to disguise the nature of where it might operate. Further specialised equipment was designed to allow the fully stowed canoes and their crews to be launched from a submarine for maximum speed and safety. By the late autumn of 1942 'Blondie' Hasler had decided his team was ready for action. Preparations were made for Operation Frankton, an attack on the blockade-runners unloading in the French port of Bordeaux, although the actual target remained a secret to the Marines. The plan entailed transporting six cockles and their crews by submarine to the mouth of the Gironde River from where the Royal Marines were to paddle the 100 kilometres to Bordeaux by night while sheltering on the riverbanks by day. On 1 December 1942 'Blondie' Hasler and his team were embarked aboard the submarine HMS *Tuna*. Only then was the nature of the target revealed to them. The passage through the Bay of Biscay was stormy and many of the men suffered from severe seasickness in the claustrophobic confines of the submarine. The raiders were eventually disembarked using the special crane and sling attached to the deck gun during the evening of Monday 7 December. Despite calm seas, one of the cockles was damaged irreparably when its hull was ripped open by a hatch cover; the crew had to remain with the submarine.

The five surviving canoes and their crews began their approach to the French coastline some 15 kilometres away. All the canoes were named after fish, including *Catfish*, *Coalfish*, *Conger*, *Crayfish* and *Cuttlefish*. Maj Hasler and his crewman, Marine Bill Sparks, led the team in his canoe, *Catfish*. As they neared the coast, they encountered a violent tide race and *Coalfish* was lost in the teeming waters together with its crew. The two marines managed to swim ashore but were promptly captured, which alerted the Germans to the likelihood of an attack despite the protestations of the marines that they had fallen from a warship out at sea. Unbeknown to Hasler, German radar had spotted the submarine, *Tuna*, when it surfaced and patrol craft of the 8th Zerstörer Flotilla began to search the river mouth. No sooner had the raiders cleared this disaster than they came across another tide race and *Conger* capsized. Although clinging to Hasler's *Catfish* saved the crew, the cockle was lost and the raiders were now down to only three canoes and their precious limpet mines after only two hours in the water and with many miles still to go to Bordeaux. In the freezing water, Hasler paddled for the shoreline where he reluctantly abandoned Cpl Sheard and Marine Moffat to their fate. They too were captured by the Germans and shot as saboteurs following Hitler's orders in the wake of the Dieppe raid that all captured commandos were to be executed rather than being treated as prisoners of war.

Delayed by these misfortunes, the remaining cockles next encountered a line of three German patrol boats sweeping the surface of the river with searchlights. By bending flat over the tops of their canoes, they managed to slip by but *Cuttlefish* with Lt J. Mackinnon and Marine Conway became separated from the main party and had to proceed alone. The turning of the tide hampered further progress. After paddling some 30 kilometres, the Marines were by now cold and exhausted. At 0630, the crews of *Catfish* and *Crayfish* came ashore at a place known as Pointe aux Oiseaux where the canoes were camouflaged and the Marines tried to sleep. As dawn broke, some French fishermen approached their position. Speaking in fluent French, Hasler persuaded them not to betray the raiding party. For the rest of the day, the Marines tried to catch some sleep under their camouflage nets as Fieseler Storch reconnaissance aircraft swept backwards and forwards along the riverbanks.

As night fell, Hasler and his three remaining companions silently slid into the channel and made good progress through the night with the help of the incoming tide and the line of buoys marking the waterway. At the Porte de Calonge opposite the vineyards of Pauillac, the raiding party found a new hiding place that again was compromised by a French man walking his dog. Once more Hasler tried to secure his silence but without any confidence and he decided to risk paddling during the early evening of 9 December just as a German patrol boat was heading directly towards their position. Having avoided this danger they paddled to their next hiding place on the Île de Cazeau where the Gironde divides into the Rivers Garonne and Dordogne. Unbeknownst to either party, the crew of *Cuttlefish*, Mackinnon and Conway, were hiding only a few hundred metres away on the same island. All the Marines were by now physically tired having paddled some 80 kilometres in three nights.

On the night of 10/11 December the weather favoured the raiders with a moderate breeze and low scudding clouds, giving a steady drizzle to mask their progress. Unfortunately, *Cuttlefish* was sunk at this time after striking an underwater obstacle. After hiding for some time with a sympathetic French couple in a village southeast of Bordeaux, Mackinnon and Conway were captured while attempting to enter Vichy France. The two remaining crews were able to arrive undetected at their final hiding place in some reed beds close to the vineyards of St Julien where they were able to sleep undisturbed throughout the day before the attack on Bordeaux. During the evening, the crews primed their limpet mines and prepared escape kits. After a final briefing the four men in their flimsy cockles set off for the docks of Bordeaux. Despite being bathed in light, Hasler and Sparks were able to approach undetected while Laver and Mills made for the eastern docks on the other side of the river. There the crew of *Crayfish* attached their limpet mines to the German merchantmen *Alabama* and *Portland*.

Meanwhile, the crew of *Catfish* slipped into the harbour basin and selected their first target, the 7,800-ton blockade-runner *Tannenfels*, which had only just arrived from Japan. Three limpet mines with eight-hour delays were fastened below her waterline next to the engine room. Hasler and Sparks then paddled upriver and attached two more to a minesweeper. They then approached a large freighter moored next to a tanker. To cover their activities, Hasler directed his canoe between the two vessels and had begun to attach his

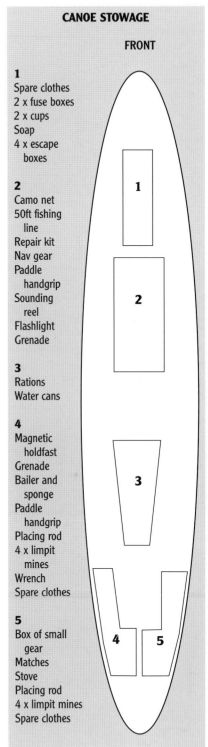

CANOE STOWAGE

FRONT

1
Spare clothes
2 x fuse boxes
2 x cups
Soap
4 x escape
  boxes

2
Camo net
50ft fishing
  line
Repair kit
Nav gear
Paddle
  handgrip
Sounding
  reel
Flashlight
Grenade

3
Rations
Water cans

4
Magnetic
  holdfast
Grenade
Bailer and
  sponge
Paddle
  handgrip
Placing rod
4 x limpit
  mines
Wrench
Spare clothes

5
Box of small
  gear
Matches
Stove
Placing rod
4 x limpit mines
Spare clothes

Above right: German prisoners are disembarked from a Landing Craft Personnel following a raid conducted by No. 2 Commando which was part of Force 133. This unit conducted offensive operations along the Dalmatian Coast from a base on the island of Vis in the Adriatic Sea to assist Tito's partisans in Yugoslavia. *CMC*

Below right: Wearing their Assault Life Jackets, the men of P Troop of 41 Royal Marine Commando are inspected on board their landing ship just prior to Operation Husky, the invasion of Sicily in July 1943. *CMC*

Below: Hill 170 – Capt Owen of 44 RM Commando recalled: 'As we advanced up Hill 170, along jungle covered features, I felt something was building up. We were hot and tired and regrettably many of us did not dig in as well as we should have done. Suddenly all hell let loose. Shells were bursting everywhere. I remember seeing a Marine hit in the pouch where he had carried a phosphorous grenade – terrible. We lost 60 men. The next day when we were burying them we were attacked again.' Over the next ten days, the Japanese made repeated fanatical attacks against Hill 170, losing over 2,000 casualties. For his heroism during the battle, Lt George Knowland was posthumously awarded the Victoria Cross, the last Commando VC of the war. *CMC*

remaining charges to the 8,600-ton *Dresden* when one of its crewmen leant over the side of the ship and shone a torch on the raiders below. After what seemed an eternity he moved on without realising the threat. Having successfully fixed the limpet mines, they paddled into the middle of the current and let it take the *Catfish* downriver back to the Île de Cazeau where they were reunited with the crew of *Crayfish*, Laver and Mills.

After sinking the cockles that had brought them so far, the two crews split up and attempted to escape from the Bordeaux area in the early hours of 12 December. As they walked northwards, their delayed action charges exploded, causing considerable damage and dismay amongst the German naval command at the ease with which the defences of Bordeaux had been penetrated by such a small band of determined raiders. Once again the German defences were bolstered with additional troops as well as artillery weapons and other military paraphernalia, causing a further drain in strength from the fighting fronts.

With no knowledge of French, Laver and Mills were unable to seek help from the local populace and on the third day they were captured. Despite still being in uniform, they were summarily shot following Hitler's notorious *Kommandobefehl*. Sheard and Moffat had drowned at the mouth of the Gironde; the latter's body finally came ashore at Brest. Wallace and Ewart had already been killed even as the limpet mines were being emplaced. Mackinnon and Conway were taken to Gestapo Headquarters in Paris where they were tortured before being executed. Only Hasler and Sparks survived and, after a harrowing trip through France and Spain, they eventually returned via Gibraltar to England some five months later. Major 'Blondie' Hasler was awarded the Distinguished Service Order and Marine Bill Sparks the Distinguished Service Cross. The Germans described Operation Frankton as the greatest Commando raid of the war.

SPEARHEAD OF INVASION

1942 was the defining year for the Commandos and for the Allied war effort in general. The Commandos had enjoyed great successes in operations large and small, from St Nazaire to Bordeaux, albeit at a considerable cost in casualties. These Commando raids had also achieved the objective of siphoning off German manpower and matériel from the Eastern Front to defend the coastlines of occupied Europe from the Arctic Circle to the Mediterranean. They were also a considerable boost for civilian morale on the Home Front at a time when there was no other means to strike back at the enemy on the Continent. But the British and Americans had now begun a strategic bombing offensive against Germany that was to cost the Nazis dear. The year had also seen the first major defeats for the Wehrmacht at the battles of El Alamein and Stalingrad. From now on, despite several reverses, the Allies went from victory to victory on every front.

It was in part to capitalise on the victory at the battle of El Alamein that the Commandos were to find a new role. In November 1942 Nos. 1 and 6 Commandos, as well as several other specialised Combined Operations units (for example No. 30 Commando), took part in amphibious landings in Algeria. Codenamed Operation Torch, American and British forces invaded the Vichy French possession to take the Germans in Tunisia from behind in a pincer with the British Eighth Army advancing from Libya in the east. Initially, the Commandos landed prior to the main assault to capture vital features and gun emplacements, but were soon committed as line infantry during the battles for Tunisia. At Steamroller Farm and the Kasserine Pass, the Commandos suffered severe casualties due in part to their lack of heavy support weapons. By April 1943 the two Commandos were ground down from an initial strength of 1,000 to just 150 men and they were

Above right: In what Brig Peter Young called ' a most hazardous procession of boats up the Chaung', 3 Commando Brigade is transported up the Daingbon Chaung in LCAs manned by sailors of the Indian Navy on 22 January 1945 to land deep behind Japanese lines to cut off their retreat down the Arakan. The units deployed were Nos. 1 and 5 Commandos together with Nos. 42 and 44 RM Commandos. *CMC*

Below right: Royal Marines struggle ashore through appalling terrain towards Kangaw; in the words of Brig Peter Young: 'There was no road. The landing was through mangrove; the paddy for about ¾ mile, leading to 170 [Hill 170 was the key objective] was swamped by the spring tides. Even the bunds didn't make proper footpaths being broken in many places. No tanks could be got ashore – or guns – the first few days but we had air support…' *CMC*

returned to Britain for refitting. It was time for a complete review of the operational role of the Commandos.

Although Commando raids continued across the Mediterranean and in the Far East, they were largely discontinued in northern Europe for fear of reprisals against the local populace. Intelligence gathering and specific sabotage missions were now the order of the day and these were the province of the SOE. During 1943 the Commandos lost two of their greatest advocates with the departure of Lord Mountbatten in August to take up a new post as commander of the allied forces in Southeast Asia (Maj-Gen Robert Laycock replaced him). As the war situation stabilised, Prime Minister Churchill lost his close personal interest in the Commandos, compounded by his disappointment in Combined Operations following the Dieppe disaster. Even so, the Special Service Brigade was greatly enlarged during the summer of 1943 to incorporate the newly formed Royal Marine Commandos. In November 1943 a new formation, the Special Service Group, was created with its own Headquarters under the command of Maj-Gen Robert Sturges RM (see box on page 48). It comprised four Special Service Brigades, with two based in Britain and one each in Italy and India. Each brigade now contained both Army and Royal Marine Commandos. Their primary role was as amphibious assault troops to spearhead the invasions of Nazi-occupied Europe.

Following the collapse of the Axis forces in North Africa in May 1943, the Allies launched Operation Husky on 10 July with landings on Sicily. Nos. 2 and 3 Commandos as well as 40 and 41 RM Commandos were tasked with guarding the flanks of the main landings and securing key objectives. There followed Operation Avalanche in September with the first landings on mainland Europe at Salerno in southern Italy. These operations came under the aegis of 2 Special Service Brigade. Thereafter, it organised Commando raids and landings on the Adriatic coast of Italy and in Albania and Yugoslavia. Meanwhile, Commando units fought throughout the campaign in Italy, including in the final decisive battle of Lake Comacchio where the Commandos gained one of their greatest battle honours and the Royal Marines their only Victoria Cross of World War II when Cpl Tom Hunter led a determined assault on an enemy position at the cost of his own life just days before the war in Europe ended.

When Mountbatten arrived in the Far East, he requested the deployment of one of the newly formed Special Service Brigades to his Southeast Asia Command. In late 1943 elements of 3 Special Service Brigade set sail for the Far East, arriving in India on 19 December. The brigade was based at Kedgaon near Poona. Its troops first saw action in Operation Screwdriver in March 1944 during the Arakan campaign in Burma. This campaign was to dominate 3 SS Brigade operations throughout the year.

In December 1944 the formation was redesignated 3 Commando Brigade under the command of Brig Peter Young. With the Japanese now in full retreat, the brigade was tasked with cutting their withdrawal route by amphibious landings behind enemy lines. On 22 January 1945, the brigade landed from assault craft with No. 1 Commando followed by No. 5 Commando and 42 RM Commando with 44 RM Commando in reserve. They occupied the dominating hill features around Kangaw and withstood repeated ferocious assaults by the retreating Japanese for the next 36 hours. With no tanks and few artillery guns in support, the Commandos resorted to hand-to-hand combat with their fighting knives. All the Commandos were heavily engaged and suffered serious casualties but the Japanese counterattacks were broken. In a Special Order of the Day, the corps commander, Lt-Gen Philip Christison, wrote: 'The battle of Kangaw has been the decisive battle of the whole Arakan campaign.' 3 Commando Brigade was withdrawn for refitting in preparation for Operation Zipper – the proposed invasion of Malaya – but the war ended before it could be implemented.

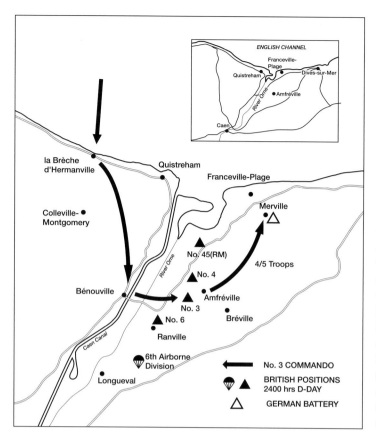

D-DAY

By the time the Special Service Group was formed in November 1943, plans for the invasion of Europe were well advanced. Operation Overlord was to be the largest seaborne assault in history and the Commandos were to be in the vanguard. 1 and 4 Special Service Brigades were tasked with seizing the flanks of the British and Canadian landing beaches of Gold, Juno and Sword in Normandy on D-Day. On 6 June 1944, No. 3 Commando landed at la Breche d'Hermanville on Sword Beach with the critical mission of thrusting inland to link up with the men of 6th Airborne Division who had captured the vital bridges over the Caen Canal and Orne River the night before. By the end of the day the task was achieved against fierce resistance, which continued over the coming weeks. Together with No. 3 Commando, Nos. 4 and 6 Commandos as well as 45 RM Commando were among the first troops to land on D-Day followed shortly afterwards by Brig Lord Lovat and his HQ of 1 Special Service Brigade. The Royal Marines were heavily involved in the initial assault with some 17,500 Marines manning the ships and landing craft at sea while the men of 41, 45, 47 and 48 RM Commandos landed on D-Day and 46 RM Commando on D-Day+1. Royal Marines also manned Centaur

tanks in an Armoured Support Group of two regiments that provided close fire support during the initial landings.

All these Commando units took part in the fierce fighting of the hedgerows in Normandy and on to the Seine River. After 83 days of combat, 1 SS Brigade was withdrawn to Britain for refitting. Between D-Day and 30 September, both SS Brigades suffered over 50 per cent casualties. Operations continued through France, Belgium and Holland and in October 4 SS Brigade began amphibious training in Buffalo LVTs (Landing Vehicles Tracked) and Weasel amphibians for operations to open the port of Antwerp. On 1 November Nos. 41, 47 and 48 RM Commandos with No. 4 Commando and four troops of No. 10 (Inter-Allied) Commando in support, landed at Westkapelle on the tip of Walcheren in the

Scheldt estuary. Manned by Royal Marines, the support craft drew the fire of the German shore batteries from the assault craft and LVTs and suffered heavy casualties accordingly. Fierce fighting continued and the Commandos suffered over 500 casualties before the Allies opened the port of Antwerp at the end of November.

On 6 December 1944 the Special Service Group was redesignated the Commando Group while the SS Brigades became Commando brigades. During the winter of 1944/45, the Commandos spent most of the time in defensive posture around Antwerp and its environs and along the Maas River as the German Ardennes Offensive battered its way towards the port. On 23 January 1945 No. 45 RM Commando was involved in a bitter battle at Montforterbeek where L/Cpl Harden, RAMC, one of the unit's medical orderlies, won the Victoria Cross. By now the British Army was chronically short of infantry and two Royal Marine infantry brigades, 116 and 117, were formed from landing craft crews that were now surplus to requirements. 116 Brigade crossed the Maas River into Germany in February but 117 Brigade did not arrive until after VE Day. In March 1 Commando Brigade spearheaded the assault into Germany with the crossing of the Rhine at Wesel with No. 46 RM Commando in the van. In April 1 Commando Brigade came under the tactical command of 6th Airborne Division and then 11th Armoured Division for the opposed crossing of the Wesel River during Operation Plunder. On the night of 10/11 April No. 3 Commando seized a railway bridge over the Aller River against fierce resistance. By 19 April 1 Commando Brigade had reached Lüneberg where it left 11th Armoured Division and came under 15th Scottish Division for what was to be its last operation of the war. No. 6 Commando followed by No. 46 RM Commando spearheaded the crossing of the Elbe River in Buffalo LVTs at Lauenburg. During this time 4 Commando Brigade remained in Holland where it mounted raids and patrols to mop up pockets of German resistance and the various garrisons that had been isolated by the Allied advance.

Since D-Day, one of the Commandos' most secretive units had accompanied the front-line troops as they advanced across northwest Europe into Germany. No. 30 Commando, subsequently designated No. 30 Assault Unit, was tasked with gathering sensitive and important intelligence and documents, particularly plans and examples of new technology

Above: Army Commandos link up with the paratroopers of 6th Airborne Division after their capture of the vital bridges over the Caen Canal and Orne River on the eve of D-Day. The Commando on the right has the classic Bergen rucksack and toggle rope and is armed with a Colt automatic pistol while the Commando on the left is wearing a Battle Jerkin and a bandolier of ammunition clips for his No. 4 rifle. The Green Berets distinguish the Commandos from the helmeted paratroopers. *CMC*

Above left: Securing the Orne: No. 3 Commando's advance to Pegasus Bridge (taken by 6th Airborne on the night of 5/6 June) and the Merville Battery.

Below left: D-Day 6 June 1944 – the HQ of 1 Special Service Brigade wades ashore on Sword Beach at Ouistreham; the tall figure in the centre of the photograph wielding a stick is Brig Lord Lovat, the commander of 1 SS Brigade, with on the right in the foreground his piper, Cpl Bill Millin, who went ashore with just his bagpipes and an F-S fighting knife while wearing a kilt that his father had worn in the Great War. *IWM – B5103*

weapons. No. 30 Assault Unit was often at the forefront of the advance and was among the first Allied troops into important towns and cities including Emden, Cologne, Kiel and Bremen, where 16 advanced Type XXI U-boats in various stages of construction at the Deschimag shipyard were captured by a team led by Lt-Cdr Patrick Dalzel-Job, RNVR. In the final months of the war and thereafter, the unit gathered a vast haul of technical intelligence as well as taking important technicians and scientists into custody.

After VE Day the Commando brigades were committed to occupation duties in Germany before returning to Britain where they were disbanded in 1946 following a decision by the Chiefs of Staff on 27 September 1945 to dispense with Army Commandos and pass responsibility for amphibious warfare to the Corps of Royal Marines. The Chief of Combined Operations, Maj-Gen Robert Laycock, had the unhappy task of making the announcement to his troops of 1 Commando Brigade:

> 'Today there is no battle in store for you… and it is with a feeling of very deep regret that it has fallen to my lot to tell you – the Commandos, who have fought with such distinction in Norway and the islands in the North, in France, in Belgium, in Holland and in Germany, in Africa and in Egypt, in Crete and in Syria, in Sicily and in Italy, on the shores and in the islands of the Adriatic, and on the beaches and in the jungles of the Arakan and of Burma – it is, I repeat, with deep regret that I must tell you today that you are to be disbanded.'

Laycock then went on to say that the famous Green Beret of the Army Commandos would die with them. After intervention from Lord Mountbatten, this at least was rescinded and the Royal Marines wear it to this day.

Below: In the dying days of the Nazi regime, No. 30 Assault Unit was at the van of the British XXX Corps and its Humber scout cars were among the first Allied troops into the city of Bremen and took the surrender of the Burgomeister on 26 April 1945. Here, No. 30 AU scout cars of B Troop rest outside the Bremen Rathaus or City Hall during the surrender negotiations. *CMC*

Left: After years of Nazi occupation, French citizens celebrate their liberation at the hands of these French members of No. 4 Commando. Besides the Commando shoulder flash and Combined Operations badge, these Commandos display the cap badge of French naval infantry. *IWM – B5279*

Below: Operation Infatuate was spearheaded by Nos. 41, 47 and 48 RM Commandos of 4 SS Brigade supported by No. 4 Commando and four troops from No. 10 (IA) Commando. After training in the specialised AFVs of the 79th Armoured Division, the Royal Marines landed on the water-logged island of Walcheren in Buffalo and Weasel amphibious tracked vehicles. These are shown here aboard a landing ship on the approach to the island, with Buffalo LVTs on the right and Weasels on the left. *CMC*

Right: No. 30 Commando was a specialised unit used to gather military and technical intelligence at the forefront of the Allied advance. By D-Day, it was known as No. 30 Assault Unit and its Royal Navy contingent was commanded by Lt-Cdr Patrick Dalzel-Job, RNVR, shown here in April 1945 wearing the relatively rare Officers Field Boots and armed with an F-S Commando dagger strapped to his thigh and over his shoulder an M1A1 Carbine with folding stock, as issued to US paratroopers. *CMC*

Below: Commando equipped with the icon of the Commandos – the Chicago piano – the Thompson submachine gun.

COMMANDO UNITS

No. 1 Commando
The former A Special Service Company became No. 1 Commando on 5 March 1941. It subsequently supplied personnel for the airborne forces. After some cross-Channel raids, it took part in the Operation Torch landings in North Africa and then deployed to the Far East in 1943. At the end of the war, it amalgamated with No. 5 Commando and was disbanded in 1946.

No. 2 Commando
Formed in March 1941, No. 2 Commando was composed of men from 34 different regiments and corps. It was reformed after its original personnel transferred to the airborne forces and then fought on the St Nazaire raid where it was wiped out. Reformed again it deployed to the Mediterranean where it fought in Sicily, Italy and Yugoslavia. No. 2 Commando was disbanded in 1946.

No. 3 Commando
Formed in June 1940, No. 3 Commando became the senior Commando unit after Nos. 1 and 2 became airborne troops. It took part in the first major raids on the Lofoten Islands, Vaagsø and Dieppe. During 1943 No. 3 Commando fought in Sicily and Italy before returning to Britain. No. 3 Commando landed in Normandy on D-Day to link up with the airborne forces. It fought at the Rhine Crossing and the advance to the Elbe. No. 3 Commando was disbanded in 1946.

No. 4 Commando
Formed in June 1940, No. 4 Commando comprised volunteers from 85 different units. It achieved fame by destroying gun batteries before the Dieppe raid. It landed in Normandy on D-Day and later fought at Walcheren. No. 4 Commando was disbanded in January 1947.

No. 5 Commando
Formed in June 1940, No. 5 Commando undertook cross-Channel raids before joining Operation Ironclad and the invasion of Madagascar in 1942. It then deployed to Burma and was amalgamated with No. 1 Commando before No. 5 Commando was disbanded in January 1947.

No. 6 Commando
Formed in the summer of 1940, No. 6 Commando personnel participated in various raids but first fought as an entity during the landings in Algeria in November 1942 – alongside US forces and using some of their equipment such as helmets and Garand rifles. It returned to Britain for the Normandy landings and subsequently fought across North-West Europe to the River Elbe. It had a special seaborne troop of raiders – 101 Troop – formed by Capt G.C. Montanaro using civilian Folboat canoes. 101 Troop later became the Special Boat Section. No. 6 Commando was disbanded in 1946.

No. 7 Commando
Formed in August 1940, No. 7 Commando was sent to the Middle East as part of Layforce in 1941. It fought in Crete in 1941, suffering heavy losses, and was then disbanded.

No. 8 Commando
Formed in mid-summer 1940, mainly from the Guards Regiments of the Household Division, No. 8 Commando suffered the same fate as No. 7 Commando.

No. 9 Commando
Formed in mid-1940, No. 9 Commando comprised many Scottish troops and, after deployment to

Gibraltar, it fought in the Italian campaign, in the Aegean and in Greece. No. 9 Commando was disbanded in 1946.

No. 10 Commando

Efforts to raise No. 10 Commando in August 1940 failed due to a lack of volunteers from Northern Command and those that did were posted to other Commandos. The unit was resurrected in January 1942 as No. 10 (Inter-Allied) Commando – *see separate box on page 36.*

No. 11 (Scottish) Commando

Formed in June 1940 from Scottish Command, No. 11 Commando gave itself the unofficial title of 'Scottish'. Like Nos. 7 and 8 Commandos, it formed part of Layforce and fought in Syria where it suffered heavy losses. It was disbanded in Cyprus in the late summer of 1941.

No. 12 Commando

Formed from British Troops in Northern Ireland (BTNI) in August 1940, No. 12 Commando BTNI first saw action in the diversionary raid on the Lofoten Islands during Operation Archery. After several successful raids up to September 1943, the unit was disbanded in December due to dwindling numbers of volunteers with the remainder being transferred to No. 9 Commando.

'No. 13 Commando'

For superstitious reasons there was no No. 13 Commando.

No. 14 Commando

Formed in 1942, No. 14 Commando was a specialised unit intended for sabotage operations in Norway and the Arctic Circle in conjunction with SOE. It was created after a raid by men from No. 2 Commando codenamed Operation Musketoon on the night of 20/21 September 1942 to attack a power station at Glomfjord. Although this was successful, several of the raiders were killed or captured. The prisoners were the first Commandos to be executed following Hitler's *Kommandobefehl* in October. No. 14 Commando was composed of two troops: one specialised in small boat operations and the other in cross-country skiing. Personnel from Nos. 12 and 14 Commandos subsequently served in Northforce and Timberforce for raids and reconnaissance missions in Norway.

No. 30 Commando

Formed on 30 September 1942 as the Special Engineering Unit, it comprised three troops with No. 33 Royal Marine, No. 34 Army and No. 36 RN or Technical – No. 35 was to be a Royal Air Force section but this was never formed. No. 30 Commando had a very specific role, to gather technical intelligence and enemy documents during Commando raids and amphibious assaults. The unit was formed at the instigation of Cdr Ian Fleming, RNVR, later the author of the James Bond books, and all its personnel underwent basic Commando training. It first went into action during Operation Torch in November 1942. Thereafter No. 30 Commando participated in most amphibious landings and was at the forefront of the Allied advance into enemy territory to gather technical intelligence.

LAKE COMÁCCHIO

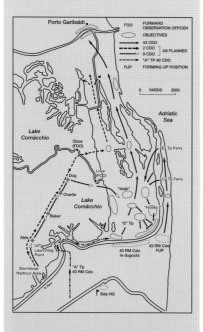

The campaign in Italy was brutal and unremitting and never lived up to Churchill's belief that the country was the 'soft underbelly of Europe'. Fighting was savage to the end and no more so than around Lake Comácchio in April 1945 when the Commandos of 2 Commando Brigade tied down the German defences on the flank of the major Allied offensive through the Argenta Gap. The amphibious assault was much hampered by weeks of drought that had lowered the water level of the lake and the assault boats could not be launched from the shore and in the words of one officer – 'For hours men heaved and dragged and pushed unwieldy craft across more than a mile of stinking glutinous mud…It was a nightmare mixture of Venice by moonlight and the end of the Henley Regatta'. However, the men of Nos 2 and 9 Commandos and Nos 40 and 43 (Royal Marine) Commandos prevailed and the attack was a great success. Comácchio became another Battle Honour for the Commandos and Gen McCreery informed 2 Commando Brigade that 'its successes in the mud and water flats round Argenta had marked the decisive phase of the battle' which led to the surrender of all German forces in Italy on 2 May 1945, a week before the collapse of Germany.

No. 40 RM Commando
Formed on 14 February 1942 as the Royal Marine Commando, subsequently A Battalion RM Commando, and from 18 October 1942 as 40 RM Commando. First saw action at Dieppe in Operation Jubilee, suffering heavy losses. Reformed and landed in Sicily in July 1943, subsequently fought in Italy and Yugoslavia. Ended the war fighting in Italy including at Comacchio. Returned to the UK in June 1945. Pronounced 'Forty Commando.'

No. 41 RM Commando
Formed on 10 October 1942, 41 RM Commando first saw action in Sicily, suffering heavy casualties. Withdrawn to the UK before landing in Normandy on D-Day. It fought at Walcheren and in the Maas River area. Returned to the UK in November 1945. Pronounced 'Four One Commando.'

No. 42 RM Commando
Formed in August 1943, 42 RM Commando first saw action in Burma in November 1944 where it fought for the remainder of war before moving to Hong Kong in September 1945 where it was stationed until June 1947.

No. 43 RM Commando
Formed on 1 August 1943, 43 RM Commando deployed to North Africa in late 1943 and first saw action in January 1944 at Anzio. It then conducted raids on the Dalmatian Islands of Yugoslavia before returning to the Italian campaign in March 1945. Returned to the UK in June and was absorbed into 40 Cdo RM in September.

No. 44 RM Commando
Formed on 1 August 1943, 44 RM Commando deployed to the Far East in late 1943 and first saw action in Burma in March 1944. It fought in the Far East for the remainder of the war. Deployed to Hong Kong in 1945 until March 1946, when it was disbanded and its personnel absorbed into 40 Cdo RM.

No. 45 RM Commando
Formed August 1943, 45 RM Commando landed in Normandy in D-Day where it fought for 83 days before returning to the UK. Deployed to Holland in January 1945, it participated in the major river crossings into Germany and ended the war at Neustadt on the Baltic. Returned to the UK in June 1945.

No. 46 RM Commando
Formed in August 1943, 46 RM Commando landed in Normandy on D-Day+1 and fought until late August when it was withdrawn from the front line after suffering heavy losses. Returned to the UK to join 1 Special Service Brigade. Deployed to Belgium in January 1945 and moved to Antwerp before fighting across the Rhine River to the Elbe River. Returned to the UK in June 1945 before being disbanded in January 1946.

No. 47 RM Commando
Formed on 1 August 1943, 47 RM Commando landed in Normandy on D-Day+1 and saw much action in France and Holland culminating in the landings at Walcheren. Moved to Germany after VE Day and returned to the UK in November. It was disbanded in January 1946.

No. 48 RM Commando
Formed in March 1944, 48 RM Commando landed in Normandy on D-Day and captured the German strongpoint at Langrune-sur-Mer where it suffered almost 50 per cent casualties. After reinforcement, it saw extensive action across North-West Europe as the Allies advanced on Germany

and fought its last action on 23 April 1945 at Biesboch in Holland. After occupation duties in Germany, it returned to the UK in November 1945 and was disbanded in January 1946.

No. 50 Commando

Formed in July 1940 in the Middle East from volunteers in Egypt and Palestine. It was amalgamated into Layforce as D Battalion before serving in the Dodecanese Islands and the battle for Crete, where it suffered such heavy casualties that it was disbanded.

No. 51 Commando

Formed in October 1940 in the Middle East with a large contingent of Jewish and Palestinian volunteers, No. 51 Commando fought the Italians in Ethiopia and Eritrea and then supported Orde Wingate, the founder of the Chindits in Burma, in organising Ethiopian irregulars into an effective force. It was subsequently absorbed into the Middle East Commando.

No. 52 Commando

Formed in October 1940 in the Middle East, No. 52 Commando saw action against the Italians in Ethiopia in January 1941 before returning to Egypt. It was then amalgamated into Layforce as D Battalion and thereafter suffered the same fate as No. 50 Commando.

Middle East Commando

Formed from the remnants of Layforce, at the insistence of Winston Churchill, to retain Commandos in the Middle East, the Middle East Commando was short-lived and, in the summer of 1942, was absorbed into Lt-Col David Stirling's 1st Special Air Service Regiment.

No. 62 Commando

This was a cover name for the Small Scale Raiding Force – *see separate box on page 37.*

Special Boat Section

The SBS was formed from the various Commando units, such as 101 Troop of No. 6 Commando, which had had conducted small-scale raids, agent insertion and reconnaissance missions using canoes and other small craft in Europe, the Mediterranean and the Far East. After the war, the role of canoe and small boat operations was continued by the Royal Marines, later leading to the Special Boat Service of today.

ROYAL NAVY COMMANDOS

Following Operation Ironclad in Madagascar, it was realised there was a need for greater control on the landing beaches to co-ordinate all the various elements such as landing craft, troop exit lanes and supply dumps. This gave rise to the creation of Royal Navy Beachhead Commandos. Each was commanded by a Principal Beachmaster with three sections each comprising two officers and 23 other ranks. All went through the standard Commando training course but at a special school at Ardentinny in Scotland. Beachhead Commandos were first used at Dieppe where they suffered heavy casualties. By the end of 1943, there were 22 RN Commandos, which were designated alphabetically – Able, Baker, Charlie, Dog, etc. Like the COPP units, the RN Commandos were at the forefront of every assault landing in all theatres of the war.

Below: The officers of Hotel Commando relax between missions at Chittagong in January 1944. These men acted as beachmasters to control all operations close to the waterline during amphibious landings and these Royal Navy Commandos served in every theatre of war. *CMC*

Above: The various national troops within No. 10 (Inter-Allied) Commando were used as interpreters and liaison officers throughout the Allied advance through Europe. These members of No. 2 (Dutch) Troop are conferring with locals at the town of Wolfhaze during Operation Market Garden on 18 September 1944. *CMC*

Right: With a Colt automatic pistol tucked into his back pocket, a Royal Marine Commando drops a bomb into a 3-inch mortar tube during fighting on the Lower Maas in Holland during April 1945. Heavy support weapons such as the 3-inch mortar became necessary when the Commandos made the transition from a raiding force to assault troops. *CMC*

Left: German troops occupying the Scheldt estuary denied the Allies the deep-water port of Antwerp for many weeks in the autumn of 1944 with a disastrous effect on the supply chain to the frontline troops. The key to the German defences was the island of Walcheren and this became the target of Operation Infatuate which was launched on 1 November 1944. The landings were provided massive fire support by Royal Navy warships and RAF bombers as well as vessels such as this Landing Craft Support (Medium) manned by Royal Marines. During the actual assault these craft gave invaluable fire support and became priority targets for the German defenders thus saving many of the landing craft carrying troops. *CEC*

Below: Men of 1 Commando Brigade move through the war-devastated town of Osnabrück on 4 April 1945. During the attack, No. 3 Commando killed 50 Germans and captured 450. *CMC*

INSIGNIA, CLOTHING & EQUIPMENT

INSIGNIA AND HEADGEAR

At the outset, all ranks within the Commandos wore their own regimental headdress and cap badge so every parade was a riot of different berets, tam-o'-shanter bonnets and forage caps of varying designs and colours. An attempt to introduce a standard form of headdress was resisted by the War Office due to its continuing antipathy towards the Commandos. This was all the more galling to the Commandos when the more recently formed Parachute Regiment was authorised to wear the maroon berets from which their nickname by the Germans of Red Devils derived. Nevertheless, the Commandos persisted and No. 1 Commando is credited with choosing the colour of the first Commando beret. Their original unit badge depicted a green salamander in a burst of red and yellow flames. Red was the colour of the despised Royal Military Police while yellow was deemed to be totally inappropriate leaving just green as a suitable colour. A local firm of tam-o'-shanter makers in Irvine, Scotland, produced the first berets and Lord Mountbatten approved the design on 1 May 1942. It gained official approval on 27 October 1942 and was issued to the Commandos immediately thereafter, although the troops continued to wear their own regimental cap badges in the new beret. In February 1946 Army Council Instruction 200 decreed that the green beret be the official head dress of the Royal Marine Commandos and it continues to be so to this day but with the Globe and Laurel cap badge and crest of the Corps of Royal Marines.

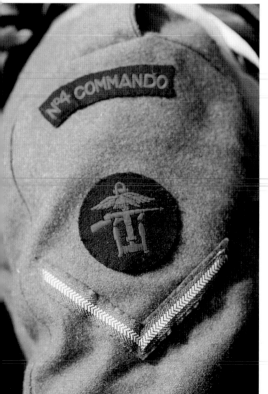

Below: The classic insignia of the Commandos with the shoulder title and the badge of Combined Operations.

CLOTHING

Initially, the Commandos wore standard British Army battledress with '37 Pattern webbing and '36 Pattern ammunition boots. Although excellent general combat items, the latter were not best suited to stealthy Commando raids because their hobnail soles were excessively noisy on tarmac or shingle beaches. Accordingly, many Commandos wore 'gym shoes' during raids, but these were hardly durable during long approach marches or withdrawals so an over-wrapper for the ammunition boot which deadened the sound on hard ground or pebbles was devised particularly for the Commandos. In time, this was superseded by the rubber soled 'S.V.' boot which was introduced in time for Operation Chariot.

The first Commando units were quick to introduce their own particular markings and insignia and these adorned their multifarious headgear and battledress blouses before a more standardised system was introduced in 1942 when the famous Green Beret was issued.

1 The shoulder title and sleeve patch of No. 1 Commando showing a salamander being consumed by fire. It was this insignia that gave rise to the colour of the Green Beret.

2 The lanyard, shoulder title and sleeve patch of Special Service units and the silver dagger of No. 2 Commando.

3 No. 3 Commando adopted a shoulder title with an integral troop number or HQ element as well as patches for each troop – D Troop shown on the left and the black disc of 5 Troop on the right.

4 Shoulder titles and lanyard of No. 4 Commando.

5 Feather hackle, shoulder title and sleeve patch of No. 5 Commando.

6 Reflecting its Scottish origins, No. 6 Commando adopted the tam-o'-shanter with the Roman numeral VI for bonnet badge and shoulder title below which is the distinctive sleeve badge of 101 Troop, the pioneers of canoe and small boat raiding.

7 Sleeve patch of the Special Service Brigade HQ personnel.

8 No. 9 Commando also featured a tam-o'-shanter but with a black hackle as a unit badge below which is the shoulder title.

9 Predictably, No. 11 (Scottish) Commando was similarly adorned with a black hackle and its own green lanyard.

10 Shoulder title of No. 12 Commando.

11 Shoulder title of the Middle East Commandos with their distinctive 'fanny' knife.

12 Shoulder title of the Commando Depot

13 Sleeve patch of the Signal Troop, Special Service Brigade.

14 Standardised shoulder titles were introduced in 1942 of a simplified design with red lettering on a dark blue background.

15 Red and dark blue were also used for the badge of Combined Operations which incorporated the Tommy gun of the Commandos with a Royal Navy anchor and RAF eagle and came in various shapes and sizes.

16 When the Commando Group replaced the Special Service Group in December 1944, a sleeve badge was introduced depicting the Fairbairn-Sykes fighting knife and this replaced the Combined Operations badge in early 1945. It is noteworthy that these last two badges continue in use to this day as the British Armed Forces become more integrated in their command structure. It is interesting to observe that almost every senior officer of the British forces in Iraq in 2003 was seen sporting a Combined Operations patch on the right shoulder as a badge of tri-service solidarity in modern warfare.

Above: The Fairbairn-Sykes fighting knife appeared in three different versions and troops carried them as they saw fit for quick and easy accessibility. This is a third pattern knife.

Right: Armed with a 9mm Sten gun, a Commando displays the standard fighting order of battledress, Bergen rucksack and cap comforter.

Far right: The Bergen rucksack was readily adopted by the Commandos following the Norwegian campaign of 1940. Originally intended to carry demolition charges, the Bergen was subsequently used by every Commando.

Right: By late 1944, the Commandos were issued with the paratroopers' camouflaged Denison smock which proved highly popular, as shown on the right. The other two Commandos are wearing the widespread sleeveless and collarless Jerkin, Leather which originated in the Great War.

Below: A sniper merges into the vegetation as he scans for a target. Sniping was a particular skill of the Commandos and snipers were used aggressively to harass the enemy at every opportunity.

Far right: A Commando corporal grabs a cup of tea as he monitors his No. 38 radio set which had a maximum effective range of one mile.

Above: A lance-corporal Bren gunner takes a smoke break while cleaning his weapon and replenishing the 28-round clips with .303-inch ammunition. The Bren gun was an excellent light machine gun which saw widespread service with the Commandos and every other British infantry unit during World War II.

Above right: While a Commando stands watch with his Tommy gun, an officer prepares demolition charges from explosives carried in his Bergen rucksack.

Right: Snipers used both binoculars and telescopes for detecting targets while concealed beneath their 3 feet by 3 feet 6 inch camouflage face veil with the No. 4 Mark 1* (T) rifle and No. 32 telescopic sight lying close by.

Opposite, Left: With a Thompson Submachine Gun M1928A1 slung over his shoulder, this Commando has the earlier version of the Bergen rucksack.

Opposite, Right: This Commando sergeant shows two of the most famous Commando weapons: the Tommy gun and Fairbairn-Sykes fighting knife tucked into his gaiter.

Main picture: Of the six Cockle canoes embarked on the submarine HMS *Tuna* for Operation Frankton, one was damaged irreparably during launching. The five remaining Cockles are depicted as they approach the mouth of the Gironde River during the night of 7 December 1942. From left to right, *Coalfish* carrying Marine Ewart and Sgt Wallace; *Cuttlefish* with Marine Conway and Lt MacKinnon; *Catfish* with Marine Sparks and Maj 'Blondie' Hasler; *Crayfish* with Marine Mills and Cpl Laver; and *Conger* with Marine Moffart and Cpl Sheard. Only Sparks and Hasler survived the raid to be hailed as the 'Cockleshell Heroes' for the successful attack against enemy shipping sheltering in Bordeaux harbour. *Reproduction courtesy of the artist, Jack Russell*

Inset: This member of the Royal Marine Boom Patrol Detachment is depicted in the uniform worn by the raiders during Operation Frankton with a dark woollen hat and disruptive pattern camouflage smock over standard battledress as well as rubberised waders with integral boots. These items were designed by Major 'Blondie' Hasler. Protruding from the collar is the tubing to allow inflation of the life preserver worn under the smock. He is armed with a silenced version of the 9mm Sten sub-machine gun and he carries a magnetic limpet mine. On his shoulder is the badge of Combined Operations and the Royal Marines flash to indicate that he was bona fide combatant. The Germans ignored such niceties and summarily executed all the raiders that they captured following the raid. *Reproduction courtesy of the artist, Mike Chappell*

Far left: A Bren gunner displays the standard equipment for amphibious landings including a fully laden Bergen with steel helmet. The white object around his chest is a life preserver or 'water wings' as it was known.

Left: The Thompson submachine gun was a popular Commando weapon throughout the war because of the power of its .45-calibre ACP round. In the early days, the 50-round drum magazine was used but it was not overly reliable and the 20-round box magazine was preferred.

Below: The Commandos were issued with a silenced version of the Sten for the quiet despatch of sentries during a raid but it was unreliable and was superseded by the specially developed De Lisle Carbine fitted with an efficient silencer.

WEAPONS AND EQUIPMENT

At the time the Commandos were formed, the British Expeditionary Force had just been evacuated from Dunkirk where it had lost all its tanks and heavy equipment. The dejected troops returned with little more at best than their helmets and rifles. All types of weapons were in short supply and the Commandos were not a high priority as the threat of invasion intensified through the summer of 1940. Nevertheless, the

Commandos scrounged whatever weapons they could, including half of the total number of Tommy guns available in Britain for the first cross-Channel raid. The Commandos have forever been associated with the Thompson submachine gun and the type illustrated (left) is the Model 1928 A1 or M1928A1 with beside it the 50-round drum magazine beloved of gangster movies which in the event was not favoured by Commandos as it was prone to jamming. They preferred the 20-round box magazines that were much easier to carry and also lighter as the Tommy gun was in any case a heavy weapon at $10\frac{1}{2}$ pounds. The principal sidearm of the Commandos throughout the war was the Colt M1911A1 .45-inch calibre automatic pistol (illustrated left) and it was issued widely to all ranks, unlike in most line infantry units where pistols were reserved for officers. This American weapon fired the .45-inch ACP round so this meant that the Commandos had to carry only two types of ammunition into battle with the other being the .303-inch round of the standard British Army infantry weapons.

At the outset, most Commandos used the .303-inch No. 3 Short, Magazine, Lee-Enfield (SMLE). From 1942 onwards this was superseded by the No. 4 Rifle. The De Lisle Commando Carbine (below) was, as its name implies, specifically designed for the

Commandos, in fact as a silenced weapon for close-quarter killing out to 400 yards during clandestine raids. The Commandos also used the silenced 9mm Sten gun but this required a different cartridge to their other weapons. It was also considered unreliable and prone to accidental discharges if dropped. Another unusual weapon used by the Commandos following the Normandy landings was the .303-inch Vickers 'K' machine gun (below) that was originally designed for the RAF for fighter planes. Accordingly, it had an extremely high rate of fire of 1,000 rounds a minute which the Commandos favoured but it consumed large quantities of ammunition – which was carried in 96-round drum magazines.

The Commandos employed snipers on a greater scale than standard units. Initially, they were issued with (below left) the Rifle, No. 3 Mark 1* (T), the T standing for Telescope, which was superseded by the No. 4 Mark 1 (T).

The Commandos were renowned for the variety of edged weapons they carried into battle of which the

Fairbairn-Sykes fighting knife was the most famous (see photo on page 30 and box on page 32). Capts Fairbairn and Sykes designed the weapon after serving in the Shanghai police in China. They became the leading unarmed combat instructors within the Commandos and the 'F-S Knife' is their enduring legacy and it remains the symbol worn to this day on the sleeves of specialised Army troops attached to the Royal Marine Commandos such as artillery and engineer personnel. The first pattern knife with its 8½-inch blade is shown in (right) and the later pattern with a 13-inch blade and scabbard (far right). The Middle East Commandos produced their own fighting knife known as the 'fanny' knuckle knife (second right). The most fearsome Commando edged weapon that was issued in the early days was also designed by Fairbairn and Sykes and was known as the Smatchett or 'Roman Sword' (third right). Another combined knuckleduster and knife was the BC41 Pattern (fourth right).

Captured German weapons were much used by the Commandos, who were permitted more leeway in this respect than line infantry units. The MP40 Schmeisser was often used in place of the inadequate Sten gun and the Panzerfaust light anti-armour weapon was preferred to the PIAT (Projector Infantry Anti-Tank), particularly for house clearing when the troops advanced into Germany.

During raids any items that were not vital to the task in hand, such as anti-gas capes and respirators, were left behind and later discarded completely. The issue steel helmet was also seen as an encumbrance and was invariably replaced by the woollen cap comforter that became another icon of the Commandos. So too were the Bergen rucksack and the toggle rope. The Bergen (right) was of Norwegian origin and initially employed to carry demolition stores during raids but Commandos quickly acquired them for their own use as they could carry an extraordinary load thanks to the A-frame that distributed the weight onto the shoulders and hips for greater comfort. The toggle rope (below right) was carried by every Commando and these could be quickly connected together to make scaling ropes or bridges across obstacles. Various assault vests were designed for the Commandos during the war and (left) depicts the 'skeleton assault harness' with bayonet frog, ammunition pouches and entrenching tool. During seaborne assaults, Commandos were encouraged to wear life preservers such as the Royal Navy pattern although one wonders whether it would be much help to a man festooned with weapons and a 60-pound rucksack. As the main British users of the .45-calibre Colt automatic pistol, the Commandos were issued with special pouches for its seven-round magazines (right).

Above: A group of Commandos reorganise before their next action wearing a variety of late war uniforms.

Left: The enduring image of the Commando raider bedecked with cap comforter, Fairbairn-Sykes fighting knife, toggle rope and Tommy gun – the tools of his deadly trade.

PEOPLE

JACK CHURCHILL (1898–1961)

Before the war Jack Churchill had been a model for Brylcream hair treatment advertisements but his good looks disguised his appetite for war and he won a Military Cross during the battle of France where he reputedly killed a German soldier with an arrow fired from a longbow. As the second-in-command of No.3 Commando during the raid on Vaagsø he won immortal fame and his nickname of 'Mad Jack' when he stood exposed on the bows of a landing craft during the assault on Maaloy Island playing the bagpipes under heavy German fire. As the boat touched ground, he casually passed his pipes to his batman, Guardsman Stretton, who handed him his Claymore and Churchill charged ashore waving his sword and 'shouting warlike cries' hotly pursued by one of his troop commanders, Capt Peter Young. Together they and No.3 Group quickly subdued the German coastal battery threatening the main landings at Vaagsø. During the action he was blown up by a demolition charge as he was 'liberating' a case of German wine. As he was borne from the field he instructed his batman to retrieve his bagpipes and the wine, which was quickly consumed – '...on the way home he was still very merry, and fortunately his wounds, if painful, were not too serious'. These exploits were witnessed by a Reuters News correspondent and gained extensive coverage in the newspapers of the time. Nevertheless, 'Mad Jack' Churchill was a truly professional soldier and he assumed

Below: With his Claymore sword at his side, Maj 'Mad Jack' Churchill inspects one of the artillery guns on the island of Maaloy that his troops of No. 2 Commando captured at the outset of the attack on Vaagsø. *IWM – N463*

Above: Three famous Commandos confer during the campaign in Normandy. From left to right, Capt Charles Head, the adjutant of No. 3 Commando, Brig John Durnford-Slater, Deputy Commander Combined Operations and Lt-Col Peter Young, CO No. 3 Commando. Peter Young was one of the most gallant and successful Commando leaders of World War 2. He ended the war as a brigadier with one DSO and three MCs. *CMC*

demands were summarily RTU'd after the action. After the demolition of the objectives, he personally orchestrated the withdrawal to the landing craft, leading knots of Commandos through burning buildings to avoid the worst of the German fire. For his leadership during the Vaagsø raid, Durnford-Slater was awarded the DSO. As the CO of No.3 Commando for the raid on Dieppe in August 1942, his force met with a similar disastrous fate as the rest of the operation when his landing craft were widely scattered following an encounter with the Kriegsmarine in mid-Channel. Of the 23 landing craft carrying No.3 Commando, only seven got to France where four were sunk or stranded on rocks but a group of his men were able to neutralise the 'Goebbels Battery' on the left flank of the main landings. In July 1943, he led the attack by No.3 Commando during the invasion of Sicily against a coastal battery on Pachino Peninsula to make up for the failure of Dieppe. He was awarded the DSO for his actions at the battle of Termoli at the Ponte del Malati that was subsequently renamed Commando Bridge; a name that continues to this day. In September, he was the commander of the Special Service Brigade during Operation Avalanche and the invasion of mainland Italy. During 1944, in the rank of brigadier, he became the second-in-command of all Commando units of the Special Service Group under Maj Gen Robert Sturges. After the Normandy landings, he commanded a tactical HQ of the SS Group, which was attached to HQ Second British Army and it is in that capacity that he is shown in the accompanying photograph with another renowned Commando, Peter Young.

ROBERT LAYCOCK (1907–1968)

After serving in the Royal Horse Guards, Capt Robert Laycock was appointed to the GHQ Middle East as an Anti-Gas Staff Officer whereupon he promptly volunteered for the Commandos and was tasked with raising No.8 Commando from the Household Cavalry and other units in London District. As a Lt Col, Laycock commanded No.8 Commando and then became deputy commander of the Special Service Brigade. As a brigadier he was sent to the Middle East in January 1941 to create a Commando formation known as 'Layforce', comprising '100 officers and 1,500 other ranks with one staff officer, a note book and eight wireless sets which nobody could work' – see Layforce and the Middle East Commandos pp. 22-25. After the failure of Operation Flipper, Laycock undertook a heroic march across the desert in company with Sgt Jack Terry towards British lines eating little more than berries until aided by some friendly Senussi tribesmen. They eventually met up with British forces after a trek of 41 days. It was Christmas Day 1941 and as he entered the officers mess, Laycock was upbraided for being an hour and 20 minutes late for Christmas dinner. Meanwhile, Jack Terry had parted company with Laycock. Throughout their wanderings, Laycock had read repeatedly from the only book he had with him which was 'The Wind in the Willows'. On reaching British lines, Terry was heard to mutter – 'Thank God I shan't have to hear any more about that bloody Mr Toad!' Within the week, Laycock was ordered to return to England to take command of the Special Service Brigade. In April 1943, the brigade was split between Laycock and Lord Lovat and the former oversaw the Commando operations for the invasions of Sicily and Italy. Laycock was instrumental in the major enlargement and reorganisation of the Commandos prior to D-Day with the creation of the Special Service Group under the command of Maj Gen Robert Sturges. It was Laycock's belief that the Commandos should be more self-sufficient with heavier integral weapons to fulfil the role of assault infantry. When Lord Mountbatten became Supreme Allied Commander in South East Asia, Maj Gen Robert Laycock succeeded him as the Chief of Combined Operations.

PETER YOUNG (1915–1988)

Like 'Mad Jack' Churchill, Peter Young was one of the legendary fighting Commandos of World War 2. As a former bank clerk, Young did not fit the image of tough Commando but he was fearless in battle and fought in virtually every theatre of operations from Vaagsø to the Arakan. He was commissioned in 1939 as a 2ND Lt in the Bedfordshire and Hertfordshire Regiment and was wounded during the evacuation from Dunkirk. After recuperation, he joined No.3 Commando and took part in the earliest Commando raids. He won the first of his three Military Crosses for his actions during the savage street-fighting in Vaagsø after his troop had completed the capture of the island of Maaloy with 'Mad Jack' Churchill. After a period on the staff at Combined Operations HQ, he became second-in-command of No.3 Commando and took part in the Dieppe Raid. With just 18 survivors of his troop on landing below the objective of the coastal guns of the 'Goebbels Battery', he managed to take his raiding force up the cliffs on a network of barbed wire which, as he put it, 'an over-conscientious German officer had inadvertently provided for them to walk on'. Young was the only Commando officer to reach his objective and bring back all his men. At one point, when they were approaching enemy machine-guns through a cornfield, he encouraged his soldiers by telling them not to worry about bullets as standing corn made an effective protection. Fortunately, he was able to withdraw to the beach with all his men. He was awarded a DSO for his part in this raid. In 1943, at Agnone in Sicily he was awarded a Bar to his MC and then, when commanding No.3 Commando in raids in Italy, received a second Bar. In 1944 he fought in Normandy, serving with distinction in the D-Day landings before being posted to the Arakan, Burma. A fellow officer recalls seeing Young's Commandos under attack from an apparently endless number of Japanese at Kangaw and sending a message asking Young if he would like reinforcements. 'No thanks,' came back the message. 'We can see this lot off all right.' And he did. In 1945 Young was promoted to command 1 Commando Brigade in Burma, and was generally acknowledged to be outstanding. From Second Lieutenant to Brigadier in six years was a remarkable achievement in itself but at the same time to be awarded a DSO and three MCs is the stuff of legends.

Below: The Small Scale Raiding Force was given the codename of No. 62 Commando because it contained many Commando personnel. One of the most legendary Commandos was Anders 'Andy' Lassen, a former Danish merchant seaman. He is shown at the extreme right of this group of the Small Scale Raiding Force undergoing training in Cumberland during the summer of 1942. Lassen was an expert with the Fairbairn-Sykes fighting knife and won the Military Cross no less than three times. He subsequently joined the Special Boat Section and was killed at Lake Comacchio in April 1945 in an action for which he was awarded a posthumous Victoria Cross, the first time that this medal was awarded to a foreign national. *CMC*

POSTWAR

The disbanding of the Commando units began in November 1945 and their personnel were either demobilised or returned to their parent regiments. Few of the latter were welcomed back with open arms as service with the Commandos was seen as a form of disloyalty in many regiments. Military careers suffered accordingly and many former Commandos chose to leave the Army in the coming years taking with them their valuable wartime expertise. Within months only Nos. 1 and 5 Commandos of 3 Commando Brigade remained in being, as garrison troops in Hong Kong. The majority of the Royal Marine Commandos were also disbanded with Nos. 40 and 43 in January 1946 and Nos. 41, 46, 47 and 48 in February. At the same time, the remaining RM Commandos were redesignated Commandos Royal Marines. Headquarters Commando Group and ancillary units such as the CBTC at Achnacarry were closed down in March. On 31 January 1946, 45 Commando RM set sail for Hong Kong to relieve Nos. 1 and 5 Commandos which were amalgamated when the Royal Marines arrived to join 3 Commando Brigade. No. 1/5 Commando was disbanded in January 1947 and the Army Commandos were no more.

Below: In the postwar years, the role of amphibious warfare has passed to the Royal Marines. During the 1970s, 3 Commando Brigade RM became specialists in Arctic warfare as well, with the role of defending NATO's northern flank in Norway; these were skills that proved invaluable during the Falklands campaign of 1982. *Royal Marines*

However, 3 Commando Brigade lived on at the direction of the Commandant General Royal Marines, General Sir Thomas Hunton, and was now designated 3 Commando Brigade RM. He also wished to reflect the theatres of operations of the wartime Royal Marine Commandos within the Special Service/Commando Brigades. Accordingly, 42 Commando RM represented the Royal Marine Commandos of the old 3 Commando Brigade which had fought in the Arakan and the Far East. 44 Commando RM was renumbered as 'Forty' to represent 2 Commando Brigade which fought in the Mediterranean and 45 Commando RM for those who fought in northwest Europe. By the end of 1946, all three Royal Marine Commando units were serving in Hong Kong. In May 1947, 3 Commando Brigade RM moved to Malta from where its units served in Palestine and the Suez Canal Zone. All three Commandos were involved in the difficult withdrawal from Palestine and the creation of the state of Israel with 40 Commando RM being the last British Army unit to leave Haifa on 30 June 1948. From a wartime strength of over 74,000 men, the Corps of Royal Marines was by now reduced to 13,000, of whom 2,200 were in 3 Commando Brigade. By 1949 the Government was anxious to reduce defence costs further and the Harwell Committee proposed that the Royal Marines be disbanded; a move fought bitterly by the Admiralty but only at the cost of more manpower.

From June 1950 to March 1952, 3 Commando Brigade deployed to the Far East for the Malayan Emergency to undertake counter-terrorism operations. All three units were widely involved in jungle warfare. They killed 171 Communist Terrorists and captured a further 50 at a cost of 30 dead. Meanwhile, 41 Commando RM was reformed on 16 August 1950 following the North Korean invasion of the Republic of Korea on 25 June 1950. Once deployed, 41 (Independent) Commando joined the US Army Special Raiding Force and conducted several classic Commando raids along the west coast of Korea. In November it came under command of 1st (US) Marine Division and fought in the epic breakout at Hagaru-ri for which it was awarded a US Presidential Citation. 41 (Independent) Commando was disbanded in February 1952.

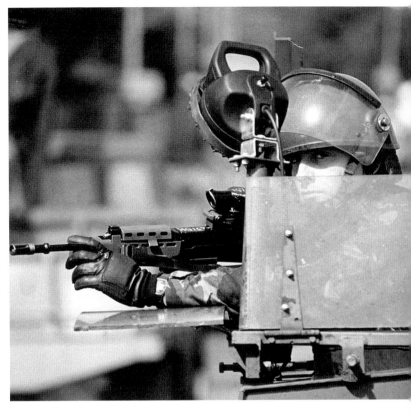

Above: The Royal Marines were among the first units to be committed on the streets of Ulster in 1969 where for the next 30 years they fought an effective counter-terrorism campaign. *Royal Marines*

For the next 20 years, the Royal Marine Commandos fought in numerous brushfire wars and counter-insurgency operations as Britain conducted its long and difficult withdrawal from Empire – Aden, Borneo, Cyprus and elsewhere, a veritable alphabet of bitter conflicts that taxed the Commandos to the full but never found them wanting. At Suez in November 1956 the Royal Marines spearheaded the Anglo-French seaborne assault to reclaim the Suez Canal after it was nationalised by the Egyptian government. 40 and 42 Commandos landed over the beaches of Port Said from landing craft in the traditional manner while 45 Commando conducted the first helicopter air assault in warfare. Another strategic innovation was the introduction of the dedicated Commando carriers, HMS *Albion* and *Bulwark*, in 1960. Each was capable of deploying a RM Commando with supporting artillery and helicopters to land the troops anywhere in the world. One was usually stationed in the Mediterranean and one in the Far East. At the same time, 41 and 43 Commandos were reactivated to expand the flexibility and capabilities of the Royal Marines.

During the 1960s the Royal Marines fought extensively in the Middle and Far East and by the end of the decade there were 633 officers and 7,515 men serving in the Corps of Royal Marines. The 1970s saw the emergence of a new conflict closer to home in Northern Ireland that was to absorb the British Army and the Royal Marines for the next 30 years. Emergency four-month and longer residential tours became a regular irksome duty to all Commandos, yet they provided invaluable training and combat experience for a generation of soldiers, sailors and marines. The 1970s saw another new theatre of operations for the Royal Marines with the commitment of 3 Commando Brigade to Norway to protect NATO's northern flank. The first deployment by 45 Commando took place in January 1970 and thereafter the Royal Marines became

specialists in Arctic warfare with regular deployments every year. In July 1974, 40 Commando was despatched to Cyprus as the British Army's rapid-deployment 'Spearhead Battalion' to protect British bases on the island following the Turkish invasion. Many tours followed to the island as United Nations Peacekeeping forces, a role that was to become ever more common in the years to come.

On 2 April 1982 Argentine troops invaded the British sovereign territory of the Falkland Islands deep in the South Atlantic. Defending the islands were just 67 Royal Marines of Naval Party 8901. They fought tenaciously, inflicting many casualties on the Argentine troops without loss to themselves, before being ordered to surrender by the civilian governor. The Falkland Islands are situated only 400 miles from the South American mainland but 8,000 miles from Britain. Any military operation to retake the islands was fraught with hazard and many military observers deemed it to be impossible. The task fell predominately to 3 Commando Brigade, augmented by the Parachute Regiment and other specialised troops. Within days of the invasion a Royal Navy Task Force sailed for the South Atlantic carrying the men of 40, 42 and 45 Commandos RM and all the supporting units of 3 Commando Brigade. Together with the Paras, they were at the forefront of the seaborne landings at San Carlos, codenamed Operation Sutton. Once 3 Commando Brigade was safely ashore, the Royal Marines began their epic 'yomp' across East Falkland towards the capital of Port Stanley in atrocious weather conditions. Both 42 and 45 Commandos fought several ferocious night battles against heavily defended Argentine positions that inevitably ended in vicious hand-to-hand combat – Mount Kent, Mount Harriet, Two Sisters, Mount Challenger – innocuous names that brought both death and glory to the Royal Marines. The Falklands War was a complete vindication of the role of the Royal Marines, if such were still required.

After the collapse of the Soviet Union and the Warsaw Pact, it was hoped that the world would become a safer place with the end of the Cold War. It was not to be. In 1990, Royal Marine units deployed to the Gulf to participate in Operation Granby to expel the Iraqis from Kuwait. After the war, the Royal Marines conducted Operation Haven to protect the Kurds along the Iraqi/Turkish border. The break-up of Yugoslavia brought yet another theatre for extended peacekeeping operations through the 1990s culminating, as the new millennium dawned, in the Kosovo campaign to curtail the ethnic cleansing of the Serbian regime of Slobodan Milosovic. The year 2000 also saw the Royal Marines deployed to Sierra Leone to restore law and order under the codename Operation Palliser.

Africa was followed by Afghanistan and Operation Jacana with 45 Commando conducting a difficult campaign against the Taliban and Al-Qaeda in the continuing war against international terrorism. Yet sterner tests lay ahead with the war to liberate Iraq from the vicious regime of Saddam Hussein. Once again the Royal Marine Commandos were in the vanguard of the assault and in the thick of the fighting throughout the campaign. Britain's Sea Soldiers were formed more than 300 years ago and today the Royal Marines are recognised as one of the world's elite fighting forces: a worthy legacy for the wartime Commandos who first wore the Green Beret with pride. But the task goes on – *Per Mare, Per Terram.*

Above: The Royal Marines are the heirs to many of the specialised Commando units of World War II that now include the Arctic and Mountain Warfare Cadre and the Special Boat Service. Another unit is the 'Comacchio Group', named after the famous 1945 battle in Italy, which is tasked with protecting the Clyde Submarine Base at Faslane in Scotland where the Royal Navy's nuclear submarines are replenished between their clandestine patrols. *Royal Marines*

Above right: Peacekeeping and peace support missions now absorb considerable time and resources within the British armed forces, such as Operation Haven in northern Iraq following the Gulf War of 1991. Here, Marines of 45 Commando RM use Supacat All Terrain Vehicles to patrol the Kurdish enclave in Iraq. *Royal Marines*

Below right: The primary role of the Marines remains assault from the sea, be it by boat, landing craft, hovercraft or helicopter. All were employed at the outset of the war in Iraq in 2003. *Royal Marines*

ASSESSMENT

The Commandos were born in the dark days of 1940 when Britain stood alone against the might of Nazi Germany. Within weeks of their formation they conducted their first daring raid against occupied Europe. Another 146 Commando raids followed before peace was achieved in August 1945 with the defeat of Nazi Germany and Imperial Japan. In each and every one of them the Commandos faced heavy odds as they set forth 'to pluck bright honour from the pale-fac'd moon' from the cold wastes of the Arctic Circle to the fetid mangrove swamps of the Arakan. In the early years of the war, the Commandos were one of the few means for the British Empire to strike back at a powerful enemy that held sway from the Pyrenees to the Urals and from Trondheim to Tripoli. Their deeds thrilled and encouraged a deprived and embattled population while the armies of America and the British Empire were formed and trained for the greatest seaborne invasion in history to liberate Nazi-occupied Europe.

Below: Men returning from Dieppe. Although the raid led to a terrible loss of life, it taught the Allies significant lessons about the size of the task they would have to undertake to invade Europe. *IWM – N463*

The Commandos played a vital role in this gigantic enterprise from small-scale raids for intelligence gathering to the tragic dress rehearsal for D-Day at Dieppe and with classic sabotage missions ranging from the destruction of the Normandie Dock at St Nazaire to the tiny force of Cockleshell Heroes that sneaked into the port of Bordeaux to sow devastation and confusion among a hated enemy. Operation Frankton epitomised the dedication and the courage of the individual raider that made up the Commandos, be they Army or Royal Marine.

Highly trained, motivated and willing to go that extra mile to achieve the objective, they were an elite fighting force but such success did not come cheap. The casualty rate was often high, not to say grievous – 50 per cent at St Nazaire, 60 per cent at Dieppe, 80 per cent for the Cockleshell Heroes. Furthermore, the Commandos faced hostile opposition from quarters other than the enemy. From the outset, there were factions in the military hierarchy that were deeply suspicious of the Commandos and not without cause. The call for volunteers for 'duties of a hazardous nature' drew a ready response from adventurous and committed men who were serving in every regiment and corps of the British Army. It cannot be denied that, by depriving the line infantry of some of the brightest and the best officers and NCOs, the British Army as a whole lacked the level of expertise and professionalism that the German Army displayed throughout World War II. Arguably this cost the British Army a greater number of casualties on the battlefield than the Commandos saved.

The Germans never felt the need for the multitude of special forces that were created by the British but this is no doubt a reflection of national characteristics. The gifted amateur prevailing in the face of fearful odds but without exceptional professionalism is a familiar and well-liked British archetype. Many of these Special Forces units were the creation of like-minded individuals, often of an eccentric nature, who were determined to fight the enemy by any means possible. Men such as 'Blondie' Hasler, 'Jumbo' Courtney and David Stirling had a vision of small bands of raiders striking far behind enemy lines to devastating effect. These achieved spectacular results in the early years of the war. The larger raids such as Vaagsø and St Nazaire were great successes, both militarily in tying down thousands of German troops and psychologically in boosting Allied morale in the dark days of the war.

Above: HQ Group during Operation Impact when No. 40 RM Commando captured Commando Bridge over the Renate Canal on 11 April 1945 during the decisive battle for Lake Comacchio in Italy (see box page 62). *CMC*

After the disaster of Dieppe, the role of the Commandos changed fundamentally from that of raiders to assault troops in opposed amphibious landings. On several occasions they were misused as standard line infantry in subsequent operations inland where they sometimes suffered heavy casualties for lack of integral support weapons and sufficient firepower. All these problems of equipment and employment were addressed in time for D-Day in June 1944 when thousands of airborne troops and Commandos, both Army and Royal Marines, spearheaded the largest seaborne invasion in history. The very success of Operation Overlord was a testament to their determination and fighting skills. These were the traits that marked out the Commandos as an elite fighting force which, despite official opposition from the outset and in the immediate postwar years, was to remain a vital component of Britain's armed forces. The concept of Combined Operations was born more than 60 years ago and it has become the standard for all military operations today. Similarly, the ethos of the Commandos is as valid today as it ever was and the Commandos of World War II would readily recognise their present day counterparts.

REFERENCE

INTERNET SITES

www.royalmarinesmuseum.co.uk
Housed in the former Officers Mess at Southsea, the Royal Marines Museum recounts the story of the Corps from its formation in 1664 to date. There is also a Combined Operations Museum at Inverarary in Scotland – www.quebec-marine.co.uk

www.djrowlands.supanet.com
As one of the foremost military artists of today, David Rowlands has covered many of the British Army's recent campaigns and produced numerous action paintings of which his 'St Nazaire' reproduced in this book on page 33 is a fine example. For more information on David Rowlands' work see his website.

www.jackrussell.co.uk
Jack Russell Gallery, 41 High Street, Chipping Sodbury, South Gloucestershire, BS37 6BA
The Gloucestershire and England wicketkeeper is also a fine artist with several important military paintings to his credit, including 'The Cockleshell Heroes' which was created with the help of Bill Sparks and is reproduced in this book on page 74–75. Prints of the painting may be obtained from the above address.

www.combinedops.com
This is a good starting point for any web search for the Commandos. In particular this site has histories of Nos. 4, 5 and 11 Commandos; the last has a fine account of Operation Flipper – the assassination attempt against General Erwin Rommel. This site also has accounts of several Commando raids and the exploits of the Small Scale Raiding Force. There are links to many other sites including:

www.4commando.org.uk
This is the site of the 4 Commando World War II Re-enactment Group whose members have a remarkable collection of original Commando uniforms, weapons, equipment and memorabilia. The group gives demonstrations at military shows across the country. Several of its members are featured in this book.

http://home.wxs.nl
There are some interesting articles at the site of the Dutch Commandos, including features on Royal Navy Commandos and the Fairbairn-Sykes Commando dagger. There are also accounts of Nos. 4 and 5 Commandos and citations for the VC winners at St Nazaire during Operation Jubilee.

www.jubilee.freehomepage.com
On Operation Jubilee.

www.guardiancentury.co.uk/1940-1949
A vivid, personal account of the No. 4 Commando raid at Dieppe.

www.nuav.net
Covers Combined Operations in Norway, as does www.combined-operations.com

BIBLIOGRAPHY

Charles Messenger, *The Commandos 1940-1946,* William Kimber, London, 1985.
Based on primary sources and exhaustive research, Charles Messenger's book is undoubtedly the best on the subject of wartime Commandos. If there is only one book that you read on the subject this must be the one.

Hilary St. George Saunders, *The Green Beret – The Story of the Commandos 1940-1945*, Michael Joseph, London, 1949.
Written in a style wonderfully evocative of the period, this was the first semi-official history of the Army Commandos of World War II. The author also wrote the official HMSO wartime publication on Combined Operations which also contains a wealth of interest.

Mike Chappell, *Army Commandos 1940-45*, Osprey Publishing, Oxford, 1996.
This book in Osprey's Elite series is an excellent introduction to the subject with detailed colour plates showing the numerous types of uniforms and equipment used by the Commandos.

Robin Hunter, *True Stories of the Commandos – The British Army's Legendary Frontline Fighting Force,* Virgin Publishing, London, 2000.
Despite its lurid title, this book is a most readable account of the Commandos during World War II and is highly recommended.

Leroy Thompson, *British Commandos in Action*, Squadron/Signal, Texas, 1987.
One of the titles in the Combat Troops in Action series, this publication contains virtually every Commando photograph in the collection of the Imperial War Museum.

James D. Ladd, *By Sea By Land – The Authorised History of the Royal Marine Commandos 1919-1997*, HarperCollins, London, 1998.
James Ladd is one of the leading authorities on the Commandos and has written several books on the subject such as *By Sea By Land*, which is a comprehensive history of the Royal Marines.

James D. Ladd, *Commandos and Rangers of World War II*, Macdonald and Janes, London, 1978.
Excellent book on WWII raiders and raiding operations.

James D. Ladd, *SBS The Invisible Raiders*, Arms and Armour Press, London, 1983.
This book is a fine account of all the numerous Commando, Royal Navy and Royal Marine

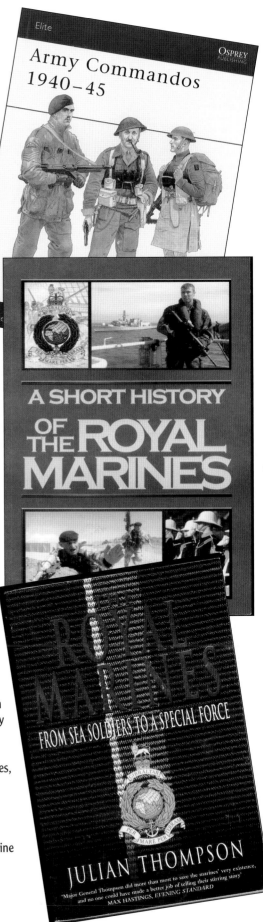

special boat sections of World War II and their eventual amalgamation into the post war Special Boat Squadron which became today's SBS.

Julian Thompson, *The Royal Marines – From Sea Soldiers to a Special Force*, Sidgwick & Jackson, London, 2000.
This is another comprehensive history of the Corps of Royal Marines written in a compelling and authoritative style as one would expect from the former commander of 3 Commando Brigade RM during the Falklands War and Visiting Professor in the Department of War Studies, King's College, London.

Peter Harclerode & David Reynolds, *Commando – The Illustrated History of Britain's Green Berets from Dieppe to Afghanistan*, Sutton Publishing, Stroud, 2001.
This book lives up to its title and contains many excellent photographs with the emphasis on post war operations.

The Globe and Laurel – The Journal of the Royal Marines.
The official journal of the Royal Marines is published six times a year and provides up to date information on the activities of the Corps.

A Short History of the Royal Marines 1664-2002, The Royal Marines Historical Society, 2002.
This is an excellent primer on the Royal Marines and is available from the RM Museum. (Royal Marines Museum, Southsea, Portsmouth, Hampshire PO4 9PX)

Left, Right and Below: Dotted across France and the world are memorials to the Commandos of World War II who gave their lives in the cause of freedom – Their Name Liveth For Evermore. *WFC*

Below left: Commando memorial at Spean Bridge. *WFC*

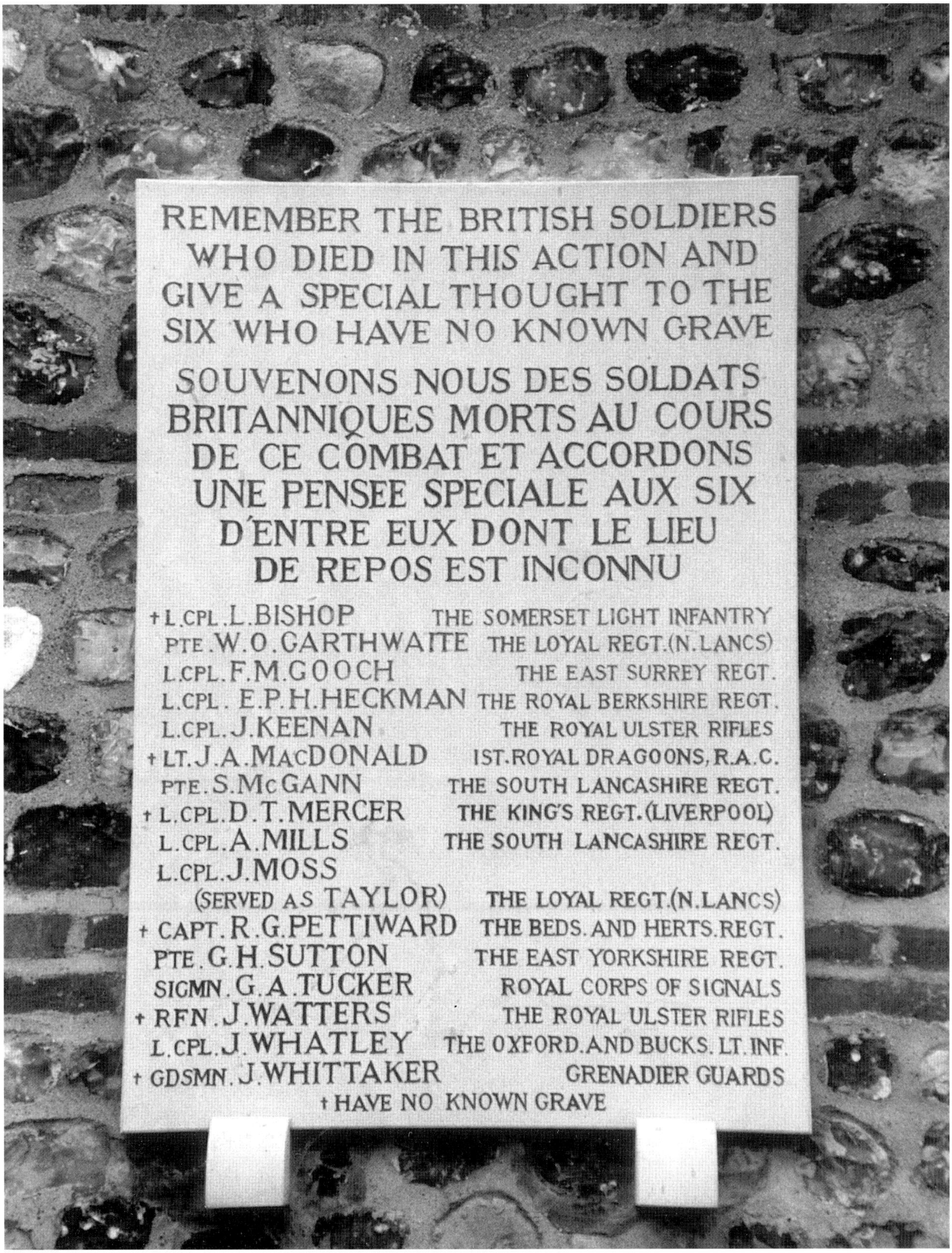

REMEMBER THE BRITISH SOLDIERS
WHO DIED IN THIS ACTION AND
GIVE A SPECIAL THOUGHT TO THE
SIX WHO HAVE NO KNOWN GRAVE

SOUVENONS NOUS DES SOLDATS
BRITANNIQUES MORTS AU COURS
DE CE COMBAT ET ACCORDONS
UNE PENSEE SPECIALE AUX SIX
D'ENTRE EUX DONT LE LIEU
DE REPOS EST INCONNU

† L.CPL.L.BISHOP   THE SOMERSET LIGHT INFANTRY
PTE.W.O.GARTHWAITE   THE LOYAL REGT.(N.LANCS)
L.CPL.F.M.GOOCH   THE EAST SURREY REGT.
L.CPL. E.P.H.HECKMAN   THE ROYAL BERKSHIRE REGT.
L.CPL. J.KEENAN   THE ROYAL ULSTER RIFLES
† LT. J.A.MacDONALD   IST.ROYAL DRAGOONS, R.A.C.
PTE.S.McGANN   THE SOUTH LANCASHIRE REGT.
† L.CPL.D.T.MERCER   THE KING'S REGT.(LIVERPOOL)
L.CPL.A.MILLS   THE SOUTH LANCASHIRE REGT.
L.CPL.J.MOSS
(SERVED AS TAYLOR)   THE LOYAL REGT.(N.LANCS)
† CAPT.R.G.PETTIWARD   THE BEDS. AND HERTS.REGT.
PTE.G.H.SUTTON   THE EAST YORKSHIRE REGT.
SIGMN.G.A.TUCKER   ROYAL CORPS OF SIGNALS
† RFN.J.WATTERS   THE ROYAL ULSTER RIFLES
L.CPL.J.WHATLEY   THE OXFORD.AND BUCKS. LT. INF.
† GDSMN.J.WHITTAKER   GRENADIER GUARDS
† HAVE NO KNOWN GRAVE

Company C, 2nd Ranger Battalion, prepares for a patrol, Ruhrberg, Germany

US RANGERS
'Leading the Way'

Ian Westwell

ORIGINS & HISTORY

The first Rangers, lightly equipped troops who 'ranged' deep in hostile territory and conducted what in modern terms are described as special operations, were primarily – although not exclusively – a phenomenon that developed in colonial America and reached their greatest expression in the wars of the mid-eighteenth century. The Seven Years War (1756–63) was truly global in scope and one of its main theatres was North America, where the French were steadily pushing southward from New France, their colonies in Canada, and thereby threatening British possessions along the New England seaboard. In attempting to stem the French tide the regular British Army was pitched into a style of fighting for which it was largely unprepared. In a densely wooded, often mountainous, terrain criss-crossed by numerous rivers, traditional set-piece battles between large formed bodies of rival troops were rare. The complex drills the ordinary soldier had learnt by rote, which also stifled any personal initiative, were far too rigid and inflexible for the conditions encountered. The French adapted their tactics to the conditions more readily by making extensive use of friendly Native Americans, and bands of French frontiersmen known as *coureurs du bois*, to conduct fast-moving hit-and-run raids, reconnaissance missions and ambushes. Their marksmanship, woodland and hunting skills, self-reliance and individual initiative proved much more suited to the terrain over which the campaign was conducted. Evidence of Britain's weakness was first revealed in July 1755 when a 1,400-strong column of British and colonial troops under Major-General Edward Braddock was virtually annihilated at the Battle of Monongahela in an ambush by 900 French and Native Americans.

Below: Major Robert Rogers (1731–95) of the British Army unit from which today's Rangers trace their lineage. In 1758 he was promoted to command His Majesty's Independent Companies of American Rangers – always known as Rogers' Rangers.

RANGERS IN COLONIAL AMERICA

Although the British were stung into creating units of light infantry from their own regular units to match the French after Monongahela, they also turned to the American colonists who had a long tradition of irregular frontier fighting. In 1675 during King Philip's War, a revolt by Metacomet of the Wampanoag tribe in Rhode Island over hunting and fishing rights, Captain Benjamin Church of Massachusetts formed a body of troops to deal with the unrest. The unit was known as Church's Rangers as its men 'ranged' far and wide to track down (and eventually kill) Metacomet. Typically, recruits to Church's Rangers and its descendants were hunters and frontiersmen, men skilled in living off the land who had often learned their skills from the Native Americans and often used them against the very same Native Americans in times of frontier unrest. Several more such units were raised during later periods of unrest, including Major John

Gorham's Company of Rangers. This New England unit first saw action during King George's War (1740–48), the North American offshoot of the European War of the Austrian Succession. Gorham's company comprised 50 or so Mohicans and frontiersmen and was chiefly involved in maintaining a British presence in Nova Scotia by quelling unrest among French settlers and Native Americans. The unit's importance was soon recognized – it doubled in size, Gorham received a regular commission in King George II's army and the Rangers received the same pay as British troops. The unit continued to serve in Nova Scotia, despite the death of John Gorham in 1751, and then participated in the French and Indian Wars under John's brother Joseph. Again it proved invaluable, taking part in the capture of Louisbourg, a key French fortress at the entrance to the St. Lawrence River, in 1758 and serving with Brigadier-General James Wolfe during the decisive Battle of the Plains of Abraham outside Quebec in 1759. Subsequently Gorham's Rangers took part in the attempt to storm Havana, Spain's chief colonial outpost in the New World, during 1762, and the following year participated in the quelling of the rebellion around Detroit led by Pontiac, leader of the Ottawa.

Although Gorham's Rangers was probably the most successful unit of the period, the founder of the most famous Ranger unit of the mid-eighteenth century was Robert Rogers (1731–95), a Massachusetts-born hunter, explorer and frontiersman, who in March 1756 was promoted to captain and given command of a unit known as the Ranger Company of Blanchard's New Hampshire Regiment. In 1758 he was again promoted, this time to major, and made commander of nine such companies, which were officially titled His Majesty's Independent Companies of American Rangers but were invariably known as Rogers' Rangers. The unit first saw action in an unsuccessful expedition to take Louisbourg in 1757 but was subsequently largely based at Fort Edward on the Hudson River some 60 miles (96km) north of Albany. It was from this base that Rogers conducted several missions that typified the Rangers' role and its dangers. In March 1758, he led a 180-strong force to reconnoitre French activity around Fort Ticonderoga, some 40 miles (65 km) north of Fort Edward. Initially moving by night, and despite appalling weather, the Rangers made good progress until confronted by around 100 Native Americans, a scouting party for a larger force of some 600 French-Canadians and other Native Americans. The Rangers ambushed the scouts, killing 40 or so, but then had to conduct a fighting withdrawal that cost 50 men.

A second operation, beginning on September 13, 1759, saw Rogers lead 200 Rangers against the pro-French Abenaki, who were encamped at St. Francis near the St. Lawrence River around 40 miles (64km) south of Montreal. The Rangers had to travel 300 miles (480km) through hostile and inhospitable terrain to reach their target. Setting out by boat from Crown Point on the west shore of Lake Champlain, Rogers' force

STANDING ORDERS
Rogers' Rangers

1. Don't forget nothing.
2. Have your musket clean as a whistle, hatchet scoured, sixty rounds of powder and ball, and be ready to march at a minute's notice.
3. When you're on the march, act the way you would if you was sneaking up on a deer. See the enemy first.
4. Tell the truth about what you see and what you do. There is an army depending on us for correct information. You can lie all you please when you tell other folks about the Rangers, but don't never lie to a Ranger or officer.
5. Don't never take a chance you don't have to.
6. When we're on the march we march single file, far enough apart so one shot can't go through two men.
7. If we strike swamps, or soft ground, we spread out abreast, so it's hard to track us.
8. When we march, we keep moving till dark, so as to give the enemy the least possible chance at us.
9. When we camp, half the party stays awake while the other half sleeps.
10. If we take prisoners, we keep 'em separate till we have had time to examine them, so they can't cook up a story between 'em.
11. Don't ever march home the same way. Take a different route so you won't be ambushed.
12. No matter whether we travel in big parties or little ones, each party has to keep a scout 20 yards ahead, 20 yards on each flank and 20 yards in the rear, so the main body can't be surprised and wiped out.
13. Every night you'll be told where to meet if surrounded by a superior force.
14. Don't sit down to eat without posting sentries.
15. Don't sleep beyond dawn. Dawn's when the French and Indians attack.
16. Don't cross a river by a regular ford.
17. If somebody's trailing you, make a circle, come back onto your own tracks, and ambush the folks that aim to ambush you.
18. Don't stand up when the enemy's coming against you. Kneel down, lie down, hide behind a tree.
19. Let the enemy come till he's almost close enough to touch. Then let him have it and jump out and finish him up with your hatchet.

Above: Rogers' Rangers Standing Orders of 1759 are still given to today's Ranger cadets.

travelled by night to avoid detection, resting during the day, and reached Missisquoi Bay undetected after 10 days. However, their numbers had been depleted by around 25 percent due to the accidental explosion of a gunpowder barrel. Rogers now hid his boats and moved towards St. Francis on foot, but two days later learned that the French had found his transports and were in hot pursuit. He nevertheless decided to continue and 12 days later reached St. Francis. Early the next morning he attacked the village and in a little more than an hour the Rangers killed more than 200 Abenaki, destroyed St. Francis, and rescued five captives for the loss of just one man. The return journey proved to be an epic of endurance. Short of supplies and harassed by the enemy, the Rangers split into several smaller groups to avoid detection. Some headed directly for Crown Point, while others made for a pre-agreed rendezvous point on the Ammonoosuck River. When Rogers stumbled in, there were no supplies as expected because the relief force had withdrawn just two hours before his arrival. A single Ranger officer and a young Native American were despatched by raft to a post known as Number Four some 100 miles (160 km) to the south and 10 days later returned with supplies. The Rangers' ordeal was over but the punitive expedition against the Abenaki had cost Rogers all but 93 of his men.

Following the end of the French and Indian Wars the Ranger concept went into decline until it was revived by both sides during the American War of Independence (1775–83). Chief among the British units to see service were the Queen's Rangers, originally a battalion of Loyalists led for a time by Rogers until his dismissal for unreliability fuelled by alcoholism in 1777. Rogers was replaced by a British officer, John Graves Simcoe, who turned the unit, which became known as Simcoe's Rangers, into a first-rate force that fought in several campaigns until forced into surrender at Yorktown in 1781. A second

Below: Colonel John S. Mosby's Confederate 43rd Battalion of Virginia Cavalry was the most successful guerrilla unit of the Civil War – so much so that part of north Virginia was dubbed 'Mosby's Confederacy'.

Above: Mosby's guerrillas in action. They tied down a great number of troops by effective harassment of Union supply lines.

battalion of Queen's Rangers was also raised and commanded by Robert Rogers' younger brother, James. It, too, saw extensive service in New York and around Lake Champlain.

Opposing the British were a number of pro-independence Ranger units raised at the instigation of the Continental Congress in June 1775. Two years later, Daniel Morgan was placed in charge of the Corps of Rangers, detachments of which fought with distinction at the Battles of Freeman's Farm (1777) and Cowpens (1781). At Freeman's Farm, part of the Battle of Saratoga, the defeated British commander, General John Burgoyne, remarked that Morgan's unit was 'the most famous corps in the Continental Army, all of them crack shots.' Morgan's exploits were matched by forces in South Carolina led by Francis Marion, known as the 'Swamp Fox' due to his elusiveness. Although not strictly Rangers, they undertook guerrilla missions that were recognizable in the tradition and proved a thorn in the side of both the British and their Loyalist allies.

RANGERS IN THE NINETEENTH CENTURY

The history of Ranger units in the nineteenth century paralleled that of the previous 100 years. Units were raised during periods of conflict and then swiftly disbanded once the fighting had ended. At the outbreak of the War of 1812 Congress ordered the raising of both foot and horse-mounted Rangers to protect the country's northern frontier from incursions by the British from Canada. Seventeen companies had been raised by the end of the war in 1815. For much of the remainder of the nineteenth century the need to protect the US frontier from outside aggression gave way to participating in the

expansion of the United States. Rangers fought in various campaigns against Native Americans, such as the wars against the Seminoles in Florida and, most famously, protected Americans living in the Mexican colony of Texas. Here, from 1823, Stephen Austin ordered the raising of an all-volunteer and unpaid mounted force that became known as the Texas Rangers. Aside from protecting American homesteaders and farmers, hunting down outlaws and maintaining the rule of law, the Texas Rangers undertook valuable scouting duties during the successful struggle to break away from Mexican rule in 1835–36 and the subsequent and successful war initiated by the United States against Mexico (1846–48) that led to the annexation of much of the southwest. Ranger units under officers such as Ben McCulloch and Jack Hays conducted forward reconnaissance missions for regular US forces during operations within Mexico.

The Texas Rangers and similar units also took part in the American Civil War (1861–65) and chiefly fought for the Confederacy. One of the earliest such units was Terry's Texas Rangers, which was raised by Benjamin Terry and Thomas Lubbock in 1861. Terry's men fought west of the Mississippi but similar units operated in the eastern theatre, most raised after the Confederate Congress enacted the Partisan Ranger Act in April 1862. Many of the units raised proved ill-disciplined and havens for criminals. Most were disbanded when the act was repealed in 1864, but some proved of continued value to the southern cause. Chief among these was the 43rd Virginia Cavalry, a unit commanded by John Singleton Mosby that was popularly known as Mosby's Rangers or Raiders. Mosby's daring exploits – raids and reconnaissance missions behind Union lines – earned him the nickname the 'Grey Ghost'. One of his most successful was a night raid against Fairfax Court House in northern Virginia during March 1863 that led to the capture of a brigadier general,

Edwin Stoughton, and severely embarrassed the Northern authorities. An attack on a Union railroad the following year caused similar embarrassment when it netted Mosby $170,000 originally destined to pay Northern troops. The Confederate raider and his band began to operate so effectively in northern Virginia that part of that state was christened 'Mosby's Confederacy' and, despite the best efforts of Northern forces, he remained at large throughout the war. He undertook his last mission on the day of the Confederate surrender at Appomattox Court House on April 9, 1865, and only formally disbanded his unit on the 21st.

The end of the Civil War was followed by a sustained westward drive that saw US citizens, many recent immigrants, settle in territories occupied by Native Americans. Clashes were inevitable, and the small peacetime US Army was quickly overstretched and not wholly suited to such a type of warfare. Once again Ranger-style units were formed to conduct scouting missions and hit-and-run raids against Native American villages. Many legendary figures of the Wild West participated in such campaigns, often as scouts, and among them were William Cody, better known as 'Buffalo Bill', and 'Texas' Jack Crawford. Larger bodies were also raised, such as the 50-strong Forsyth's Scouts raised by Major George Forsyth in 1868, but by the late 1880s the need for such formations was all but over due to the completion of the pacification programme directed against the Native Americans. The end of the Native American Wars left the Rangers and similar bodies with little to do. Some, such as the Texas Rangers continued to undertake law enforcement duties, but they had no obvious military role and the concept remained dormant for some 60 years until the outbreak of World War II.

REVIVING THE RANGER CONCEPT

The origin of the modern US Rangers lay with the Commando forces raised in Britain from 1940. President Roosevelt's enthusiasm for this type of force was communicated to the Chief of Staff of the US Army, General George Marshall, and he sent Colonel Lucian K. Truscott Jr. to England in early 1942 to evaluate the potential of Britain's Commando force and investigate the raising of similar US units. Not all the branches of the US armed forces were enthused by the idea. The Navy in general, and the Marine Corps in particular, felt that they had little to learn from the British and argued that they already had the training and capabilities to conduct the types of operation undertaken by the Commandos. This to some extent was true, as the Marine Corps was somewhat reluctantly raising specialist raider-type units to conduct such missions, but these Marine Raider battalions were largely needed in the Pacific, where the Japanese were posing a more immediate and ongoing threat.

Truscott, who was attached to the British Combined Operations staff under Lord Louis Mountbatten while in England, reported back to Marshall in late May and recommended the formation of a US Commando-type unit. The chief of staff concurred and the relevant orders to raise an 'American Commando' were issued on June 1. However, the chief of the general staff's Operations Division, Major General Dwight D. Eisenhower, pointed out that the name Commando was very much associated with the British and requested that a more American name be used for the new unit. Truscott remembered the exploits of Rogers and his men and suggested that Ranger would be a fitting alternative. With a name settled on, it was now necessary to find and train the officers and men for the reborn Rangers. The most immediate and accessible source of recruits were the US forces already stationed in Britain.

Above: General Ben McCulloch (1811–62) – once of the Texas Rangers – was killed at the Battle of Pea Ridge, Arkansas, in March 1862, while in command of the Confederates' west wing. His early war experiences were as a Texas Ranger, and as the captain of a Ranger company in the Mexican War; he would become Chief of Scouts to General Zachary Taylor. Known for his daring exploits, his reputation ensured his prominence during the Civil War. He was promoted general – the first Confederate to be elevated to this position from civilian life – and on August 10, 1861, he beat the forces of Brig. Gen. Nathaniel Lyon at Wilson's Creek in southwest Missouri. Fighting under Van Dorn at Pea Ridge, his troops overran a battery of Union artillery. McCulloch rode forward to get a better view of the enemy line, was shot from his horse and died instantly.

Left: John S. Mosby (1833–1916) after promotion to brigadier general.

READY FOR WAR

The officer designated to found the new Ranger unit was Major William O. Darby, an aide to Major General Russell P. Harte, commander of the US 34th Infantry Division and, from January 27, 1942, the head of the US Army Northern Ireland. Darby, an Arkansas-born West Point graduate whose chosen army career was in the artillery, was stationed at Carrickfergus, some 20 miles (32 km) north of Belfast, but had already requested more active assignments. On June 8 he was ordered to form a Commando-style unit but in the early summer of 1942 the US forces in Britain were small compared to what they would become by 1944. Nevertheless Darby set about raising suitable recruits from what was available locally. These were the two divisions that comprised the US V Corps, the 34th Infantry and 1st Armored, and various support units.

COMMANDO TRAINING AT ACHNACARRY

Over the following days Darby interviewed potential recruits, both officers and men, and by the 19th, the day that the 1st Ranger Battalion was officially activated, he had a pool of some 2,000 personnel to work with. These were quickly whittled down to around 570 men – 20 percent above the official establishment figure of 26 officers and 447 other ranks – but Darby expected many volunteers to fall by the wayside during training. The raw materials Darby had to work with were of many backgrounds and came from across the United States. The largest group, some 60 percent, had been serving with the 34th Division, and were mainly from Iowa, Minnesota and Nebraska. A further 30 percent were drawn from the 1st Armored Division and the remaining 10 percent were mainly support troops from V Corps' medical, logistical and signal units. On the 25th Darby and his recruits were inspected by General Robert Laycock, the commander of the British 1st Special Service Brigade, an experienced Commando group under whose direction the Rangers would receive their initial specialist training.

Above: Corporal Franklin M. Koons (nicknamed 'Zip') was the first US soldier to kill a German in World War II during the landings at Dieppe in August 1942.

The Rangers transferred to the west coast of Scotland three days later and were based at Achnacarry Castle, a few miles north of Fort William close to Loch Arkaig. Achnacarry was home to the British Commando Training Depot and its commanding officer, Lieutenant-Colonel Charles Vaughan, was tasked with directing the Rangers' training programme. Vaughan, a long-serving officer with recent experience of the Commando raids on the Lofoten Islands and Vaagsø in northern Norway, had created a demanding and realistic course. The programme he had devised consisted of three parts and was undertaken by both officers and men. First, speed marches over the area's rugged mountains and valleys, which grew from three to 16 miles (5–25 km), coupled with timed obstacle courses built up the Rangers' strength and stamina. Next, they were shown how to use the weapons and equipment appropriate to lightly equipped raiding

forces. Finally, they were taught the tactical skills they would need to carry out their specialist role, such as scouting and patrolling, silent killing, mountaineering, river-crossing and street-fighting. Three-day exercises were used to evaluate the Rangers. By the end of the first week Darby's original 20 percent surfeit of recruits had turned to a 10 percent deficit as many men fell by the wayside and were returned to their original units.

Above: Training was a major part of the Rangers' life throughout the war, with the emphasis on physical exercise and realistic battle conditions. At the start the training took place alongside their British counterparts – the Commandos – in Britain (as here in August 1942).

The Achnacarry training ended in late July and on August 1 the Rangers retraced their steps to Fort William to begin the next state of their preparations – amphibious warfare training directed by the Royal Navy. This was conducted at HMS *Dorlin*, a shore establishment near Acharacle on the coast of Argyll and ideally placed to make use of the adjacent Western Isles. The six Ranger companies were billeted in pairs at Glenborrodale, Glencripesdale and Roshven, while Darby set up his headquarters at Shielbridge. Early training centred on Kentra beach close to *Dorlin*, where the British had established a realistic course to test the Rangers' abilities with assault boats. Other skills developed included navigation, cliff assault and raids on coastal batteries. Once again, three-day exercises were used to put theory into practice.

BLOODING AT DIEPPE

It was during this period that a handful of Rangers gained first-hand experience of real combat. Operation Jubilee, the raid on the port of Dieppe on August 18–19, was designed to test the strength of the German defences in northern France and the feasibility of seizing a port, which was seen as an essential prerequisite for any future large-scale invasion of Nazi-occupied Europe. Although the bulk of the forces committed to Jubilee were drawn from the Canadian 2nd Division, it was planned as an all-arms operation, one involving 237 warships and some 74 squadrons of aircraft. A number of

This page: More views of training emphasising the skills needed to become a Ranger – physical endurance; climbing skills; unarmed and armed combat. Most of the early photos, such as these, were taken in Scotland as British Commando instructors (seen far right) put the Rangers through their paces – including jumping off the remarkable 20-foot (6m) barrier on the Commando assault course in Argyll (below right) with full pack, M1917A1 helmet and M1 rifle! Many of the Rangers' exercises were conducted using live firing to ensure the most realistic possible training environment. The preponderance of training photos of Rangers – and all special forces – against action shots is caused by the very nature of their missions. They tended to take place at night or in low light conditions, often in situations where a Press or Service photographer would have been a hindrance.

DIEPPE

The first American ground forces to see action against the Germans, three Rangers were killed (*) and several captured. Those of the 1st Ranger Battalion who took part were: 1-Lt. Leonard F. Dirks, 1-Lt. Robert Flanagan, 2-Lt. Charles M. Shunstrom, 2-Lt. Edwin V. Loustalot*, 2-Lt. Joseph H. Randall*, Capt. Roy A. Murray, S/Sgt. Gino Mercuriali, S/Sgt. Kenneth D. Stempson, S/Sgt. Lester E. Kness, S/Sgt. Merritt M. Bertholf, Sgt. Albert T. Jacobsen, Sgt. Alex Szima, Sgt. Dick Sellers, Sgt. Edwin C. Thompson, Sgt. Harold R. Adams, Sgt. John J. Knapp, Sgt. Kenneth G Kenyon, Sgt. Lloyd N. Church, Sgt. Marcell G Swank, Sgt. Marvin L. Kavanaugh, Sgt. Mervin T. Heacock, Sgt. Theodore Q. Butts, Sgt. Tom Sorby, T/4 Howard W. Henry*, T/5 Joe C. Phillips, T/5 John H. Smith, T/5 Michael Kerecman, T/5 William S. Brinkley, Cpl. Franklin M. Koons, Cpl. William R. Brady, Pfc. Charles F. Grant, Pfc. Charles R. Coy, Pfc. Charles Reilly, Pfc. Clare P. Beitel, Pfc. Donald G Johnson, Pfc. Donald L. Hayes, Pfc. Edwin R. Furru, Pfc. Erwin J. Moger, Pfc. Howard T. Hedenstad, Pfc. Howard W. Andre, Pfc. James C. Mosely, Pfc. James O. Edwards, Pfc. Owen E. Sweazey, Pfc. Pete M. Preston, Pfc. Stanley Bush, Pfc. Walter A. Bresnahan, Pfc. William E. Lienhas, Pfc. William S. Girdley, Pvt. Don A. Earwood, Pvt. Jacque M. Nixon.

Commando units were also deployed as was a small detachment of Rangers – 44 men and five officers under Captain Roy Murray. Also on hand was Truscott, who acted as an observer.

The bulk of the Rangers were attached to the two British Commandos that were earmarked to neutralize the German coastal batteries to the east and west of Dieppe. Forty Rangers including Murray were assigned to No. 3 Commando under Lieutenant-Colonel J.F. Durnford-Slater and this force sailed from Newhaven on the south coast of England late on the 18th. Their mission was to come ashore at two beaches codenamed Yellow 1 and Yellow 2 some five miles (8 km) to the east of Dieppe and then silence the cliff-top battery at Bruneval, which had been designated 'Goebbels'. The Commandos and Rangers crossed the English Channel in 27 slow-moving wooden landing craft known as Eurekas as part of a flotilla that included *Steam Gun Boat No. 5*, with Durnford-Slater and Murray on board, *Motor Launch 348* and an anti-aircraft vessel.

The plan was soon in disarray. Four of the Eurekas turned back because of engine failure and the remainder then ran into a small German convoy some 8 miles (13 km) from their target at around 0347 hours on the 19th. In the subsequent firefight many of the Eurekas suffered heavy damage, were sunk or dispersed, and the steam gun boat was virtually wrecked. Durnford-Slater and Murray were therefore unable to play any further part in Jubilee. Only one Eureka reached the target area on schedule but its men could do little more than direct harassing fire against Goebbels battery before withdrawing after some 90 minutes. Six other Eurekas did make a landing but they were 25 minutes late and the troops came ashore in daylight. Some 50 men, including a handful of Rangers, were soon pinned down by heavy fire and were unable to make any progress inland. One of the Rangers, Lieutenant Edwin Loustalot, was mortally wounded, becoming the first US soldier to be killed in European land fighting during World War II. The remainder of the party were eventually taken prisoner.

The attack on the coastal battery codenamed 'Hess' some six miles (10 km) to the west of Dieppe was led by Lord Lovat's No. 4 Commando, which included six Rangers (four sergeants and two corporals), and proved much more successful. Their crossing in

HMS *Prince Albert*, a converted ferry, was uneventful and two assault parties, known as Group One and Group Two, were successfully landed around Varengeville-sur-Mer. Lord Lovat led Group Two ashore at a beach codenamed Orange 2, which lay some 2 miles (3 km) from Group One's target, Orange 1. This pincer attack against Hess was conducted with surprise and great speed and the defenders were quickly overwhelmed and the battery neutralized. One of the Rangers, Corporal Franklin Koons, became the first US soldier to kill a German in combat and his sniping skills during the action earned him a Military Medal, which was presented by Lord Louis Mountbatten, head of Britain's Combined Operations. By 0730 the action was over and Lovat's men were withdrawn without difficulty.

The action against Hess was the only clear-cut success of the whole controversial operation. The main landing by the Canadians stalled on the beaches and ended in heavy losses – some 3,400 men or close to 70 percent of those engaged – but Jubilee did highlight shortcomings in equipment and tactics for amphibious warfare. The Rangers also suffered in this learning process. Darby recorded seven officers and men missing in action – either killed or taken prisoner – and seven injured. Consequently four officers and 39 men returned from the Dieppe raid and their experiences were used to improve the battalion's amphibious training. Despite Jubilee's failure, the Rangers' role in the operation made front-page news in the United States. The *New York Post* led with the banner headline 'We Land in France' while the *New York World Telegram* somewhat optimistically proclaimed that 'US Troops Smash the French Coast'.

PREPARING FOR OPERATION TORCH

The Rangers' time at HMS *Dorlin* came to an end shortly after the Dieppe raid and they moved from the west to east coast of Scotland. At Dundee, they were partnered with the British No. 1 Commando to undertake joint training that emphasized techniques for neutralizing all manner of coastal defences, such as batteries and pill boxes. The programme lasted until September 24, when the 1st Battalion boarded a train that took it to Glasgow. The Rangers were assigned to the US II Corps and attached to the US 1st Infantry Division. Both the division and Darby's men had been earmarked to play a leading role in the forthcoming invasion of North Africa, Operation Torch, which was scheduled to open in early November. Between September 29 and October 25, the Rangers honed the skills they had been taught over the previous months and were given some final lessons on the best way of loading both themselves and their equipment into assault craft of various types. On the 26th the months of preparation came to an end. After travelling to Gourock, a few miles west of Glasgow, the battalion boarded three former Glasgow–Belfast ferries, the *Royal Scotsman*, *Royal Ulsterman* and *Ulster Monarch*, which had been commandeered by the Royal Navy as amphibious assault transports and were preparing to take them to North Africa.

Above: Another view of 'Zip' Koons, who gained fame for his fighting at Dieppe; note the 1st Rangers shoulder flash.

Left: 1st Ranger Battalion exercise on a wet autumn day in Scotland, October 31, 1942 – one of a series of photographs taken on this exercise (see also pages 18, 19 and 68).

Above and Opposite: Landing craft training, Scotland October 31, 1942.

Left: Well it started fine! Preparing kit for their next exercise, men of 1st Rangers, October 9, 1942.

IN ACTION

OPERATION TORCH – THE INVASION OF NORTH AFRICA

The 1st Ranger Battalion was assigned to Major General Lloyd Fredendall's Centre Task Force for Operation Torch. Fredendall's overall role was to seize the port of Oran in Algeria in a widely dispersed three-pronged assault and, aside from the Rangers, his command included the US 1st Armored and 1st Infantry Divisions. Darby's men were assigned to spearhead the easternmost of Fredendall's three landings by combat teams drawn from the 1st Infantry Division on beaches near the small port of Arzew some 25 miles (40 km) east of Oran. Darby's chief task was to neutralize two Vichy French coastal batteries that could potentially devastate the assault craft carrying the two of the 1st Division's regimental combat teams that were scheduled to land at three beaches codenamed Z Green, Z White and Z Red in Arzew Bay to the immediate southeast of Arzew itself. One battery, known as Fort de la Pointe, was sited at the harbour's northern edge and contained three coastal guns surrounded by barbed wire and behind which lay a small French fort with walls about 20 feet (6 m) high. The second and potentially more threatening target, the Batterie du Nord, containing four 105 mm guns, was on high ground north of the fort and overlooked both the harbour and Arzew Bay. Darby formulated a plan of attack after studying air photographs of his objectives and the area surrounding Arzew. He opted to split his command into two groups and assault the batteries simultaneously, thereby capitalizing on the element of surprise. A smaller group under Major Herman Dammer was ordered to sail directly into Arzew harbour to tackle the Fort de la Pointe while the larger party under Darby himself was to come ashore some four miles (6 km) north of the Batterie du Nord and attack it from the rear.

Late on November 7, as the Centre Task Force's ships sailed eastward some 15 miles (24 km) offshore toward Arzew Bay and rounded Cap Carbon, *Ulster Monarch* and *Royal Ulsterman* with Darby's four Ranger companies – C, D, E and F – on board dropped out of the convoy and followed the coastline due south to the small landing beach north of the Batterie du Nord that had previously been identified from the air photographs. Nearing their target under cover of darkness and a sea fog, the Rangers embarked in 10 Landing Craft, Assault, which were backed by a pair of Landing Craft, Support. One of the assault craft became stuck in its davits, pitching its occupants into the waters below. All were quickly rescued and the remaining craft headed for shore, although they had to be guided in by the captain of the *Ulster Monarch*, who had spotted that they were initially heading in the wrong direction. This last-minute course correction allowed the Rangers to reach their allocated beach, land undetected save for a surprised and easily captured French sentry, and then quickly scale the cliff that

Below: Lieutenant Colonel William O. Darby on a speed march with his men, December 5, 1942, North Africa (see biography page 81).

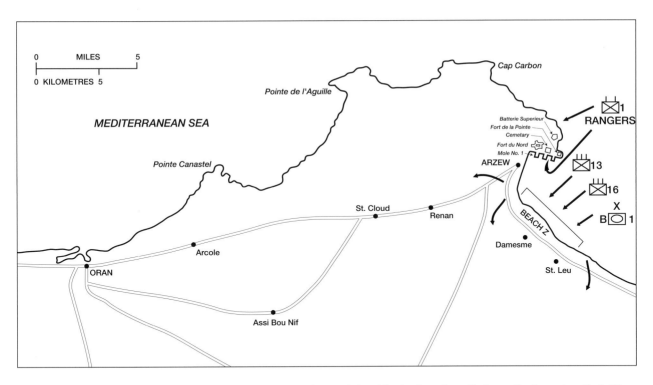

Above: The Rangers' landings at Arzew, North Africa, November 8, 1942. It wasn't the largest operation the Rangers would take part in during the war, but it was handled efficiently and the objectives were taken.

barred their exit from the beach. Darby's assault group moved towards its objective by following the coast road to within two miles (3 km) of the battery and then followed a wadi that led to the ridge line on top of which lay the Batterie du Nord and a smaller supporting defensive work called the Fort du Nord.

As Darby made his way toward his target, the two Ranger companies that had remained with the main invasion force sailing toward Arzew disembarked into five assault craft from the *Royal Scotsman* at 0100 hours on the 8th. Christened Dammer Force, the men of Companies A and B headed for shore in silence. Finding the boom that might have delayed their attack open rather than closed as expected, they sailed undetected and on schedule into the harbour – but on the wrong course. A swift realignment brought them back on track and they made their way between the outer jetty and main pier as planned. Moments later the assault craft reached a low but slanting seawall and their ramps came down, leaving the Rangers to scramble noisily over the slippery sea defences with some difficulty and then make their way to the battery. Surprise was total despite the noise. Three Vichy French soldiers were captured at gunpoint as the Rangers made their approach and the barbed wire surrounding the Fort de la Pointe was swiftly cut. The attackers bounded over a low wall, fired a few shots to make their presence known, and within 15 minutes had captured the guns and around 60 prisoners.

Darby now commenced his assault against the Batterie du Nord. Company D with four 81 mm mortars was deployed in a convenient ditch some 500 yards (500 m) from the battery to provide covering fire while Companies C, F and E approached its northern perimeter and began cutting paths through the 14-foot (4 m) wide barbed wire entanglements that skirted the position. As this task was being completed the Vichy French opened fire with several machine guns that threatened the momentum of the attack. Darby called down mortar fire and, after just eight highly accurate rounds, the French fire died away and the Rangers stormed into the compound. Some headed for the battery's control tower, others thrust bangalore torpedoes into the barrels of the coastal

Right and Opposite: Operation Torch — the assault craft, November 8, 1942. The photo on page 23 is on either *Ulster Monarch* or *Royal Ulsterman* and shows 81mm mortar rounds being loaded into an assault craft preparatory to the attack. Note the US flag and white armbands (see also photos on page 24). These were worn to identify friendly forces during the attack.

Opposite, Below: Physical exercise on board the transport during the journey to North Africa, November 5, 1942.

Below: Training continued, even in Africa; this shows Rangers preparing to assault a gun position, December 12, 1942. Most of the Rangers spent the end of 1942 and the beginning of 1943 attached to 5th Army Invasion Training Center at Arzew where they took part in exercises as demonstration troops. This is part of the area assaulted in earnest on November 8. Note the fixed bayonets: the Rangers often used the M1 rifle and M1905 bayonet.

guns, while others stormed though the position's main entrance. The bulk of the garrison had taken shelter in an underground powder store and, after being threatened by grenades and bangalore torpedoes thrown down its ventilator shafts, they surrendered. The battery was securely in Darby's hands by 0400 hours at a cost of two Rangers killed and eight wounded and he was able to signal his success to the invasion fleet lying offshore.

As the main landings got underway around Arzew the Rangers conducted various mopping-up operations around the batteries and harbour. At dawn Darby turned his attentions to the Fort du Nord. Vichy machine guns opened fire as he was attempting to persuade the garrison to surrender by telephone but Darby was able to secure the fort commander's agreement as Ranger mortar fire struck the position and silenced the fire. Darby and a small party of his men moved towards their objective but once again machine guns opened up on them and a Ranger company decided to force the issue by assaulting the fort. Some men were halted by its moat but others stormed across the drawbridge and broke through the main gateway. The garrison surrendered immediately and the Rangers marched them away to the Batterie du Nord.

Above: The official caption identifies this as forcing the doors on a building captured during the fighting on November 8. The general lack of interest exhibited by the troops shows that the action was over by this time. Note the white identification armbands in this and the photograph below.

Meanwhile, after neutralizing the Batterie de la Pointe, Dammer Force fanned out to occupy key points, such as the small oil refinery north of the harbour, and dealt with Vichy snipers who were harassing the Rangers. A hillside cemetery between the two forts was cleared before dawn and then the Rangers dealt with similar resistance in the harbour area, chiefly around the piers and warehouses, and silenced a battery of 75 mm field guns firing on Allied shipping.

Most of the Ranger companies remained in Arzew over the next three days to complete its pacification and maintain order, but two were detached to aid units from the 1st Infantry Division as its regimental combat teams pushed southeast and southwest from their landing beaches. Lieutenant Max Schneider's Company E moved out on the afternoon of the 8th to support the 1st Battalion, 16th Infantry Regiment's

push along the coast road running southeast from Arzew. The rendezvous took place at 0700 on the 9th and Schneider was ordered to move down the road towards the town of La Macta. Some 800 yards (700 m) east of Port-aux-Poules the company was hit by light fire from concealed positions on a low ridge. This was brushed aside and, after a successful enveloping attack just a mile from La Macta, Schneider's men captured their objective. Company C was first tasked with defending the headquarters of the 1st Division at the village of Tourville on the 8th but then aided the 1st Battalion, 18th Infantry Regiment, in its assault on St. Cloud some 12 miles (20 km) southwest of Arzew. The Rangers established blocking positions south of the town under cover of darkness but at dawn on the 9th were hit by intense enemy fire at close range. The company commander, Lieutenant Klefman, was killed but the St. Cloud garrison surrendered during the afternoon. Both detached companies returned to Arzew on the 10th.

The Rangers' role in Operation Torch, which had cost them a mere four killed and 11 wounded and led to the capture of several hundred prisoners, ended with the actions at La Macta and St. Cloud, and Darby's men were not initially involved in the subsequent, somewhat badly handled Allied drive eastward toward German-held Tunisia. For the next three months they were attached to the Fifth Army Invasion Training Center at Arzew, honing their own skills particularly in night fighting and teaching seaborne assault techniques to other units. At the end of January 1943 the battalion underwent some reorganization: Company D gave up its mortars and regained its purely assault role, while an entirely new Company G was formed from more than 100 fresh volunteers. The spell at the training centre ended at the beginning of February. On the 1st the battalion boarded 32 Douglas C-47 transports at Oran and was flown to Youks-les-Bains airfield near Tébessa close to the Algerian–Tunisian border.

Above: Full marching order for 1st Rangers as they march past agaves on December 5, 1942.

Below left: This is a photograph closer to the action. It shows Rangers in position on the Batterie du Nord on November 8 following the brief battle for Arzew. Note the M1919A4 Browning .30 machine gun, the standard support weapon for the Rangers.

THE BATTLE FOR TUNISIA

After landing, the Rangers moved to the headquarters of General Lloyd Fredendall, commander of the US II Corps, which lay a little to the east of Tébessa, and Darby was briefed on his next operations. The proposed missions had two aspects. First, to conduct a reconnaissance in strength to identify the Axis divisions, both Italian and German, that were retreating into central Tunisia from neighbouring Tripolitania along the coast by way of Gabès. Second, they were to mask the redeployment of Allied units away from southern and central Tunisia, to meet a thrust by Colonel-General Jürgen von Arnim's Fifth Panzer Army from Tunis and Bizerte in the north of the country, by conducting hit-and-run raids and aggressive patrols to mislead the enemy as to the real strength of the opposition they faced. Three raids were planned – against Italian positions some five miles (8 km) from Station de Sened, against the Djebel el Ank, and Medilla. Observation of the enemy at Sened revealed that the Rangers faced troops from two of the Italian Army's better formations – the *Centauro* Division and the Bersaglieri.

Darby began the first raid on February 11, setting out towards Sened, which lay some 32 miles (56 km) from the Rangers' encampment at Gafsa, at the head of half of the 1st Battalion – Companies A, E and F. The first 20 miles (32 km) were by truck and jeep but then the raiders dismounted at a front-line Free French outpost and conducted the final approach on foot. By dawn on the 12th they had covered some 8 miles (13 km) more and lay just four miles from their target. Darby ordered his men to hide up during daylight to avoid detection from enemy ground observers and reconnaissance aircraft, and laid plans for the attack. The final approach to Sened began at around midnight, and at 600 yards (550 m) distance Darby ordered his men into a skirmish line for the assault. The Rangers had so far been undetected but some 200 yards (200 m) from the target, the Italians opened fire with machine guns. Nevertheless, the attack caught most of Sened's garrison by surprise as Darby's men swept into the positions. Aided by mortar fire, the Rangers quickly overcame any opposition. Many of the Italians fled, but around 50 were killed and many more wounded. The Rangers, who had one man killed and 18 wounded, also captured 10 prisoners from the 10th Bersaglieri Regiment. With dawn on the 12th less than three hours away, Darby now ordered a rapid withdrawal. His command was divided into two columns, one of which included the wounded, and both set off on the 12-mile (20 km) trudge back to friendly lines. Both groups returned without further loss – the faster column arrived at dawn on the 12th and the slower with the wounded during the following day.

Sened was an operation of the type that had brought Robert Rogers' fame in the eighteenth century and its success was recognized by the awards given to the 1st Battalion. Darby, four of his fellow officers and nine enlisted men received the Silver Star; the Italians who had faced the

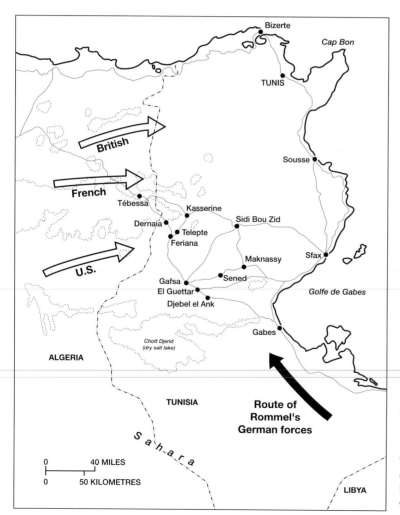

Below: The advance towards Kasserine, Tunisia 1943.

Rangers took to calling them the 'Black Death'.

However, the Rangers were unable to capitalize on their success at Sened as the other planned raids were cancelled due to a major two-pronged German attack that was launched against the Kasserine Pass in central Tunisia. Devised by Field Marshal Erwin Rommel, who had recently returned to North Africa after an illness, the intention was for armoured units to strike through the pass that ran through the Western Dorsale range, capture the Allied base at Tébessa and then turn northwards to encircle the Allied forces battling in northern Tunisia. The Rangers, who were acting as a rearguard, pulled out of Gafsa on the 14th and three days later they moved into position to cover the eastern entrance to Dernaia Pass, a second route south of Kasserine that also led to Tébessa. The Rangers were strung out over two miles (3 km) of front in hill-top positions some four miles (6 km) from the vital Gafsa–Kasserine road at Feriana from where a route branched westwards through the Dernaia Pass towards Tébessa. Axis troops were advancing along the Gafsa–Kasserine road and the Rangers were ideally placed to report on these troops' movements. The Germans did not assault Dernaia directly but kept it under periodic artillery fire and launched various probes and reconnaissance operations. The Rangers also conducted patrols and had firefights with the enemy but there were no major attacks to deal with, although one company was flung into the battle for Kasserine on the 22nd.

The Rangers remained at Dernaia Pass until March 1, when they were withdrawn from the front line and went into camp at Djebel Kouif. On the 13th they set out for Gafsa, some 50 miles (80 km) southeast of Dernaia, once again and reached the town three days later. Gafsa was the juncture of two important roads that led northeast and southeast through passes to the coast of central Tunisia and was to be the springboard for attacks by Patton's US II Corps after the end of the fighting at Kasserine. The northern advance towards Sfax by way of Sened and Maknassy was led by the US 1st Armored Division, while the US 1st Infantry Division and the 1st Rangers were tasked with capturing Axis-held El Guettar, from where roads lead northeast to Sfax and southeast to Gabès. The Rangers were ordered to probe El Guettar to discover the strength of the defences and on March 18 they moved against their objective under cover of darkness only to find that the oasis had been abandoned.

With El Guettar as a forward base, II Corps' attack towards the coast could develop and the Rangers were ordered to seize the commanding heights of Djebel el Ank, which overlooked the routes to Sfax and Gabès. These enemy positions were only five miles (8 km) from El Guettar, but were too strong to attack frontally, so Darby pulled his men back to Gafsa and launched them on a 12-mile (20 km) flanking march late on the evening

Above: Troop movement during the Battle of Sened. An extremely successful use of the Rangers saw the Italian troops at the Station de Sened in a surprise attack. Darby and thirteen other Rangers received Silver Stars for the action.

of the 20th. The lightly equipped Rangers made good progress, although the accompanying combat engineers with their heavy mortars found the going more difficult. By 0600 on the 13th Darby was ready to assault the enemy positions. The attack commenced, with the Rangers neutralizing enemy strongpoints one by one, often at bayonet point, despite facing heavy machine-gun and artillery fire. Two hours later the combat engineers began dropping mortar rounds on the remaining Axis emplacements. The main battle ended successfully in the early afternoon, when the US 1st Infantry Division's 26th RCT arrived to occupy the djebel, but the Rangers continued mopping-up operations until 1400 hours, when Darby was able to report the capture of both the heights and 200 prisoners.

The swift loss of Djebel el Ank brought about a series of counterattacks from the Germans, who immediately attacked the high ground stretching in a curve from the Djebel el Ank in the north to Djebel Berda, some five miles (8 km) south of the El Guettar–Gabès road, that was now occupied by the 1st Infantry Division. On the 24th the Rangers were moved to aid two battalions of the division's 18th Infantry Regiment which were struggling to beat off German counterattacks against their positions on the Djebel Berda. Darby's men initially settled down on the djebel's Hill 772 but all of the battalion bar Company D were flung into action against a German attack on the isolated battalions. For three days the Rangers fought on, often surrounded, but their action allowed the two battalions to withdraw in good order. The Rangers were relieved by units of the US 9th Infantry Division and withdrawn from the fighting around El Guettar on March 27, although the battle continued for several days. The 1st Battalion received a Presidential Unit Citation for this action some 12 months later.

Darby now found his battalion divided to undertake patrolling duties as the campaign in Tunisia entered its final phase. Two companies were stationed at Gafsa, two at Madjene el Fedj, some 25 miles (40 km) north, and two at Sidi bou Sid, a further 35 miles (56 km) to the north.

The last Axis forces in North Africa finally surrendered on May 13 but the Rangers had already departed to prepare for their next operation. On April 17 they had moved by road and rail to Nemours, close to Oran in Algeria, where the battalion established a base and training facilities. Two days later Darby, who had requested the expansion of the Rangers, was informed that he was to oversee the creation of two new battalions and that they had to be ready for action in six weeks. Darby decided to split his existing battalion into three two-company groups and use these experienced men as the core of the new units. As a 2nd Battalion had been activated in the United States on April 1, Companies A and B consequently formed the basis for the 3rd Rangers under Major Herman Dammer, Companies E and F went to the 4th Rangers under Major Roy Murray, while Companies C and D were used to rebuild the 1st Battalion under Darby. With time pressing, Darby scoured North Africa for potential recruits and candidates were despatched to Nemours to undergo training with Dammer. The two new units were formerly activated on May 21 but were given the title Provisional until June 21. The whole command, which was reinforced by the 83rd Chemical Mortar Battalion (equipped with 4.2-inch mortars), was designated the Ranger Force (Provisional) but was more commonly known as Darby's Rangers.

THE INVASION OF SICILY

Darby's Rangers had been detailed for a leading role in Operation Husky, the Anglo-US invasion of Sicily. The Rangers were earmarked to spearhead landings by the US Seventh Army under General George Patton at two points on the island's west coast – the towns of Licata and Gela. As the invasion drew near, Darby moved with the the 1st and 4th

While the Rangers were preparing for the invasion of Sicily, in the United States and United Kingdom other cadres were preparing. These photographs were taken on a wet February 26, 1943, at the Commando Depot (later the Commando Basic Training Centre), which had been established at Achnacarry Castle, near Fort William, in the Highlands of Scotland in March 1942. The depot was commanded by the formidable Lt-Col Charles Vaughan (see *Spearhead 10 Commandos*) who is in both photographs.

Above: Top brass at the Commando Depot watching 29th Rangers parade: from left to right in the front — Capt Joy, depot adjutant; J.M. Pate, Minister of War Transport; Maj Gen. Gerow; Brig. Robert Laycock, chief of the Special Service Brigade; and Lt-Col. Vaughan.

Left: Major-General Gerow talks to Sgt John O'Brien of the 29th Rangers. Nearest the camera is Lt-Col. Vaughan. (See also pages 44–45 for further information on 29th Ranger Battalion.)

Battalions to the vicinity of Algiers to link up with the 1st Infantry Division once again, while Dammer moved his command to camps around Bizerte in northern Tunisia to support Major General Lucian Truscott's US 3rd Infantry Division.

The 1st and 4th Rangers boarded the landing ships USS *Dickman*, HMS *Albert* and HMS *Charles*. They were to act as a spearhead force to tackle Axis defences at Gela before the main landing by the 1st Infantry Division began. Estimates suggested that the target and its environs were defended by three fixed shore batteries, a battery of 77 mm field guns, two mortar companies and more than a score of machine-gun positions. Darby planned for his two battalions to land directly opposite Gela, to the left and right of a 2,000-yard (1,800 m) pier that jutted out into the harbour from the dead centre of the coastal town. The 1st Rangers were to land to the north of the pier and then swing westward to neutralize a fort, while the 4th Rangers swung eastward to deal with other coastal defences. Half an hour after the initial assault the 1st Battalion, 39th Engineers, was scheduled to land on the 1st Rangers' beach to be followed at 30-minute intervals by the 83rd Chemical Mortar Battalion and a second battalion of engineers respectively. The 1st Battalion engineers, fighting as infantry, were ordered to fill the vacuum left by the flanking attacks of the two Ranger battalions.

At around 0130 hours on July 10, the Rangers clambered into their 48 assault craft from their landing ships, a task made difficult because of 40 mph (64 km/h) winds and rough waters, and headed for their forming up point some five miles (8 km) from their dropping-off point. The final run in, which took some 30 minutes, began at 0245. The enemy were alert to imminent attack but their fire, although heavy and directed by searchlights, was largely inaccurate and the Rangers made directly for shore with little difficulty. As expected the pier was primed for demolition and its central section was demolished just as the the attackers passed, but few casualties were caused and the assault waves made for shore, some arriving five minutes early. Many boats reached their allotted target without difficulty but others beached on sandbars and the Rangers had to wade ashore. Some made it easily but others, particularly in the 4th Battalion, became casualties when they ran into barbed wire and a minefield. The two battalions next moved through the edges of Gela, meeting only light resistance from occasional snipers, and then began the task of neutralizing the flanking defences. Aided by salvoes from the cruiser USS *Savannah*, the 1st Battalion quickly overcame the defenders of the fort, while similar successes were achieved by the 4th Rangers.

These missions complete, Darby reassembled his forces on the beaches and led them into Gela to form a perimeter to protect the ongoing unloading of troops and supplies. At around 0700 hours the Italians pushed tanks of their Gruppo Mobile E into the town and these were beaten off thanks to a single 37 mm anti-tank gun managed by Darby and Captain Charles Shunstrom, bazookas and satchel

Below: Gela was a significant target on the east of Seventh Army's landings on Sicily. The Rangers secured their objective, threw a perimeter around the city and held it against counter-attacks. This is the cathedral on July 11, 1943, the day after the landings.

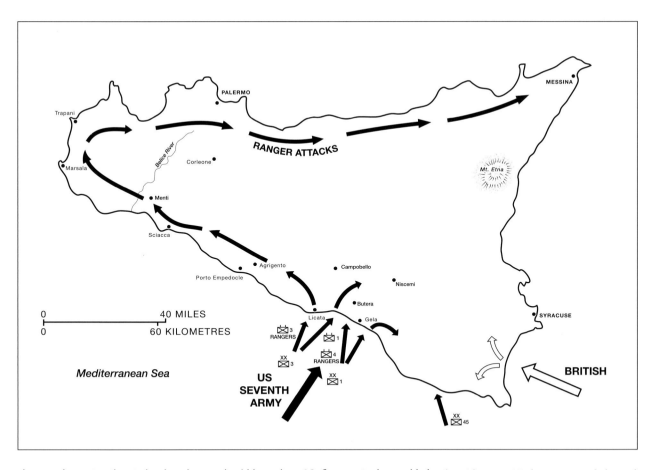

Above: The Rangers' Sicilian campaign, which started at Gela and Licata and ended on the coast opposite the toe of Italy.

charges. A greater threat developed around midday, when 18 German tanks rumbled toward the town supported by elements of the Italian *Livorno* Division. Once again the attack was repulsed by the Rangers, who bolstered their own meagre fire power with rounds from the mortars, a number of captured 77 mm field guns, and offshore naval support. A third attack by a battalion of enemy infantry stalled some 2,000 yards (1,800 m) from the town thanks to the massed firepower of the 83rd Chemical Mortar Battalion. By early afternoon Gela was firmly held by the Allies and the Axis troops were withdrawing into the high ground around the town.

On the 12th Darby was ordered to advance towards San Nicola and Monte Delta Lapa, mountains that rise precipitously out of the coastal plain and guard the entrance to a pass some four miles (6 km) northwest of Gela that leads to Licata and its invasion beaches. As the 1st Infantry Division battled inland for the town of Niscemi, Darby moved against the enemy holding the peaks with a command reinforced by the engineer and mortar units that had landed with the Rangers two days previously and a newly attached armoured infantry detachment. The armoured infantry and engineers assaulted San Nicola while the two Ranger battalions struck against Monte Delta Lapa. Under cover of darkness the Rangers climbed the steep-sided peak but ran into a hail of artillery fire from concealed batteries. The attack stalled and only regained its momentum when Darby called down fire support from the *Savannah* that proved highly accurate. The Rangers took some 600 prisoners during the battle and linked up with the 3rd Division, which had been pushing southwards from Licata, the following day.

Darby's next task was to assault the inland town of Butera, some 4,000 feet (1,200 m) above sea level and eight miles (12 km) inland due north of Gela. Fire support was provided by 18 self-propelled 75 mm howitzers and the *Savannah*. The advance, a two-pronged attack, commenced under cover of darkness shortly after midnight. Some of the troops moving directly on Butera pushed forward at a rapid rate, forcing Darby to halt the imminent artillery bombardment. Although German officers attempted to force the Italians to fight, they had little success and the small party of Rangers occupied the town with unexpected ease.

While Darby was securing Gela and battling for Butera, Major Herman Dammer's 3rd Rangers had landed on beaches some three miles (5 km) west of Licata to the north of Gela, paving the way for the arrival of the US 3rd Infantry Division's 7th Regimental Combat Team. The first waves came ashore unhindered at 0400 on the 10th but quickly ran into sporadically heavy machine-gun and artillery fire from enemy positions on high ground. These were soon overcome and the battalion turned eastwards, moving along a ridge that ran directly into Licata itself. The town was quickly occupied and the battalion remained there until the morning of the 12th, when it advanced inland to Campobello to the north. Dammer's Rangers next moved via truck and on foot to first Naro and then Favara in the van of a northwards sweep to clear the coast of the enemy. From Favara the troops moved westwards towards the town of Agrigento, which was held by a sizeable Italian garrison.

The plan to capture Agrigento involved a regiment of the 3rd Division moving directly on the target while the Rangers tackled a high peak known as Montaperto, from where Axis artillery could fire down on any force moving on the town, as the first stage of a flank march around Agrigento. Some three miles (5 km) out of Favara the Rangers, who were attempting to clear a roadblock barring their way forwards, were struck by intense artillery fire, but they were able to break through the Italian defences and capture some 165 prisoners within the hour. The main attack on Montaperto opened on the morning of July 16 and, despite enemy artillery fire, the Rangers scrambled up the peak's steep slopes supported by their mortars. This fire forced the Italian gunners to abandon their artillery pieces and a fortuitous round also hit the battery's ammunition dump. Montaperto was quickly occupied and Dammer's men then swept over an adjoining piece

Below: S/Sgt Francis P. Padrucco of 1st Rangers was awarded the Silver Star for his actions during the assault on Gela, Sicily. His left arm carries the 1st Ranger Battalion's shoulder flash; next the white 5 and A displayed on a blue field against a red background denoting Fifth Army; finally his staff sergeant's stripes.

of high ground, where the enemy had command and observation posts. Here, the Italians surrendered without a fight.

After the capture of Montaperto the Rangers again moved southward in the direction of Porto Empedocle, a coastal town lying just north of Agrigento. From positions in an almond grove some 2,000 yards (1,800 m) from the town, the battalion, minus one company left to guard the left flank and rear, launched a pincer attack from east and west at around 1430 on the 16th. While the the two companies under Dammer attacking from the east quickly overcame pockets of resistance, three companies under Major Alvah Miller had to fight hard to crush German troops holding a walled cemetery and coastal defence positions. Porto Empedocle was declared secure by 1600. On the 17th the 3rd Battalion established a camp near Montaperto but during the following day moved to Raffadalio north of Agrigento, where it remained for a week and then rejoined the rest of Darby's command, which was now based at Ribera, a few miles farther north.

Some seven days after the landings and initial exploitation phase of Husky, the Allies had control of several linked and expanding beachheads and were poised to drive through Sicily toward their ultimate objective – Messina. Patton's US Seventh Army in the western half of island was detailed to support the main drive by General Bernard Montgomery's British Eighth Army in the east. However, Montgomery encountered stubborn resistance that slowed his advance to a crawl and Patton, facing lesser opposition, decided to strike out for Palermo on the island's northwest coast rather than relieve some of the pressure faced by the British. Several units, part of a newly activated Provisional Corps under Major General Geoffrey Keyes, were committed to the drive on Palermo. Darby was given command of Force X, which comprised the three Ranger battalions, the 39th Regimental Combat Team, and a battalion of 155 mm guns, and ordered to follow the coast road that looped round the northeast of the island.

Darby initially left his Ranger battalions close to Ribera and late on July 20 set off to locate the 39th RCT. After passing through Sciacca, he located the unit at Menfi at 0300 hours the following day and the advance along the coast began two hours later. The objective was to capture Castelvetrano and then march on Marsala

Above: By July 21, 1943, the Rangers had reached the capital of Sicily – Palermo.

on the island's west tip before swinging due east to reach Palermo. The RCT successfully overcame Axis forces defending the line of the Belice River and Castelvetrano fell on the 22nd, the day that other US troops entered Palermo. With Palermo secured, the RCT, reinforced by the 1st and 4th Rangers, swept though northwest Sicily, taking Marsala and then liberating Trapani on the north coast some 40 miles (64 km) west of Palermo. Within a few days, Force X and the accompanying 82nd Airborne Division were in position around San Guiseppe to the south of Palermo, marking the end of the liberation of western Sicily. Force X was immediately disbanded.

While the 1st and 4th Battalions were placed in reserve and established a camp at Corleone to the south of Palermo, the 3rd Battalion, which had been held back at Menfi during the drive to clear western Sicily, moved up to the front and was attached to Truscott's 3rd Infantry Division for a second time. The division was pushing towards Messina on the northeast tip of the island and had reached Sant'Agata di Militello on the sole coastal road, Highway 113, between Palermo and Messina and some 50 miles (80 km) short of its objective. The 3rd Battalion, soon joined by Darby and a 1st Battalion company, served with the division's 7th Regimental Combat Team and was pitched into battle against German rearguards in the Caronie Mountains who were attempting to protect the ongoing withdrawal of forces from Messina to the Italian mainland by way of the Straits of Messina. On August 12 the Rangers first stormed the high ground of Popo di Marco, four miles (6 km) southwest of Capo d'Orlando, and then aided the drive of the 7th RCT towards Naso on Highway 113. The next target was Patti, some 35 miles (56 km) from Messina. For this operation the Rangers fought alongside the division's 15th Regiment. While the regiment pushed on the objective by launching an amphibious assault, the Rangers moved inland by truck to San Angelo di Brolo and launched a similarly successful attack from the mountains. The Rangers' next target was Monteforte, which was taken with the aid of a detachment of pack howitzers transported by mules. By dawn on the 16th Darby was holding high ground above the town of Sanbruca, just four miles (6 km) west of Messina, and poised to move against the final Allied objective. The following day, once the Germans had completed their largely successful evacuation to mainland Italy, the Rangers marched into the coastal city, marking the end of the 38-day campaign.

Several Allied units were withdrawn from the Mediterranean theatre after the capture of Sicily to prepare for the D-Day landings in June 1944. Although Rangers were destined to play a key role during Operation Overlord, these were not part of Darby's command as both he and his men were earmarked for the forthcoming invasion and occupation of the Italian mainland. On August 18 Darby and his three battalions were gathered together and moved back across the island to Palermo to rest, receive replacements and prepare for their next task – the forthcoming assault on the Italian mainland. During their time at Palermo Darby's command was expanded to include a Ranger Cannon Company consisting of four half-track-mounted 75 mm guns under Shunstrom.

OPERATION AVALANCHE – THE SALERNO LANDINGS

On September 3 Montgomery's British Eighth Army launched Operation Baytown, crossing the Straits of Messina from Sicily and making unopposed landings at Reggio di Calabria on the very tip of the Italian mainland. Six days later, just hours before Italy announced an armistice, the Allies launched the two other prongs of their invasion of southern Italy. Operation Slapstick saw the British 1st Airborne Division put ashore from warships at the port of Taranto in the southeast, while General Mark Clark's US Fifth Army began Operation Avalanche, a larger assault against beaches in the Gulf of Salerno, some 45 miles (72 km) south of Naples on the west coast. Salerno was chosen in preference to a large-scale landing on the more distant Adriatic coast as Allied aircraft on Sicily could only guarantee cover over the former area, the nearby extensive port facilities at Naples were seen as a potentially valuable prize and it placed the Allies on the most direct route northwards to Rome.

The Rangers' role in Avalanche was to act as a flank guard to the main amphibious

Below: Operation Avalanche – the landings at Salerno on September 9, 1943 – saw the Rangers used as a flank guard for General Mark Clark's Fifth Army. The landings at Salerno were the largest amphibious operation of the war up to that date and were strongly resisted by the Germans. The counter-attacks of September 12–14 came close to pushing the Allies into the sea. It was only the weight of fire from offshore and the Allied air bombardment that enabled the beach-head to remain secure.

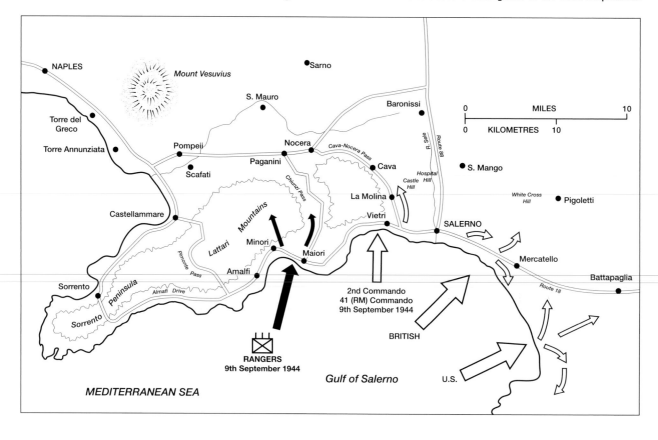

assaults of Clark's British X Corps and US VI Corps by securing the 25-mile (40 km) length of the Sorrento Peninsula and the Lattari Mountains, which divide the Gulfs of Naples and Salerno. Darby's command, which was temporarily attached to X Corps, was to land at a point some 10 miles (16 km) northwest of the more northerly of the two main landing sites and around seven miles (10 km) west of Salerno itself. Once ashore the various battalions were to push inland and establish blocking positions in the 3–4,000-foot (1,000 m) mountains to control the various passes through which any German reinforcements from the Naples area would have to travel to reach the main invasion beaches. The target area had three main passes – Cava–Nocera at the eastern, inland extremity of the peninsula, which was the most direct route from Naples to Salerno and though which Highway 18 snaked; the Chiunzi Pass some 5 miles (8 km) west of Cava–Nocera; and the Pimonte Pass, a tunnelled route that ran north-south to Castellammare on the southern shores of the Gulf of Naples. A fourth route, the Amalfi Drive, also circled around the peninsula's coastline by way of Sorrento and Castellammare and was another potential, if more circuitous, path for German troops heading for Salerno. The capture of the high ground would allow the Rangers to spot enemy troop movements in the surrounding lowlands and call down naval gunfire from Allied warships in the Gulf of Salerno on any potential targets by radio.

The Rangers were transported to a 1,000-yard-long (900 m) narrow stretch of beach around Maiori on the peninsula's southern coast in three Landing Ships Infantry (LSI) and five Landing Craft Infantry (LCI), guided to their objective by a British destroyer. Because of a shortage of landing craft – sufficient to land just one battalion at a time – the first assault wave was placed in the LCIs, while the follow-on units were shuttled to shore in the Landing Craft Assault carried by the LSIs. The 4th Rangers led the way, landing in the dead centre of the beach at around 0320 hours on September 9. Complete surprise had been achieved and the battalion quickly established blocking positions on either side of the beachhead and neutralized coastal defences in the vicinity of Capo d'Orso near Maiori, while the next waves, comprising the 1st and 3rd Rangers, were brought ashore in quick succession and then pushed rapidly inland towards the Chiunzi Pass.

Within three hours of landing the Rangers had accomplished their primary mission. Speed and surprise had enabled them quickly to overpower what limited opposition they encountered. By 0800 hours the 1st and 3rd Rangers were digging in on Monte St. Angelo di Cava and Monte di Chiunzi, 2,500–3,000-foot (900 m) heights on the eastern edge of the pass, while the accompanying 509th Parachute Infantry Battalion took up position on 4,000-foot (1,200 m) Monte Ceretto on the western edge of the pass. Daylight revealed that the Rangers indeed had panoramic views of the surrounding low ground, particularly the towns of Pagani and Nocera, and could easily bring down naval and artillery fire on any German forces heading for Salerno along Highway 18 or by rail through Nocera. As these units consolidated their positions, the 4th Battalion pushed westward along the Amalfi Drive and then moved northward through the Pimonte Pass to take Castellammare. The peninsula and its passes were effectively barred to the Germans by the 12th.

The German response to the Rangers' landing was swift. The 4th Battalion was soon pushed out of Castellammare and withdrew westward to Vico Equensa by way of the coastal Amalfi Drive. As they retreated the troops destroyed bridges and sections of raised roadway to slow their pursuers. The battalion held on to its positions around Vico Equensa for the next two weeks in the face of frequent German attacks but then withdrew along the coast road to the peninsula's south coast. New positions were established around Pimonte and the nearby route that ran directly northwards through the Pimonte Pass to Castellammare. The battalion faced German pressure on two fronts – from west to east

Above and next page: After Salerno, the Rangers fought effectively on the Italian Front – so much so that the 1st and 3rd Battalions received a Presidential Unit Citation (see box page 37). This sequence of photographs taken on November 10, 1943, shows Company D, 3rd Ranger Battalion, on patrol.

along the Amalfi Drive and from north to south through the Pimonte Pass – but the local terrain greatly aided its defence. The road in the pass ran through an 800-feet-long (250 m) tunnel and the Rangers dug in at its southern entrance and on the high ground either side. A 75 mm gun mounted on a half-track was sited on the tunnel's entrance and this, coupled with various other strongpoints, ensured that the Germans could not force their way through the pass. The Amalfi Drive, with the sea on one side and mountains on the other also provided ideal defensive terrain and, once again, the Germans were denied an alternative route to Salerno as the Rangers took up strong positions some two miles west of Amalfi.

Darby had expected his mission to last perhaps just a few days, certainly no more than a week, yet his Rangers had to remain in the hills for 21 days. The rapid breakout from Salerno by Clark's Fifth Army never materialized as the Germans fought stubbornly to throw the Allies back into the Mediterranean. As the pressure at Salerno mounted, it became even more imperative that the Rangers slow the flow of enemy reinforcements moving south from Naples. Thanks to excellent observation on the high ground overlooking Highway 18 and first-rate ship-to-shore communications, accurate gunfire from a British battleship, two cruisers and a shallow-draught monitor significantly reduced the flow of German reinforcements to the Salerno beaches. However, the Rangers had to contend with sometimes acute shortages of supplies, particularly food and ammunition, during their stay in the mountains and had to beat off numerous localized German counterattacks, while enduring frequent artillery and mortar bombardments.

The Allied breakout from Salerno finally began on the 20th. Clark's VI Corps first drove eastward in a looping attack toward Naples and, three days later, was joined by X Corps, which pushed directly northwards along Highway 18 towards the port. Able to observe this latter push, Darby ordered his men to strike for Pagani, close to Nocera at the northern end of the Chiunzi Pass, and also reoccupy Castellammare. With the Germans abandoning their positions in a staged withdrawal to the line of the Volturno River north of the port, the Rangers made steady progress by way of Pompeii and Mount Vesuvius in support of the US 82nd Airborne Division. Naples was liberated on October 1 and the Rangers moved in. Darby's casualties in the passes and subsequent advance totalled 13 killed and 21 seriously wounded in the 1st Battalion, seven killed, one missing and 14 wounded in the 3rd Battalion, and eight killed, eight missing and 21 wounded in the 4th Battalion. The 1st and 3rd Rangers received Presidential Unit Citations for their staunch defence of the Chiunzi Pass.

WINTER FIGHTING IN THE APPENNINES

The occupation of Naples proved to be no more than a brief respite for the Rangers. On October 3 they ended their attachment to X Corps and came under the direct command of the US Fifth Army. Just three days later Darby was ordered to prepare two of his battalions for renewed combat by the end of the month. By the 12th the Allied advance towards Rome had faltered along the Volturno River in an area some 40 miles (64 km) north of Naples that Kesselring had ordered defended to the utmost in order that he could prepare even stronger defences – the Gustav or Winter Line – along the Garigliano and Rapido Rivers. The Ranger battalions moved back south to the Sorrento Peninsula and established a camp at San Lazzaro, where they spent some two weeks resting, training and receiving replacements.

By the end of October the Allies had reached the Bernhard or Reinhard Line, an outer defensive zone covering the approaches to the Gustav Line that ran almost directly north–south across the central Italian mainland some 10 miles (16 km) east of Monte Cassino. It was here that the Rangers returned to combat. The 4th Battalion was the first to leave San Lazzaro and on November 1 joined the Fifth Army's US 3rd Division on the Volturno, where they helped secure a crossing over the river; the 1st Battalion left its base late on the 8th and completed the 30-mile (48 km) journey by truck to link up with the US 45th Division around Venafro at 0130 hours the following day. It was later joined by the 3rd Battalion, which was initially held back at San Lazzaro to integrate its larger body of replacements, and then both took part in fighting southwest of Venafro, serving successively with the US 45th and 36th Infantry Divisions.

The 1st Battalion immediately moved into position. Venafro, some 12 miles (20 km) due east of Cassino, was surrounded by commanding heights that provided excellent positions for spotting enemy troop movements. The Rangers occupied Monte Corno, supported by the 83rd Chemical Mortar Battalion and the Ranger Cannon Company, while the 509th Parachute Infantry Battalion took charge of the adjacent Monte San Croce. On the 11th the mortars and cannon company supported a successful attack by the paratroopers on the ridge that ran between the two peaks and gave them an uninterrupted view of the German-occupied village of Concacasalle. The 1st Rangers, joined by the 4th Battalion from the middle of the month, spent several weeks in the mountains. There were no major battles, but the Rangers conducted patrols and reconnaissance missions, and used their mortars to harass the Germans around Concacasalle. The weather was bitterly cold and the conditions, allied to frequent enemy shelling, ensured that the two Ranger units suffered a steady stream of casualties. The 3rd Battalion had also suffered during the fighting. It was tasked with leading the assault to take Monte Rotondo and the village of San Pietro on high ground along the eastern edge of the plain that leads to Cassino, but was stopped some 800 yards (700 m) outside the village. When this advance stalled, the battalion was transferred to Ceppagna close to Darby's other two units.

The Rangers' time around Venafro came to an end in mid-December. The 1st and 4th Battalions departed for Lucrino Station on Pozzuoli Bay to the west of Naples on the 14th, and the 3rd followed six days later. The various units were badly depleted, having suffered casualty rates of around 40 per cent during their time in the mountains due to the prolonged combat and the adverse weather. During the Christmas period they were allowed to relax and reorganize. Darby had recently been promoted to full colonel during a visit to Clark's headquarters at Caserta north of Naples and his various units were redesignated the 6615th Ranger Force (Provisional) on January 16, 1944. Aside from the 1st, 3rd and 4th Rangers, this formation included the 509th

---

**PRESIDENTIAL UNIT CITATION
1ST AND 3RD RANGER BATTALIONS**

The 1st and 3rd Ranger Battalions, with the following attached units:
319th Glider Field Artillery Battery;
Headquarters Battery, 80th Airborne Antiaircraft Battalion;
Battery D, 80th Airborne Antiaircraft Battalion;
Battery E, 80th Airborne Antiaircraft Battalion;
Battery F, 80th Airborne Antiaircraft Battalion;
Medical Detachment, 80th Airborne Antiaircraft Battalion;
Company H, 504th Parachute Infantry Regiment;
2nd Platoon, Company A, 307th Airborne Engineer Battalion,
are cited for outstanding performance of duty in action during the period 10th to 18th September 1943.

These units, comprising a single Ranger force, landed at Maiori, Italy, with the mission of seizing high ground controlling Chiunzi Pass and securing the left flank of the Fifth Army in its push northward into the plain of Naples. The position held by this force was vital not only for flank security, but also for observation of the plain and of the German supply routes and communications lines to the Salerno battlefront.

During this period, the Ranger force was subjected to almost continuous mortar and artillery fire and was repeatedly attacked by a determined enemy. Hostile forces were estimated to outnumber the Rangers and attached units by approximately eight to one, but despite superior enemy numbers, the Ranger force heroically fought off every attempt to dislodge it.

Because of its limited strength and the large area assigned to it for defense, the force held the line thinly, marked with strongpoints with gaps covered by fire.

Several major counterattacks were repelled during the period and numerous enemy patrols were stopped, often in bitter, close-in fighting, with the Ranger force using its mortars, artillery, automatic weapons, and grenades with devastating effect.

The officers and men of these units fought without rest or relief and with limited food and water supplies. The continuous nature of the enemy fire and activity was such as to try the men to the limits of their endurance.

Although overwhelming enemy forces drove almost constantly at the sparsely held positions, the determination and courage of the 1st and 3rd Ranger Battalions and their attached units offset the enemy superiority in numbers and made possible the successful accomplishment of a vital mission.

Official:	Dwight D. Eisenhower
Edward F. Witsel	Chief of Staff
Major-General	
The Adjutant General	

Above: Italy, January 1, 1944 – 80 men of 1st Ranger Battalion line up to receive decorations from Brigadier-General Theodore Roosevelt.

The Anzio landings, part of a plan to force the Gustav Line, took place on January 22, 1944. Training for them involved three weeks of amphibious practices and physical exercise.

Right: January 14, 1944. Men of 2nd Platoon, Company A, 1st Rangers do their usual log exercises.

Above right: January 16, 1944. Soldiers of 3rd Ranger Battalion photographed at Baia in front of the landing craft that will take them to the Anzio landings. By the 29th all but six of the 767 men from the 1st and 3rd Battalions were either dead or prisoners.

Far right: January 14, 1944. 1st Rangers load into British LCAs for beach-landing manoeuvres near Naples.

Above: November 10, 1943: a medic treats a leg wound sustained during a skirmish by Pfc John Brady of the 3rd Ranger Battalion.

Above right: Operation Shingle – the landings at Anzio by US and British forces under the command of General Lucas. This map shows the Rangers' part in the battle.

Below right: 1st Ranger Battalion troops board vessels at Baia.

Parachute Infantry Battalion, the 83rd Chemical Mortar Battalion, Company H, 36th Engineer Regiment, and the half-track-mounted Ranger Cannon Company. The regrouping was a prelude to what was to be Darby's fourth and final amphibious assault – Operation Shingle, the landings by the Anglo-US VI Corps under Major General John Lucas at Anzio some 40 miles (64 km) south of Rome, which were supposed to break the stalemate at Cassino by establishing a threatening beachhead behind the German lines and forcing them to retreat northwards.

ANZIO – THE RANGERS' NEMESIS

After some three weeks of vital amphibious training for the new recruits arriving at Pozzuoli, the Rangers boarded their assault vessels anchored off Baia on January 20 in preparation for the 120-mile (190 km) voyage northwards to Anzio. The transports comprised *Princess Beatrix*, *Winchester Castle*, a pair of landing craft, tank, a single landing ship, tank, and HMS *Royal Ulsterman*, which had seen service with the Rangers during the Arzew landings and whose presence was seen as a favourable omen. The Anzio operation opened early on January 22, with the Rangers undertaking the spearhead role by landing on beaches at Anzio itself. The 1st and 4th Rangers came ashore first, beginning at 0200 hours, and quickly fanned out through Anzio with some making for Nettuno to the east. Opposition was extremely light and the engineers accompanying Darby's command set about clearing beach obstacles and mines, while landing craft returned with the 3rd Battalion. The port was secured by 0800 hours and throughout the day the Rangers extended their perimeter by linking up with the British 1st Infantry Division at Peter Beach to the north of Anzio and the US 3rd Infantry Division at X-Ray Beach around Nettuno.

For the next two days, the beachhead expanded slowly as more and more Allied troops poured ashore. The Rangers held the central sector of the perimeter, a flat area bisected by drainage ditches and dotted with woodland between one road running due north from Anzio to Carroceto and another from Nettuno to Padiglione. It quickly became apparent that the Germans, who were rushing reinforcements into the area while Lucas failed to capitalize on the element of surprise, held the high ground overlooking the Allied positions and could rain down artillery fire on the Anzio plain at will. The Rangers initially engaged in patrol work but for the most part kept to their foxholes. However, on the 25th Darby was ordered to support an advance by the British 1st Division towards Carroceto. The 4th Battalion led the way, having to negotiate numerous drainage ditches, while the remaining two battalions initially remained in reserve. Support was provided by a US paratrooper battalion and a detachment of tank destroyers. While the British faced stubborn resistance at Carroceto, the Rangers had to deal with snipers, enemy mortar fire, and frequent firefights. However, the subsidiary role at Carroceto was only a prelude to a much more ambitious operation to break out of the beachhead.

By late January Lucas, who was under increasing pressure from his superiors to act decisively, felt compelled to launch a major breakout from Anzio. This called for a simultaneous two-pronged effort on the night of the 28th, one by British forces in the direction of Campoleone from Carroceto and the second to the east by the US 3rd Division. The Rangers, supported by the US 504th Parachute Infantry Regiment, were tasked with leading the 3rd Division's attack, which was directed towards the town of Cisterna. The plan was for the Rangers to advance under cover of darkness some four miles (6 km) beyond the northeast sector of the existing Allied perimeter, capture Cisterna and then hold it for a few hours until larger forces arrived on the scene. Cisterna was of considerable importance to the ongoing Italian campaign as it was a hub of communications running southeast from Rome to Monte Cassino. In German hands

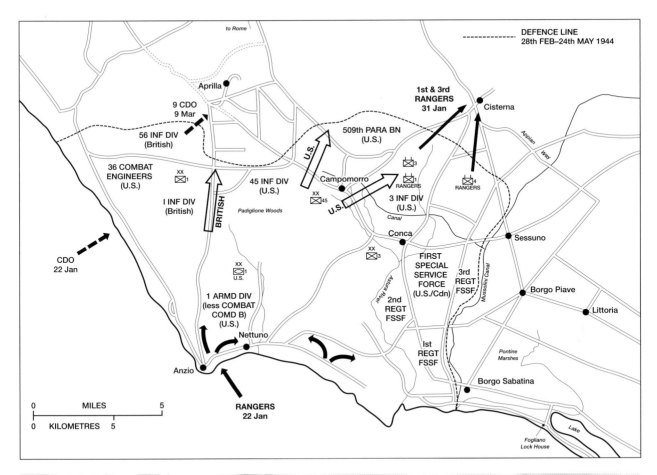

DEFENCE LINE
28th FEB–24th MAY 1944

to Rome

Aprilla

9 CDO
9 Mar

56 INF DIV
(British)

36 COMBAT
ENGINEERS
(U.S.)

XX
1

I INF DIV
(British)

45 INF DIV
(U.S.)

Padiglione Woods

BRITISH

509th PARA BN
(U.S.)

Campomorro

U.S.

XX
45

U.S.

Canal

1st & 3rd
RANGERS
31 Jan

Cisterna

XX
3

XX
1
RANGERS

3 INF DIV
(U.S.)

XX
4
RANGERS

Appian Way

Conca

XX
3

FIRST
SPECIAL
SERVICE
FORCE
(U.S./Cdn)

Sessuno

3rd
REGT
FSSF

Mussolini Canal

Borgo Piave

Littoria

CDO
22 Jan

XX
1
U.S.

1 ARMD DIV
(less COMBAT
COMD B)
(U.S.)

Nettuno

Anzio

RANGERS
22 Jan

Astura River

2nd
REGT
FSSF

1st
REGT
FSSF

Pontine
Marshes

Borgo Sabatina

Fogliano
Lock House

Lake

MILES
0   5

KILOMETRES
0   5

Above: A German casualty lies next to his Kübelwagen, Anzio.

Right and Below right: As a footnote to Anzio, these two photographs, taken June 21, 1944, show a guerrilla band formed of escapees from a German prison train. A number of these men were Rangers who had been captured during the attack on Cisterna. They escaped and operated behind enemy lines disrupting enemy communications before reaching their own forces.

Below: Burying the dead during the Italian campaign.

Highway 7 and the railway that ran through Cisterna were used to ferry troops to the Gustav Line; if the town was in Allied hands then the severing of these two arteries might lead to a German withdrawal from Cassino and facilitate a rapid drive on the Italian capital.

The plan was for the Rangers to crawl forward from the existing front line in virtual single file along a ditch, the Fossa di Pantano, which was an offshoot of the western branch of the Mussolini Canal and ended just two miles (3 km) short of Cisterna. They would then debouch onto the open land outside the town and follow the line of the road running between it and Nettuno by way of the village of Isola Bella to their objective. It was a tricky plan, but one that the Rangers were trained for and experienced enough to accomplish, and intelligence indicated that the local opposition was expected to be light. However, events conspired against the Rangers even before they opened their attack. Returning from a planning meeting shortly before commencing their unit's spearhead attack against Campoleone, several British officers took a wrong turning and were killed in a German ambush. Consequently a new unit had to be assigned the task and its officers briefed on what was expected of them. This inevitably caused a delay and the twin-pronged offensive did not open until the night of the 29th — some 24 hours later than intended. In the interim the Germans had moved forces into the area of Cisterna in preparation for launching a major counterattack on the Anzio beachhead. Rather than facing just elements of the *Hermann Göring* Division, the Rangers were now also confronted by units from the 26th Panzergrenadier and 715th Infantry Divisions.

Unaware of these developments, the Rangers opened the advance on Cisterna late on the 29th. The advance was led by the 1st and 3rd Battalions, which had infiltrated between the opposing front lines, seemingly without being spotted, by 0100 hours on the 30th. The 4th Battalion and the Ranger Cannon Company, tasked with clearing the Anzio–Cisterna road for follow-on forces, moved off at 0200 hours but had advanced just 800 yards (700 m) before being hit by heavy enemy fire. As dawn broke the difficulty of the situation became evident — the leading two battalions were well short of Cisterna and were fighting in isolated companies and platoons against a much stronger enemy force. Worse, the 4th Rangers was first delayed by heavy fighting at Isola Bella and then brought to a complete halt at Femina Morta well short of the other battalions. News also reached Darby that the commander of the 3rd Battalion, Major Alvah Miller, had been killed by a shell fired by a tank.

The Rangers' predicament became clearer at around 0830 hours. The 1st Battalion's commander, Major Jack Dobson, radioed that he was surrounded some 800 yards short of Cisterna and that German fire was causing heavy losses among his troops in their open positions. The 3rd Battalion was in a similar situation. The 4th Battalion and units of the US 3rd Infantry Division struggled to relieve the trapped Rangers but were unable to break through. By early afternoon, the 1st and 3rd Battalions — what remained of them — were at the end of their tether. Some Rangers fought on until killed, others, many of them wounded, surrendered, and a handful withdrew to friendly lines. The 4th

Battalion itself was effectively surrounded but held on until relieved on the morning of the 31st. Supported by other troops it finally captured Femina Morta, but this was a trifle compared to the virtual annihilation of the 1st and 3rd Battalions.

The crushing reverse at Cisterna effectively wiped the three Ranger battalions from the US order of battle in Europe. Only six of 767 men from the 1st and 3rd Battalions managed to escape from the killing fields outside the town; the remainder were either dead or prisoners. Some 500 captured Rangers were paraded through central Rome by the Germans, an event recorded on film for propaganda purposes. After the battle the 4th Battalion was in little better shape but still saw further action at Anzio, chiefly in helping to blunt a counterattack against the beachhead perimeter in early February, and then, following the breakout and liberation of Rome in late May and early June, it operated at the Fifth Army's patrolling school at Civitavecchia to the north of the Italian capital. The remnants of the 1st and 3rd Battalions, the handful who had survived Cisterna and support personnel who had not taken part in the fighting – about 150 in total – had already been withdrawn and sent to Camp Butner, North Carolina, in early May. Some became instructors at infantry training schools, while others were reassigned to the US-Canadian 1st Special Service Force's 1st Regiment. The 1st and 3rd Battalions were officially deactivated on August 15 and the 4th followed on October 26.

RAIDING OCCUPIED EUROPE

While Darby's battalion was fighting in North Africa, a short-lived Ranger unit was activated back in England to conduct pinprick raids along the coast of occupied Europe. In September 1942, with the departure of Darby's unit for North Africa imminent, plans were laid for the creation of a new Ranger battalion from US personnel stationed in Britain. On December 20 the 29th Provisional Ranger Battalion came into existence at Tidworth Barracks in Wiltshire and was commanded by Major Randolph Millholland.

Below: It wasn't only in Britain that Rangers were being selected and trained. This photograph (and that opposite) are of Fort Jackson, South Carolina, on April 22, 1943, as Ranger recruits undergoe live fire training. Established on June 2, 1917, the new Army Training Center was named in honour of Major General Andrew Jackson, the seventh president of the United States. The first military unit to be organized here was the 81st 'Wildcat' Division. In 1939 Fort Jackson was organized as an infantry training centre. Four firing ranges were constructed, and more than 500,000 men received some phase of their training here. Today the camp is the largest and most active Initial Entry Training Center in the United States Army, providing training to almost 50 percent of the men and women who enter the service each year.

Above: The 'German Village' at Fort Jackson, sees another Ranger course undergoing live fire training, April 22, 1943.

Officers and men were volunteers drawn from the US 29th Infantry Division and 18 members of the 1st Battalion were detached to train the new recruits. As with previous Ranger units, the 29th moved to Achnacarry for Commando training and then on to Spean Bridge to learn amphibious assault techniques. The programme was completed by February 1943 and the Rangers moved to Dartmouth where they were attached to No. 14 Commando for the following six weeks.

Unlike other Ranger units, the 29th Battalion conducted hazardous small-scale raids, usually involving one or two men accompanied by British Commandos. These were nuisance missions against Occupied Europe, chiefly along the coast of Norway and northern France, and were not always successful. One of three such raids against Norway involving the 29th Battalion, code named Roundabout, took place on March 23, when five Rangers, three British and five Norwegian Commandos came ashore at Landet with the intention of attacking enemy shipping. However, the mission ended prematurely when the raiders were discovered by German sentries. In May the battalion moved to Bude, Cornwall, and then to HMS *Dorlin* during July. The 29th Rangers' last operation was code named Pound. A party of 18 men from No. 12 Commando and two Rangers landed on the island of Ushant off the west coast of Brittany during the night of September 3–4 to attack a German radar station. A German sentry (possibly two) was killed and then the raiders returned home unscathed. Pound was the unit's last action due to the imminent arrival of the 2nd and 5th Rangers from the United States and the scaling down of British Commando raids across the Channel. After the Ushant raid the battalion spent time at Dover but was deactivated while based at Okehampton, Devon, on October 15 and its personnel returned to the 29th Division.

The Rangers practised opposed landings from the sea from the earliest days in Scotland in August 1942 – as these photos show. Still wearing their British-style M1917A1 helmets, the men of 1st Rangers practise on a cold Scottish loch the skills that were to prove so effective in Normandy less than two years later. By the time of the Normandy landings, the Allies in general and their special forces – Rangers, Commandos, etc – in particular had a great deal of practical experience in amphibious warfare and landing on defended coasts. On top of this, they had specialist equipment – especially all forms of landing craft – that gave them the technological edge.

PREPARING FOR OPERATION OVERLORD

The brief service of the 29th Provisional Battalion in 1942 and the deactivation of the 1st, 3rd and 4th Battalions in 1944 did not signal the end of the Rangers' involvement in World War II. On March 11, 1943, while Darby's 1st Battalion was fighting in Tunisia, a directive had been issued to form a 2nd Battalion, which was activated at Camp Forrest, Tennessee, under the command of Lieutenant Colonel William Saffarans on April 1. Some 2,000 volunteers were evaluated and about 500 accepted for training under the watchful eyes of ex-1st Battalion officers and non-commissioned officers. Saffarans and three other commanders came and went, but in June Major James Rudder took command, and the battalion commenced specialist training. In September, its men went through the Scouts' and Raiders' School at Fort Pierce, Florida, where they learned to work with small assault craft and boats. Next the battalion moved to Fort Dix, New Jersey, to practise advanced tactical techniques. Deemed ready for active service, the battalion sailed for England on the liner *Queen Elizabeth* on November 21.

The 2nd Rangers was soon joined by a further battalion as US planners felt that two such specialist units would be needed for the invasion of Occupied Europe. The 5th Battalion was activated at Camp Forrest on September 1 and in November followed the 2nd Battalion through Fort Pierce and then, from the 20th, trained at Fort Dix. It sailed for England in January 1944.

Main photograph: Live fire opposed landing exercise in Scotland, August 1942.

Inset, Left and Right: Wire was a major obstacle on defended beaches. Bangalore torpedoes were the chief anti-wire weapon. Photos are of 29th Battalion.

Meanwhile, once in England, the 2nd Battalion was initially stationed at Bude, north Cornwall, and continued to concentrate on training, although individual Rangers served with British Commando parties during several small cross-Channel raids. Many of these were designed to gain intelligence or as nuisance raids to mislead the Germans as to where the Allied invasion would take place. On the night of December 26–27, 1943, for example, two Rangers took part in Operation Hardtack 4, which was designed to assess the beach defences at Ault, south of the Somme Estuary and some distance from the Normandy area. On the 28th the battalion moved to Titchfield Barracks and subsequently underwent cliff-assault training in the Isle of Wight. It returned to Bude in February 1944 and in April spent some weeks at the Assault Training Centre at Woolacombe in north Devon before moving to Dorchester in Dorset on the 27th.

The 5th Battalion under Major Max Schneider arrived at Liverpool on January 18 and was initially based at Leominster before spending time at the Commando Training Depot at Achnacarry in March and the Assault Training Centre in April. Further periods of training followed, but on May 5 the two battalions were united at Dorchester and a day later Rudder was placed in command of what was named the Provisional Ranger Group. By the end of the month the battalions had moved to their final marshalling area around Swanage for embarkation in preparation for their spearhead role on D-Day.

Left: Practice night landing, January 1944.

Right and Below: It could almost be Normandy – the pill boxes and gullies of Omaha, and the cliffs of Pointe du Hoc. In fact the photos are taken on the north coast of Devon, England, around Bude. The wide expanse of sand, with dunes and some cliffs provided the Rangers and other Allied forces with the perfect place to hone their landing techniques . . . and, of course, maintain their physical fitness thanks to the ubiquitous pole routine.

Right: The attack on Pointe du Hoc – a brave and brilliantly executed special force attack in no way belittled by the fact that the Germans had not positioned their guns in the casemates.

LEONARD LOMELL

Lomell was a first sergeant with Company D, 2nd Rangers, and, although wounded in the initial landings at the base of the Pointe du Hoc on D-Day, he scaled the cliffs and played a key role in the mission, winning the Distinguished Service Cross for the destruction of three 155 mm guns:

'... Jack Kuhn [also to win the DSC] and I went down this sunken road not knowing where the hell it was going, but it was going inland. We came upon this vale or little draw with camouflage all over it, and lo and behold, we peeked over this hedgerow, and there were the guns. It was pure luck. They were all sitting in proper firing condition, with ammunition piled up neatly, everything at the ready, but they were pointed at Utah Beach, not Omaha. There was nobody at the emplacement. We looked round cautiously, and over about 100 yards away in a corner of a field was a vehicle with what looked like an officer talking to his men.

We decided that nobody was here so let's take a chance. I said; "Jack, you cover me and I'm going in there and destroy them." So all I had was two thermite grenades – his and mine. I went in and put the thermite grenades in the traversing mechanism, and that knocked out two of them because that melted their gears in a moment. And then I broke their sights, and we ran back to the road, which was 100 yards or so back, and got all the other thermites from the remainder of my guys manning the roadblock, and rushed back and put the grenades in traversing mechanisms, elevation mechanisms, and banged the sights. There was no noise to that. There is no noise to a thermite, so no one saw us...'

ASSAULTING THE POINTE DU HOC

The Ranger Group was attached to the US 29th Infantry Division's 116th Regiment for Operation Overlord and was detailed to undertake one of the the most hazardous missions conducted on D-Day. Omaha Beach was overlooked by the commanding cliffs of the Pointe du Hoc to the west and intelligence had identified a six-gun German coastal battery being installed on the cliff-top that could sweep the beach and target any invasion fleet. The garrison was estimated at 200 men from the 716th Coastal Defence Division.

The Pointe du Hoc assault opened at 0540 hours on June 6, 1944, with a bombardment of the cliff-top from the battleship USS *Texas*, which was followed by an attack from 19 A-20 Boston medium bombers from the US Ninth Air Force. Those Rangers earmarked to lead the attack, 225 men from Companies D, E, F of the 2nd Battalion under the direct command of Lieutenant Colonel Rudder, had a difficult approach. They boarded their Landing Craft, Assault (LCAs) from two transports, *Amsterdam* and *Ben-my-Chree*, amid rough seas. It was expected that the journey to shore would take around three hours but the LCAs were buffeted by high waves and the troops and crews were quickly drenched or convulsed by seasickness. Two of the three accompanying heavily laden supply craft sank. Worse, one of the landing craft, *LCA.860*, with 20 Rangers from Company D aboard was also lost, although the men were rescued by a motor launch and returned to England. Finally, a navigation error by the commander of the leading LCA, that with Rudder on board, led the flotilla towards another promontory, Pointe de la Percée, three miles (5 km) to the east of the objective. Rudder spotted the error but the course correction delayed the attack for some 40 minutes. This had far-reaching repercussions. First the slow-moving LCAs had to sail westwards parallel to the coast and only 100 yards (100 m) or so offshore to reach the Pointe du Hoc, and in doing so came under close-range enemy fire. Second, the naval bombardment by the *Texas* ended exactly on schedule as it was believed that the Rangers had landed successfully and on time. The loss of fire support allowed the defenders to emerge from their bunkers and man their positions. Two destroyers, the USS *Satterlee* and HMS *Talybont*, used their main armament to rectify the situation but their weight of shell was obviously much less than that of the battleship. Finally, the remainder of the 2nd Battalion and the whole of Schneider's 5th Rangers were supposed to land in direct support of Rudder when the latter fired flares to signals to signify a successful landing. Because of the delay no flares were seen at the expected time and at 0700 Schneider adopted the pre-agreed alternative plan. The codeword Tilt was issued and the LCAs carrying a battalion and a half of Rangers swung away from the Pointe du Hoc and made for the western end of Omaha Beach.

Rudder's three companies, which had lost 40 men during the approach, landed on the narrow beach below the cliff and quickly discovered that their problems were far from over. Aside from the alert defenders, much of their specialist climbing equipment was unusable. The DUKWs with turntable ladders were unable to cross the crater-pocked landing site, and many of the rocket-propelled grapnels for their climbing ropes were useless as the saturated ropes were far too heavy to be fired to the top of the cliff. Nevertheless the attack continued; some grapnels were still operable and the Rangers had their sectional ladders to hand. Others simply resorted to climbing the cliff by hand, seeking out footholds in the cliff face. Despite intense German fire and the severing of several ropes that pitched Rangers to their deaths, Rudder's men inched their way upwards. At 0730 the commander received a radio message, 'Praise the Lord,' indicating that some of his men had reached the summit and were fighting inland towards the coastal road running between Grandcamp-les-Bains to the west and Vierville-sur-Mer to

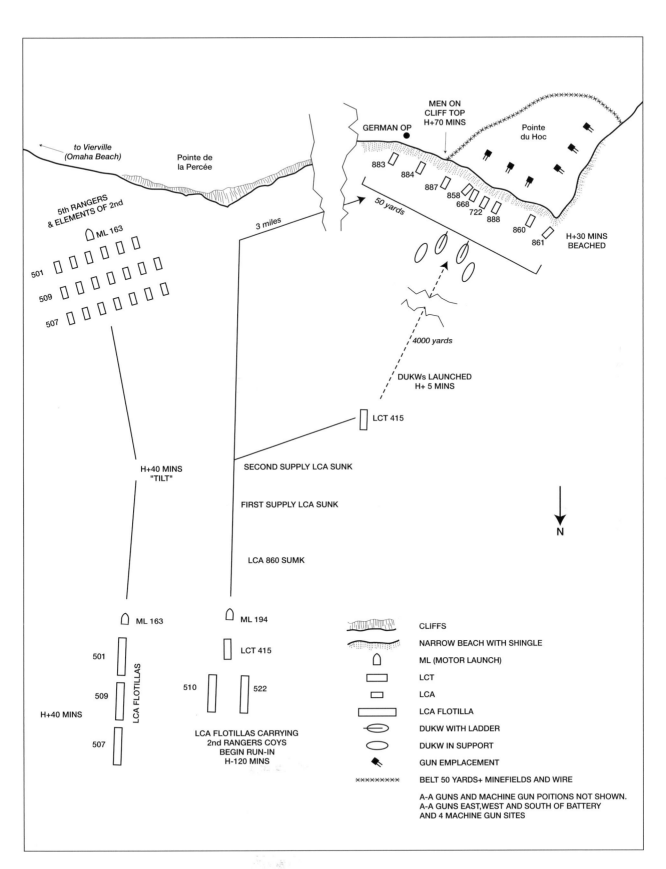

to Vierville
(Omaha Beach)

Pointe de
la Percée

MEN ON
CLIFF TOP
H+70 MINS

GERMAN OP

Pointe
du Hoc

883

884

887

858

668
722
888

860

861

H+30 MINS
BEACHED

50 yards

5th RANGERS
& ELEMENTS OF 2nd

ML 163

501

509

507

3 miles

DUKWs LAUNCHED
H+ 5 MINS

4000 yards

LCT 415

H+40 MINS
"TILT"

SECOND SUPPLY LCA SUNK

FIRST SUPPLY LCA SUNK

LCA 860 SUMK

N

ML 163

ML 194

501

LCT 415

509

510

522

H+40 MINS

507

LCA FLOTILLAS

LCA FLOTILLAS CARRYING
2nd RANGERS COYS
BEGIN RUN-IN
H-120 MINS

CLIFFS

NARROW BEACH WITH SHINGLE

ML (MOTOR LAUNCH)

LCT

LCA

LCA FLOTILLA

DUKW WITH LADDER

DUKW IN SUPPORT

GUN EMPLACEMENT

xxxxxxxxx   BELT 50 YARDS+ MINEFIELDS AND WIRE

A-A GUNS AND MACHINE GUN POITIONS NOT SHOWN.
A-A GUNS EAST, WEST AND SOUTH OF BATTERY
AND 4 MACHINE GUN SITES

Above: It would be only on D+2 that relief came and prisoners could be taken away. Note the Stars and Stripes prominently displayed. This was to stop friendly fire problems – some Rangers were lost to Allied tank fire on D+1.

Left: Aerial view of Pointe du Hoc. Heavily bombarded by Allied aircraft in the days preceding D-Day, and by the battleship *Texas*, nevertheless the position was difficult to assault, thanks to the 100 ft (30 m) cliffs and a tenacious defence. It was even more difficult to hold: short of men (Rudder was down to 70 effectives) the Rangers performed heroics in the face of German counter-attacks.

Far left: The way up the Pointe – photograph taken D+2 when the way up was being used for supplies. Note the joined toggle rope. Compare this photograph with those of the re-enactment on pages 66 onwards.

Above: US troops land on Omaha Beach: the scene of the worst casualties on D-Day – over 2,000. The 5th Rangers and three companies of the 3rd (the other three were attacking Pointe du Hoc) landed on the west of Omaha.

the east. Reports also indicated that resistance was less than expected, chiefly because the naval and air bombardments had not only turned the Pointe du Hoc into a shell-cratered wasteland but had also dazed and demoralized many of the defenders. The Rangers now sought out the coastal guns but only discovered their emplacements. The mystery was solved at around 0900 when the guns were discovered about 880 yards inland, hidden under camouflage and waiting to be installed in their final positions. While these guns were destroyed, Rudder sent a message to his superiors shortly after midday: 'Located Pointe du Hoe [*sic*]. Mission accomplished. Need ammunition and reinforcements. Many casualties.' It was no more than the truth; his command, split into small groups with an estimated effective strength of 100 men, was facing severe German counterattacks, and the supply situation was critical as much-needed ammunition had been lost on the sunk supply craft.

If Rudder's men were not to be overwhelmed, it was essential that the 5th Rangers fight their way off Omaha Beach and head westwards for the Pointe du Hoc, but Schneider's men, like all the US forces committed to Omaha, were facing a difficult task. Their landing was well executed and there were few casualties but the men had to seek shelter behind a low sea wall to avoid murderous enemy fire. With the landings on Omaha in clear jeopardy, the assistant commander of the 29th Division, General Norman Cota, turned to Schneider's men at around 1000. Fearing his troops would never get off the beach, he issued a terse order: 'Lead the way, Rangers.' Individual platoons now began to move forward and seek a way inland between minefields and various other obstacles and were eventually able to reach a road running parallel to the coast some 1,000 yards (900 m) inland and leading to Vierville, which lay on the western edge of Omaha and blocked the direct route to the Pointe du Hoc. By nightfall, the bulk of the 5th Battalion was holding the western fringe of Vierville but was still short of its objective, although a platoon from Company A was able to swing south of the town and reach Rudder. During the 7th Rudder's men beat off several counterattacks, partly aided by naval support, received some much-needed supplies and had their strength boosted by a second platoon from the 5th Rangers. At 1700 hours that afternoon he was ordered to strike out towards Vierville to link up with a relief column comprising Companies A, B, and C of the 2nd Rangers, the whole of the remaining 5th Rangers and 150 men from the 116th RCT. Despite having tanks in support, this force was halted by artillery fire near St. Pierre-de-Mont, forcing Rudder to hold out for a second night. A second relief attempt was mounted on the morning of the 8th. The 5th Rangers and two battalions from the 116th Infantry pushed forward from around St. Pierre-de-Mont and finally reached Rudder's perimeter, thereby ending the battle for the Pointe du Hoc. Both battalions subsequently moved into Grandcamp. The action had cost Rudder 135 casualties but earned his unit a Presidential Unit Citation, an honour also granted to the 5th Battalion. Over the following days both battalions helped in the capture of Grandcamp and dealt with pockets of German resistance around Grandcamp and Isigny.

FROM NORMANDY TO VICTORY

After a spell integrating replacements and providing security details during June and July, the 2nd and 5th Battalions' next major role was to exploit the Allied breakout of the Normandy bridgehead that followed the success of Operation Cobra in late July. Once Patton's Third Army had successfully funnelled through the bottlenecks at Avranches and Pontaubault that led from southwest Normandy into northeast Brittany, it then spread out on a wide front, with two corps detailed to seize Brittany and the numerous ports defended by the German XXV Corps. Moving on a narrow front Major General Troy Middleton's US VIII Corps struck westwards towards Brest along the peninsula's north coast and southwest towards Rennes, while Major General Walton Walker's US XX Corps headed due south to St. Nazaire to seal off Brittany from the rest of France.

The US forces pushed forward quickly, with the US 6th Armored Division making rapid progress towards Brest. The division, which had moved through Pontaubault on August 2, reached the port four days later but failed to force the garrison, 30,000 troops of the German II Parachute Corps under General Hermann Ramcke, to surrender. The heavily defended port had to be taken by a formal siege, carried out by the US 2nd, 8th and 29th Infantry Divisions, Allied aircraft and warships, French Resistance units and the two Ranger battalions. Operations only commenced on August 25, being delayed because of the need to capture St. Mâlo. Brest was ringed by around 75 major concrete emplacements and these had to be taken one by one often using flamethrowers, satchel charges and shaped charges to pierce their armour. The Rangers were flung into the battle to neutralize several key defences. It took Rudder's 2nd Battalion several days of hard fighting between September 5 and 9 to seize the Lochrist battery but the Rangers eventually captured some 1,800 prisoners. The 5th Battalion helped capture Le Conquet after a two-hour fight and stormed La Mon Blanche with less difficulty, but its attack on Fort de Portzic, which opened on the 17th, lasted for two days, though its fall signalled the end of German resistance. Brest, the town and its harbour facilities in ruins, surrendered on the 18th.

After Brittany both battalions moved eastwards, participating in the Allied drive towards the German border and performing a number of functions. The 5th Battalion acted as a headquarters security force for General Omar Bradley's Twelfth Army Group in Belgium during October and November. In December it linked up with the US 6th Cavalry Group of Patton's Third Army and conducted various small-scale actions against enemy-held towns. After a spell attached to the US 95th Infantry Division in January 1945, the battalion joined the 94th Infantry Division on February 9, taking over a large section of the front near Wehingen.

It was during this period that the 5th Rangers undertook an operation more suited to its skills. On February 23, the unit pushed out from the bridgehead over the Saar River and fought its way to a point three miles (5 km) behind German lines to seize high

Right: Company C, 2nd Ranger Battalion, prepares for a patrol. Note the variety of equipment – all wear the M1941 field jacket but with various bits of webbing and different footwear. The man in the centre rests his BAR on the ground.

Below right: 6th Rangers in the first wave attacking Dinagat, October 17, 1944.

Below: The patrol goes out near Heimbach, Germany, March 3, 1945.

ground overlooking the supply road linking Irsch and Zerf two days later. Isolated and outnumbered, the battalion fought on alone until relieved by elements of the US 10th Armored Division on the afternoon of the 27th. Holding the roadblock cost the battalion around 90 casualties but it killed an estimated 300 German troops, wounded 500 and took another 300 prisoner, earning a Presidential Unit Citation for the action. The fighting aided the drive of armour towards Trier, allowing elements of the US XX Corps to reach the River Rhine.

The 5th Rangers spent March in Luxembourg integrating replacements for the losses suffered during the Irsch–Zerf action but then conducted security roles, such as guarding prisoners and overseeing affairs in liberated towns. In May, in one of the battalion's last actions, it served with the US 3rd Cavalry Group in the drive on Austria through southern Germany and secured largely undefended bridges over the Danube River.

The 2nd Battalion also moved eastwards after the fall of Brest, advancing through Belgium and then undertaking a period of training in Luxembourg during October. Returning to combat, the Rangers were attached to the US 28th Infantry Division and took part in the battle to clear the Hürtgen Forest. In December Rudder was promoted and transferred to take command of the US 109th Infantry Regiment, part of the US 28th Infantry Division, and Major George Williams took charge of the 2nd Battalion, which operated in a defensive role during the German Ardennes offensive. In January 1945 the weakened battalion was pulled out of the line and set up camp at Schnidthof in Germany, where replacements were integrated into the unit. In February the battalion served with the US 102nd Cavalry Group and participated in the crossing of the Roer River during March. April saw the battalion performing security details.

Germany's surrender heralded the demise of the two battalions. In May, following the completion of various internal security duties, the 2nd Rangers established a base at Dolreuth in Czechoslovakia, where it was reduced to zero strength in June and formally deactivated at Camp Patrick Henry, Virginia, on October 23. The same fate befell the 5th Battalion. Based at Ried, Austria, in May and June, it was reduced to zero strength and formally deactivated on October 22 at Camp Miles Standish, Massachusetts. The end of the two battalions did not, however, signal the end of Ranger participation in World War II.

RANGERS IN THE PACIFIC

Although the bulk of the Ranger battalions served in the European theatre, the need for a similar force to operate against the Japanese in the Pacific was recognized by the commander of the US Sixth Army, Lieutenant General Walter Krueger, in the penultimate year of the war. In spring 1944, with the invasion and liberation of the Philippines becoming a real possibility, a lieutenant colonel and former provost marshal of Honolulu, Henry A. Mucci, took charge of the 98th Field Artillery Battalion, which had seen action on New Georgia and was earmarked for conversion. The unit soon lost its 75 mm howitzers, while those men not wishing to convert to Rangers were transferred out and replacements integrated into the new structure. As the necessary intensive training programme continued near Port Moresby, the 6th Ranger Battalion was officially activated at Hollandia, Dutch East Indies, on September 24, 1944.

The 6th Rangers went into action a few weeks later as part of the preliminary stages of the invasion of Leyte and thereby become the first US troops to return to the Philippines since the Japanese occupation in 1942. The battalion's mission was to neutralize radio and radar stations on three islands that covered the main route to the landing beaches on Leyte. They were also to set up navigation lights to guide the main invasion fleet to its ultimate target. On October 17, 1944, three days before the main

Above: Company E, 6th Rangers, board assault craft October 17, 1944.

Opposite, above: Men of Companies B and E, 6th Rangers, going ashore behind an armoured bulldozer, Santiago Island, Luzon, January 20, 1945.

Opposite, below left: Guerrillas meet up with Rangers on Dinagat Island, October 18, 1944.

Opposite, below right: Raising the Stars and Stripes on Dinagat.

assault, part of the battalion's headquarters company and its Company D came ashore on Suluan Island, while most of the remainder of the unit landed on the larger island of Dinagat. At Dinagat, the Rangers disembarked from their five Auxiliary Personnel Destroyers into landing craft and began their run to shore at around 0930. Despite problems caused by reefs, all of the assault companies were ashore on the island's northwest coast by 1230 and patrols were searching for the small enemy garrison. While the sweeps of Suluan and Dinagat continued, the rest of the headquarters company and Company B assaulted Homonhon Island during the following day. The detachments on Suluan and Homonhon quickly achieved their objectives and then headed to Dinagat, the largest of the three islands, to link up with the main party. For the next few weeks the battalion conducted patrols out of the coastal village of Loreto, observing Japanese ship movements and air attacks, and mopping up isolated pockets of resistance, but on November 14 the Rangers sailed for Leyte.

The 6th Battalion fought on Leyte for several weeks and fulfilled several roles. In the second half of November and December, the Rangers acted as guards for the Sixth Army headquarters at Tanuan and Tolosa and also protected a Seebee construction unit building an airfield at the former location. They next participated in the invasion of Luzon, the main island of the Philippines. Landings at Lingayen Gulf by Krueger's Sixth Army began on January 9, 1945, but the Rangers did not spearhead the assault and came ashore during the 10th and 11th. For the next few weeks the battalion acted as guards for the Sixth Army's headquarters but also undertook more aggressive operations – two companies landed on Santiago Island at the northwest entrance to Lingayen Gulf to establish a radar station, while other detachments launched reconnaissance patrols into Luzon's mountainous and jungle-covered interior.

However, the most renowned Ranger operation of the campaign took place at the end of January after Mucci attended a meeting at Dagupan, the Sixth Army's headquarters, on the 27th and was ordered to free an estimated 500 US captives from a Japanese prison camp some 10 miles (16 km) east of Cabanatuan in the island's central plains. Many of the prisoners were survivors of the Japanese capture of the Philippines in 1942 and it was feared that they would either be moved or executed before they could be liberated by the forces committed to the ongoing ground offensive. Mucci felt that the infiltration of the whole battalion some 30 miles (48 km) behind enemy lines would be far too risky so selected his Company C under Captain Robert Prince and the 2nd Platoon of F Company for the raid – just 121 men. Filipino guerrillas were available to guide the Rangers to their target, while members of the Alamo Scouts, a specialist reconnaissance formation created by Krueger and named after the famed mission in his home town, San Antonio, Texas, kept the compound under observation.

The raid opened at 0500 hours on the 28th, when trucks transported the Rangers from their base at Calasio by way of Dagupan to Guimba, where they disembarked from their transporters. They next marched a few miles eastwards to Lobong, where they were met by 80 local guerrillas under Captain Eduardo Jonson. As darkness fell the raiders set off for their objective, negotiating the jungle paths leading eastwards three miles (5 km) south of Baloc. After crossing the Cabanatuan–San José road they plunged farther eastwards, crossing the Talavera River around midnight and then reached the Cabanatuan–Rizal road at 0400 hours on the 29th. Two hours later Mucci and his men halted at Balincarin, five miles (8 km) north of the camp, where they ate and rested – they had covered 25 miles in 24 hours. Mucci was joined by Captain Juan Pajota, who added 90 armed guerrillas and 160 porters to the raid. Pajota was also able to provide the carts that would be needed to move the sick and weakened prisoners back to friendly lines. At 1600 hours Mucci led his men due south towards Plateros, where he met two Alamo Scouts. They informed him that Cabanatuan was guarded by 500 Japanese troops

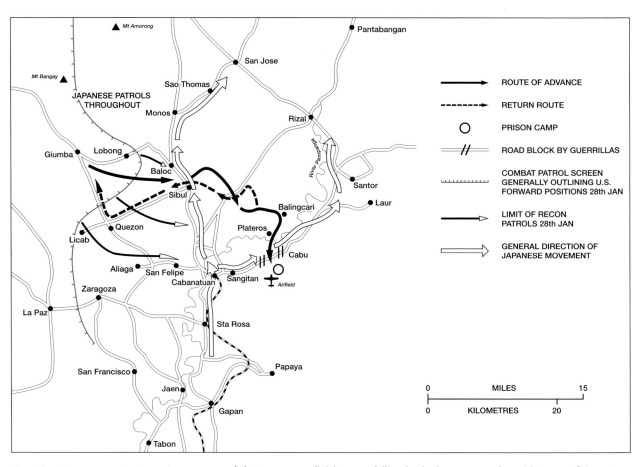

Above: The mission to rescue the prisoners from Cabanatuan.

and that an enemy division was falling back along a second road between Cabanatuan town and Rizal that ran close to the compound near Cabu. Mucci gained permission from Sixth Army headquarters to delay his attack until the next day to allow the enemy division to depart.

The raid devised by Mucci was complex, involving several distinct forces. Jonson's guerrillas and a six-man Ranger bazooka team established a blocking position at a point on the road some 800 yards (700 m) southwest of the camp to stop any Japanese advancing from Cabanatuan town. Similarly, Pajota's guerrillas set up positions on the same road but at Cabu bridge a mile (1.6 km) northeast of the compound to prevent the arrival of any of the 800-strong enemy garrison based at the latter town. Other guerrillas were detached to sever the camp's telephone lines to isolate it from outside help. Company F's 2nd Platoon under Lieutenant John Murphy infiltrated into positions close to the compound's eastern perimeter; its job was to neutralize two emplacements and a pair of observation towers at the moment when Company C began its attack through the main gate on the northern perimeter, which was also close to the huts holding the US prisoners. Speed was essential as any delay might have allowed the Japanese to execute their captives.

After leaving Platero during the afternoon of the 30th, the Rangers and guerrillas crossed the Pampanga River. The guerrillas then took up their blocking positions and the Rangers pushed on to the camp without being detected. The attack opened at around 1945 and was heralded by the cutting of the telephone lines and Murphy's diversionary assault on the eastern perimeter. Company C, in positions just 20 yards from the main gate, then attacked, rapidly killing sentries and men resting in nearby barracks. The

company's various assault sections now split up to carry out various tasks and fanned out through the complex: four tanks and two trucks were destroyed; radios were smashed; the prisoners released and helped out of the compound. The raid was completed in a mere 30 minutes; Prince fired a single red flare to start the withdrawal. Ranger casualties had been remarkably light with just a few men wounded but a medical officer, Captain James Fisher, was mortally wounded by a mortar fragment and a second man, Roy Sweezy, fell victim to friendly rifle fire. A mile outside the now-burning camp, the captain fired a second flare, which was the signal for the two blocking parties to abandon their positions. Jonson had no difficulties and fell in behind the withdrawing Rangers and liberated prisoners, but Pejota took around an hour to extricate his men from a bitter firefight with an unexpectedly large Japanese force of 2,000 men from Cebu.

The withdrawing column first renegotiated the Pampanga River, where carts were waiting for the sick and wounded, and then reached Plateros, where Fisher succumbed to his wounds the next day in the temporary field hospital he himself had previously established. The column began the next stage of journey back to friendly lines at 2130, and, as more and more carts were made available, passed through Balincarin. Flank and rear guards were deployed to slow the pursuit of the Japanese and, although the column moved slowly on a course that paralleled but was south of that used to reach the prison camp, Mucci was fortunate in that he would not have as far to go as expected because, on the morning of the 31st, he learned that the front line had been pushed beyond Guimba and Lobong since he had left for the operation. The Rangers' first contact with Sixth Army units occurred at Talavera town, where ambulances and other transports were gathered to move the sick and wounded to nearby hospitals at Guimba. Some 513 prisoners had been brought out of captivity while two Rangers had been killed and 10 wounded. The Cabanatuan raid was a classic Ranger operation and earned the gratitude of MacArthur who remarked that: 'no incident of this war has given me greater satisfaction than the Ranger rescue of these Americans.' Aside from the acclaim of the popular press back home, those involved received other awards. C Company and F Company's 2nd Platoon earned Presidential Unit Citations. Mucci and Prince received the Distinguished Service Cross, every

Above: Escorting PoWs released from Cabanatuan prison on Luzon, Philippines, January 1945.

Below: January 30, 1945. Donald A. Adams of 6th Rangers and Abe Abraham, ex-PoW.

MERRILL'S MARAUDERS

An American Ranger-style force, the 5307th Composite Provisional Unit was formed in India in 1943 and trained under the direction of Orde Wingate, the Chindit leader. Nicknamed 'Merrill's Marauders', after their leader, Brigadier-General Frank Merrill, they campaigned brilliantly, earning a Presidential Unit Citation. Outnumbered, without heavy weapons, they defeated the veterans of the Japanese 18th Division who had conquered Singapore and Malaya in 1941. They disrupted enemy supply and communication lines, and finally captured Myitkina Airfield, the only all-weather airfield in Burma. While in Burma they trained Gurkhas and Kachins, such as those illustrated here.

Below right: US-trained Gurkha Ranger on guard at Myitkina, January 18, 1945.

Below: Gurkha and Kachin training session underway at Myitkina.

other officer the Silver Star, and every enlisted man the Bronze Star.

The Cabanatuan mission was also the high point of the 6th Battalion's participation in the Pacific campaign, but the unit continued to operate in the Philippines until the end of the war. A variety of operations were conducted, chiefly hit-and-run raids, reconnaissance, and clearing Luzon's highland interior. Such operations were conducted by individual companies. In April, for example, one was used to block a Japanese withdrawal from the eastern sector of Luzon, while beginning in May another was sent on a long-range mission into the north of the island. This involved the battalion's Company B infiltrating some 200 miles (320 km) behind enemy lines to reach Appari on the island's north coast and then aid an assault landing by the US 11th Airborne Division. After the landings the Rangers operated with the paratroopers as they pushed southwards from Appari down the valley of the Cagayan River to link up with the US 37th Infantry Division in what was one of the last major attacks of the campaign.

Following the Japanese surrender in August 1945 the battalion was earmarked for occupation duties, although 139 men had already been demobilized on August 20. The remainder left Luzon for Japan on September 15 and landed at Honshu's Wakayama Beach 10 days later. The battalion established a base that was christened Camp Fisher, after the doctor killed in the withdrawal from Cabanatuan, but its occupation duties were neither onerous nor prolonged. At the end of November the battalion paraded for a final time before Krueger and it was formally deactivated on December 20, thereby ending the story of the Rangers in World War II.

AWARDS

Unit	Award	Location	Date
1st Rangers (1)	Presidential Unit Citation	El Guettar	1943
	Presidential Unit Citation	Salerno	1943
2nd Rangers (2)	Presidential Unit Citation	Pointe du Hoc	1944
	Croix de Guerre	Pointe du Hoc	1944
3rd Rangers (3)	Presidential Unit Citation	Salerno	1943
4th Rangers (4)			
5th Rangers (5)	Presidential Unit Citation	Pointe du Hoc	1944
	Croix de Guerre	Pointe du Hoc	1944
	Presidential Unit Citation	Irsch–Zerf	1945
6th Rangers (6)	Presidential Unit Citation	Cabanatuan (7)	1945
	Presidential Unit Citation	Philippines	1944–45

Notes

1 Participated in six campaigns, including four amphibious assaults.
2 Participated in five campaigns, including one amphibious assault.
3 Participated in four campaigns, including three amphibious assaults.
4 Participated in four campaigns, including three amphibious assaults.
5 Participated in five campaigns, including one amphibious assault.
6 Participated in three campaigns, including one amphibious assault.
7 Awarded to Company C and 2nd Platoon, Company F.

DARBY'S FAREWELL

The 1st, 3rd and 4th Rangers were officially deactivated in late 1944 following their return to the United States and in April 1945 Darby penned a heart-felt letter (in the event shortly before his own death) to those who had survived the battles in Europe:

'... As your commanding officer, I am justly proud to have led such an outstanding group of American fighting men. Never was I more sad than on the day of our parting. Never was I more content than being with you on our many exciting operations. You trained hard, you fought hard, and always you gave your best regardless of discomfort or danger. From the great Allied raid at Dieppe through the exacting, bitter campaigns culminating with the Anzio beachhead battles, the 1st, 3rd, and 4th Ranger Battalions have performed in a capacity unsurpassed by the highest traditions of the American Army. Your record speaks for itself.

We – the living Rangers – will never forget our fallen comrades. They and the ideals for which they fought will remain ever present among us, for we fully understand the extent of their heroic sacrifices. We will carry their spirit with us into all walks of life, into all corners of America. Our hearts join together in sorrow for their loss; but also our hearts swell with pride to have fought alongside such valiant men. They will never be considered dead, for they live with us in spirit ...

No better way can I sum up my feelings of pride for your splendid achievements than to state this: Commanding the Rangers was like driving a team of very high-spirited horses. No effort was needed to get them to go forward. The problem was to hold them in check. Good luck, Rangers, and may your futures be crowned with deserving success.'

INSIGNIA, CLOTHING & EQUIPMENT

Above right: Rangers' shoulder flashes. The first (left)was designed by Sgt. Anthony Fleet in 1942. Each of the six battalions wore an unofficial scroll like this one – made official in 1987. The lozenge shape (middle) was only worn by members of 2nd and 5th Rangers. The third (right) was used by 29th Rangers. Underneath is the unofficial flash of 'Merrill's Marauders'.

Right: Re-enactment view of Operation Torch uniforms – M1942 herringbone twill suits, M1 helmets, M1928 haversacks, and gasmasks carried slung across their chests. The man on the right carries an M1 .30 cal rifle; the one on the left an M1928A1 Thompson submachine gun. Note US identification armbands.

Below: Corporal 'Zip' Koons displays his 1st Ranger Battalion shoulder flash.

The Rangers who saw service in World War II generally wore uniforms and carried weapons that were standard throughout the US Army. However, as the text below reveals there were exceptions to this that grew out of their specialist role and, with regard to uniform, because of their initial attachment to British units. Members of the various battalions also wore standard rank insignia and the like but did adopt a range of unit cloth badges that marked them out as Rangers.

INSIGNIA

The insignia most used to identify members of the six main Ranger Battalions during World War II was the scroll worn singly on the wearer's upper left shoulder. This was originally an unofficial design created for the 1st Battalion in late 1942 by Sergeant Anthony Fleet but it was later copied by the other battalions and gained acceptance with the US military authorities. Fleet's badge comprised a very dark blue/black scroll-shaped background with white lettering enclosed in a edging in the form of a thin red line. The title 'Ranger' appeared in the centre with the unit's number to the viewer's left and the abbreviation 'BN' for battalion on the right. The cloth patches were generally manufactured locally and were not always readily available so it is not uncommon to see photos of Rangers without the device.

During Operation Torch in North Africa in November 1942, the 1st Battalion wore special badges to indicate their nationality to the opposing Vichy French, as it was thought that they were less likely to fire on US troops. A detachable US flag was worn on the left shoulder and a plain white band was worn about midway between the elbow and shoulder of one, or sometimes both, arms.

In contrast to the more common scroll device, the short-lived 29th Provisional Ranger Battalion wore an entirely different scroll comprising a small red shoulder tab with the words '29th Ranger' in mid-blue lettering. This was sometimes worn above the emblem of the US 29th Infantry Division, a green-edged circle divided into blue and grey halves by an S-shaped curve, from the ranks of which the battalion's recruits were drawn.

A second cloth shoulder insignia was officially approved for all of the Ranger battalions in July 1943, although it appears only to have been worn by the 2nd and 5th Battalions, and began to appear the following September. It consisted of a lozenge-shaped piece of light blue cloth with gold-yellow edging and the title 'Rangers' in the centre rendered in the same colour. An unofficial version of the design with two gold-yellow edges was worn by members of the 5th Battalion from September 1943 but was replaced by the prescribed version after a couple of months. Both symbols were nicknamed the Blue Sunoco as they bore a close similarity to the corporate logo of the

Above: Wet weather gear in Scotland, October 31, 1942. Note the 'new' M1 helmet rather than the British-style M1917A1. The original rubberised cotton ponchos soon gave way to resin-coated nylon fabric. They didn't have hoods – just a drawstring – or sleeves – snap fasteners allowed them to be gathered around the arms. All had metal grommets to allow them to be used as tent shelters.

US Sunoco Oil Company and, unlike the scroll, sometimes appeared on both shoulders. The 2nd and 5th Battalions abandoned their Blue Sunoco designs during the summer of 1945, only after the war in Europe had ended, when they adopted the standard scroll.

During the assault on the Pointe du Hoc the Rangers of both battalions had field identification symbols painted onto the back of their helmets. These consisted of a gold-yellow lozenge with the battalion number in black in the centre. Officers were further identified by a short, broad vertical white band running behind the lozenge, while non-commissioned officers had a similar device but running horizontally.

CLOTHING

For the most part the Rangers wore standard US military dress throughout the war. When training in Scotland, they were mostly seen in the one-piece herring-bone work suit in olive drab. The British-style M1917A1 helmet was used during this period but was replaced by the ubiquitous M1 during the latter part of 1942. For operations in North Africa, Rangers wore serge olive drab trousers, wool shirts of a similar colour, the M1 helmet and web gaiters and in warm weather they generally fought in this shirt-sleeve order. However, as desert nights can be cold, they were often seen dressed in the M1941 jacket, a waist-length single-breasted design, that proved only moderately successful in combating the night-time temperatures. It was not uncommon for Rangers to wear extra items of clothing – pullovers, scarves and the olive knit cap or beanie – for additional warmth. The jacket issued to members of armoured units, a waist-length design with knitted collar and cuff, was also highly prized as it had a warmer lining and offered greater protection from the weather. However, for the most part, the Rangers soldiered on with the M1941 through Sicily, Italy and D-Day, but many adopted the M1943 woollen field jacket when it became available as this design offered better protection against the winter weather encountered during the final stages of the campaign in Europe.

For its operations in the Pacific the 6th Rangers mostly wore the lightweight M1943 herring-bone fatigues and for the Cabanatuan raid its headgear comprised the M1941 field cap.

Probably almost uniquely, some Rangers also wore British battledress for a time. The party of men who fought at Dieppe in 1942 had much the same uniform as the Commando units to which they were attached and the same was true of members of the 29th Ranger Battalion when they participated in raids against Occupied Europe.

WEAPONS

The Rangers were essentially fast-moving light infantry and generally lacked support weapons that were more powerful than light/medium machine guns, mortars and bazookas. Their small arms were generally standard issue and comparable to those carried by other US infantry units. If their firepower needed to be boosted, they were supported by units or detachments that could provide the necessary weapons.

Pistols, Rifles and Sub-machine Guns

When the 1st Battalion arrived in Scotland for training, the men were equipped with the M1903A1 bolt-action Springfield rifle but this was quickly replaced by the .30-calibre Garand M1 semi-automatic from the autumn of 1942 and this became the mainstay of the individual Ranger's firepower for the remainder of the war, although some hung on to the Springfield for a time. Among these men were snipers, one of whom was attached to the headquarters of each platoon, who continued to use a modified version of the M1903 Springfield, the A, fitted with a telescope sight such as the M73B. When it became available, the Rangers also adopted the shorter M1 carbine. The most popular sub-machine gun was the excellent .45 calibre M1 Thompson, which was originally held at battalion level and issued to individual Rangers when necessary. The Rangers used the 50-round drum magazine in their early days but it proved cumbersome and was replaced by the 20- or 30-round box magazine. The most popular pistol was M1911A1 automatic.

Machine Guns

The first Ranger battalions were issued with 23 .30-calibre tripod-mounted Browning M1919A4 light machine guns. These were wholly satisfactory weapons, capable of firing around 500 rounds per minute from 250-round belts, but not entirely suited to Ranger-style operations as they were comparatively heavy and not easy to move around the battlefield at speed. More practical for giving direct close support during an attack was the M1918A2 Browning Automatic Rifle (BAR). This was operated by a single Ranger

Above: T/Sgt. John S. Rembecki does some paperwork in camp in England, October 1942. Note the early war equipment – British-style M1917A1 helmet.

Right: This close-up shows a detail of the front of the M1926 US Navy lifebelt, worn under an assault vest.

Below: Rear view of the two soldiers seen on page 67. Note the five-magazine pouch for the Thompson and the waterbottle of the man on the right, and the M1923 cartridge belt of man at the left..

Far right: A re-enactment of the Pointe du Hoc mission. Note the extremely light combat gear carried – he has little more than a water bottle and a Thompson. Note the Airborne jump boots that were often used by Rangers.

Above: January 20, 1943 – a Ranger exercise in North Africa.

Right: Going over the rail of the transport to the assault craft, November 8, 1942.

Opposite: Speed march training, 1st Rangers North Africa, December 5, 1942. At right, Corporal Chester Fisches of Clinton, Idaho, carries his rifle over his shoulder. He is bareheaded in the heat, and wears the shirt sleeve order so often seen in North Africa, wool shirt, trousers, boots, M1938 webbing gaiters. He has an M1923 rifleman's, s web cartridge belt and an M1 rifle. At left, is similarly clad Private Edward T. Calhoun of Campbelleville, Kentucky.

SCALING THE POINTE DU HOC

The three companies of the 2nd Ranger Battalion under Lieutenant Colonel James Rudder tasked with scaling the 100-foot (30 m) cliffs of the Pointe du Hoc faced one of the most difficult tasks of D-Day. Aware that speed was essential to their success, they were issued with various ingenious devices that were designed to lessen the difficulties of reaching the summit of their target as quickly as possible.

The Rangers came ashore in several LCAs (Landing Craft, Assault) that had each been fitted with three pairs of rockets. One pair was capable of throwing a ¾-inch (7 mm) diameter rope attached to a grapnel to heights of around 200 feet (70 m); the second deployed similar rope lines but these were fitted with 2-inch wooden toggles every foot or so; and the third pair launched light rope ladders that had rungs every two feet. However, many of the ropes became thoroughly sodden during the final approach to the beach and proved far too heavy to be lifted to the cliff-top when fired. When these devices failed, the Rangers resorted to smaller hand-held versions with a range of around 100 feet (30 m) and some of these did reach the summit. The LCAs also carried self-assembly ladders ashore. These consisted of 4-foot (1.2 m) tubular sections that could be fitted together to complete a 112-foot (34 m) ladder. For the Pointe du Hoc assault the Rangers pre-assembled 16-foot (5 m) sections to hasten the process of completing the ladders once they were at the base of the cliffs.

The most extraordinary items of equipment available to the Rangers were specially customized DUKW amphibians. Although these were normally deployed to carry troops or supplies, on D-Day the Rangers were accompanied by two DUKWs fitted with turntable-mounted extendable ladders capable of reaching heights of around 100 feet (30 m) that had been acquired from the London Fire Brigade. The top of each ladder was fitted with a pair of Lewis guns designed to give the climbers a measure of fire support. Although the converted DUKWs had performed to expectation on exercises before June 6, on the actual day they failed at the first hurdle. They were unable to reach the foot of the cliffs due to their inability to cross the narrow shell-blasted beach that was littered with large sections of the cliff that had been detached by the pre-landing naval bombardment.

Since much of the specialist climbing equipment was unsatisfactory for the intended task, the Rangers resorted to other methods. Some were able to use ordinary climbing ropes or put together sections of toggle ropes, several of which were cut by the Germans as the Rangers scaled the heights, while others resorted to gouging out hand and foot holds in the face using their hands and combat knives. In the event many Rangers were killed or wounded in the climb and a good number needed several attempts to reach the summit.

Right: Three more re-enactment views of Rudder's 2nd Rangers assaulting Pointe du Hoc. Note in particular the '2' in an orange diamond on the back of the helmet identifying the unit. This was seen with the 2nd and 5th Rangers. While the ladder looks efficient, in fact the Rangers found the specialist climbing equipment did not work as planned (as described in the box above). Note also the rear of the US Navy lifebelt on man at left, and the US assault vest worn by the two lower men (in two different colours).

who might carry up to 12 20-round magazines on the specially designed M1937 belt. Although the BAR was fitted with a bipod, it was not uncommon for Rangers to remove the stabilizing device to reduce the weapon's weight and make it easier to wield.

Mortars

The Rangers relied on two main types of mortar. Typically, a battalion was issued with six of the larger calibre 81 mm M1 types and three times as many of the smaller 60 mm M2 version of the weapon.

Anti-tank Weapons

For tank-killing the earliest Ranger battalions relied on the generally unsatisfactory British-designed .55-calibre Boys anti-tank rifle fitted with a five-round magazine. The official establishment called for a battalion to have 20 of these weapons but their obsolescence was evident even in the early stages of the war and the Rangers came to rely on the 2.36-inch M1 rocket-launcher, the famed bazooka, which packed a much better punch, not only for attacking tanks but also for neutralizing fixed defences.

Grenades and Demolitions

As with other equipment, the Rangers were issued with standard anti-personnel grenades. Among these were the M6 fragmentation grenade and the more unusual M6 CN-DM devices filled with tear or vomiting gas. Rifle grenades were also available. For example the M1919 Springfield could be fitted with the M1 launcher to fire the M9 anti-tank grenade. Rangers were trained in the use of bangalore torpedoes, which were primarily used for clearing paths through minefields or cutting barbed wire entanglements. They consisted of 1½-inch or 2-inch diameter 8-foot tubes filled with 10 or 12 lb of explosives. Depending on the width of the obstruction, several sections could be fitted together in much the same way as a socket bayonet is fixed to a rifle and an igniter fitted to the end nearest the user. A nose plug was fitted to the front portion to allow the whole device to be pushed more easily through any obstruction. The Rangers also employed the pole charge on occasion. This close-quarters device was used for pushing through the observation slits and fire ports of pill-boxes and consisted of a pair of Mk IIIA1 percussion grenades fixed to a length of tent pole.

PEOPLE

WILLIAM O. DARBY (1911–45)

Darby had a conventional upbringing in Fort Smith, Arkansas, and secured a place at West Point in part thanks to the intervention of a local member of Congress, Otis Wingo. A member of the class of 1933, he had an exemplary record as a student and on his graduation was commissioned as a second lieutenant in the 1st Battalion, 82nd Field Artillery Regiment, which was part of the 1st Cavalry Division and based at Fort Bliss, Texas. Over the following years Darby attended various training courses and gained sufficient leadership skills to be promoted to captain on October 1, 1940. In 1941 he gained his first experiences of amphibious assault techniques when he attended exercises in Puerto Rico and at the New River training facility in North Carolina. During November Darby was ordered to Hawaii but had not arrived by the time of the Japanese surprise attack on December 7 and, following the US declaration of war, he was ordered to report to Major General Russell Hartle's 34th Infantry Division, which sailed for Northern Ireland on January 15, 1942.

Hartle was made commander of the US Army Northern Ireland on the 27th with Darby as his aide, but the young officer was looking for a more active role and on

Left: Fort Jackson, April 24, 1943, sees more PE. The men are wearing the distinctive field hat so popular with Merrill's Marauders.

Below left: October 8, 1944. 6th Rangers march to its embarkation point in New Guinea preparatory to assault Dinagat Island. This photograph gives a good idea of the tropical clothing – herringbone fatigues and camouflaged helmet covers.

Below: Lt-Col. W. O. Darby in the field, North Africa, December 12, 1942.

WORLD WAR II RANGER COMMANDERS

1st Battalion
Major William O. Darby (**1**)
Major John Dobson (**2**)

2nd Battalion
Lieutenant Colonel William C. Saffarans
Major L. E. McDonald
Lieutenant Colonel James E. Rudder
Major George S. Williams

3rd Battalion
Major Herman Dammer
Major Alvah Miller (**3**)

4th Battalion
Major Roy Murray

5th Battalion
Major Owen H. Carter
Lieutenant Colonel Max Schneider
Lieutenant-Colonel Richard Sullivan

6th Battalion
Lieutenant Colonel Henry A. Mucci
Major Robert Garrett

29th Provisional Ranger Battalion
Major Randolph Millholland

(**1**) died of wounds, posthumously promoted brigadier-general
(**2**) badly wounded at Anzio
(**3**) killed at Anzio

Below: Darby epitomised the Rangers of the early war years and it was his drive that ensured they were prepared to a high standard and performed as expected. An exceptional leader, Derby was decorated a number of times – here he wears the the ribbon the British Distinguished Service Order presented to him for heroism above and beyond the call of duty. He is seen after Anzio, when his command was wiped out, as CO of 179th Infantry Regiment, part of 45th Infantry Division, before he took on a staff role.

June 8 he was appointed to lead a new unit, which was to become the 1st Ranger Battalion. Between the summer of 1942 and early 1944 Darby was the dominant figure in the Rangers. He took part in several major operations – Operation Torch, the Tunisian campaign, Sicily, Salerno, and Anzio, and oversaw the expansion of his command from one to three battalions. Darby received numerous awards, including a Silver Star for the Sened night attack, a Distinguished Service Medal for the action at El Guettar, and a Distinguished Service Cross for the landings at Gela in Sicily. In the autumn of 1944 he received several other awards, among them the Legion of Merit, the Croix de Guerre, the Soviet Union's Order of Kutuzov, Third Class, and the Oak Leaf Cluster to the Purple Heart. However, Anzio marked his last action with the Rangers. Following the virtual destruction of all three battalions in late January 1944, he was left without a command and on February 16 was assigned to the US 45th Infantry Division's severely understrength 179th Infantry Regiment, leading it for the next two months. Thanks to the intervention of General Mark Clark, Darby was assigned to the Operations Division of the War Department General Staff and left Anzio for Washington during April. Over the following several months he undertook staff duties that were not particularly to his liking but his requests for a return to a more active role were initially turned down.

Darby nevertheless continued to request a transfer and finally gained permission to return overseas on March 29, 1945. He had a roving commission to study the effectiveness of air support during ground operations and decided to return to Italy to join the 10th Mountain Division under Major General George P. Hayes, formerly Darby's commander when he had served with the 99th Field Artillery Regiment during 1940–41. Shortly after Darby's arrival the division's assistant commander was wounded and Darby, with Hayes' support, was able to take his place. In late April, the division was attacking up the east side of Lake Garda in the north of Italy and on the late afternoon of the 30th after the defeat of a German counterattack, Darby decided to go forward to inspect one of the numerous tunnels through which ran the lakeside road and where the enemy advance had been blocked. All seemed quiet as he left a command post at a hotel in Torbole, but as Darby was preparing to board a waiting jeep a shell landed within 10 yards. Darby's heart was hit by a small fragment and he died of his wounds within a few minutes without regaining consciousness. On the same day he died, Darby's name appeared in a list of officers who had been recommended for promotion. Secretary of War Stimson broke with existing practice and Darby's name remained on the list. He was posthumously promoted to the rank of brigadier general. Darby's undoubted leadership skills were perhaps best summed up by General Lucian Truscott, who was moved to write shortly after his death that he had 'Never in this war… known a more gallant, heroic officer.'

Above: A conference aboard the *Winchester Castle*, January 1944. From left to right: ship's captain S. F. Newdigate; Lt-Col. William P. Yarborough, CO of 509th Parachute Infantry Battalion; and Lt-Col. Roy A. Murray, CO of 4th Ranger Battalion.

HENRY MUCCI (1911–97)

Henry Andrew Mucci, a graduate of the West Point Class of 1936, had been present at the attack on Pearl Harbor in December 1941, when he was the provost marshal in Honolulu. When in 1944 he took charge of the newly formed 6th Ranger Battalion at the age of 33, he quickly gained two nicknames: 'Little MacArthur', because he smoked a pipe similar to that used by the commanding general in the theatre, and 'Ham', an affectionate play on his initials that reflected his sometimes theatrical style of leadership. However, Mucci was a strict disciplinarian, supremely fit, and ambitious for his new battalion. He led it with distinction during the Philippines campaign, most notably during the rescue mission at Cabanatuan in early 1945. After the war, Mucci returned to his hometown, Bridgeport, Connecticut, and received a rapturous hero's welcome from 50,000 local citizens for his leadership of the Cabanatuan operation. Following a failed attempt to be elected to Congress, he later became a representative for an oil company from Canada and worked in the Far East, although there were rumours, which he strenuously denied, that he was actually an undercover operative for the Central Intelligence Agency. He died aged 86 after suffering complications from a hip fracture that occurred while swimming in rough seas near his final home in Melbourne, Florida.

JAMES E. RUDDER (1910–70)

Texas-born Rudder attended the John Tarleton Agricultural College in 1928 and 1929 but then studied at Texas A&M University, graduating with a degree in industrial education. He was subsequently commissioned second lieutenant in the US Army Reserve, while working as a teacher and football coach at Tarleton. He was called up in 1941 and two years later, as a lieutenant colonel, was assigned to command the 2nd Ranger Battalion. On D-Day he led the crucial and difficult assault on the Pointe du Hoc, a successful operation but one that saw Rudder wounded twice. He led the battalion over the following six months during operations to liberate northwest Europe and was then transferred to command the 109th Infantry Regiment, which saw action during that winter's Battle of the Bulge. By the war's end Rudder was a full colonel and had been awarded numerous medals, including the Distinguished Service Cross, Legion of Merit, Silver Star, and the French Legion of Honour with Croix de Guerre and Palm. Rudder was the mayor of Brady, Texas, between 1946 and 1952, and for a year was vice-president of the Brady Aviation Company. In early 1955, he became a commissioner overseeing the Veterans' Land Program and held the post for the next three years, before becoming vice-president of Texas A&M. In 1959 he became the university's president and in 1965 became president of the entire A&M system, a position he held until his death. In his later years Rudder was successively promoted to brigadier general and major general in the US Army Reserve and in 1967 his distinguished career was crowned by President Lyndon Johnson awarding him the Distinguished Service Medal.

LUCIAN K. TRUSCOTT JR. (1895–1965)

Texas-born Truscott was a leading figure in the creation of the Rangers and had a distinguished career as a senior field commander during World War II. He joined the US Army in 1917 and spent his early years as a cavalry officer before being attached to the 13th Armored Regiment in 1940. In May 1942 he was promoted to the rank of brigadier general and assigned to the Allied Combined Operations staff under Britain's Lord Louis Mountbatten. During this period he analysed the Commandos and recommended that the United States raise a similar force, a decision that led directly to the creation of the Rangers. Truscott oversaw their first operation – the raid in force on Dieppe in August – but was then transferred to other assignments. As commander of the 3rd Infantry Division, which fought alongside the Rangers on occasion, he took part in the invasions of Sicily, Salerno and Anzio in 1943. In February 1944 he took command of the VI Corps at Anzio and subsequently led it during the invasion of southern France. In December 1944 he returned to Italy to take charge of the Fifth Army during the final stages of the campaign. After a spell as commander of the US Third Army in Bavaria he returned to the United States in 1946 and retired the following year.

Above: Brigadier General Truscott on July 2, 1943, when in command of US 3rd Infantry Division.

Right: 1st Sgt Warren E. Evans – the official caption notes him as 6ft 4in in height, 24 years old, native of Aberdeen, South Dakota, ex-football player – being congratulated by Brigadier-General L. K. Truscott, August 1942.

POSTWAR

KOREA – RANGER HOPES DASHED

The swift disbandment of the six Ranger battalions at the end of World War II reflected the general scaling down of US armed forces and a growing emphasis on nuclear deterrence in the era of the Cold War at the expense of conventional forces. However, the value of specialist ground troops became apparent with the outbreak of the Korean War in June 1950. The US Army's Chief of Staff, General J. Lawton Collins, visited South Korea and on his return to the United States recommended the formation of so-called Marauder Companies. A formal request was issued on August 29, on the basis that each company should comprise five officers and 107 men skilled in reconnaissance and behind-the-lines missions and be attached to individual divisions. Following a suggestion that the new units would be better named Airborne Ranger Companies, volunteers from the 11th and 82nd Airborne Divisions assembled at Fort Benning, Georgia, where Colonel John Van Houten had been placed in charge of the newly activated Ranger Training Center (Airborne). The first four companies completed their six-week training course on November 11. In total 15 Airborne Ranger Companies were activated from late October 1950 to late February 1951 but only six served in Korea; the remainder stayed in the United States or were stationed elsewhere overseas, chiefly West Germany and Japan.

Below: March 6, 1951– a Ranger patrol briefing.

The companies that fought in Korea from December 1950 undertook a range of missions, such as intelligence-gathering, raids and ambushes to collect prisoners, and as spearhead infantry. Mostly these were small-scale and hazardous affairs – one recruit remarked that, 'for the Rangers in Korea, fighting outnumbered and surrounded was routine' – but the Rangers were occasionally involved in larger operations. The largest occurred on March 23, 1951, when the 2nd and 4th Airborne Ranger Companies parachuted alongside the 187th Airborne Regimental Combat Team in the vicinity of Munsan-ni to block the retreat of North Korean and Chinese troops from Seoul, the South Korean capital,

Above: M16 rifle at the ready, a camouflaged 75th Ranger walks point on an operation in Tuyen Duc province, March 4, 1970.

which had just been liberated by UN forces for the second time. The action, the only such airborne mission of the war, was not wholly successful and many of the enemy forces escaped the attempted encirclement.

By mid-1951 the seesaw war of movement in Korea had ended and both sides established fixed positions along what the UN forces christened the Main Line of Resistance. It was not a happy time for the Rangers; there were undoubted problems with logistical support as they relied on the divisions they served with for supplies, and doubts were expressed on the worth of such units in a static war. In July 1951 orders were issued to deactivate the various companies. Those in Korea were disbanded on August 1, while those serving elsewhere followed between September and December. The Ranger Training Command was inactivated on October 17 but hopes that the Rangers might rise again came with the creation of the Ranger Department the same month. Its role was to train officers and non-commissioned officers who could pass on Ranger skills to others when they were returned to their parent formation.

THE COLD WAR AND VIETNAM

From the late 1950s the leading members of NATO began programmes to develop special forces capable of operations deep behind enemy – Warsaw Pact – lines. Capable of acting wholly independently, they were composed of very small units that were known as Long Range Reconnaissance Patrols (LRRPs) or, in the case of the United States, Long Range Patrols (LRPs), and their chief function was reconnaissance and intelligence-gathering. The first LRPs were raised to test the concept, appearing in around 1958, and two companies were formally activated in West Germany on July 15, 1961. They had a checkered career, being deactivated four years later, re-attached to a new unit, and then transferred back to the United States in 1968.

Renewed impetus to develop the LRP idea came with the commitment of US ground forces to Vietnam, where the need for specialist units to conduct a whole range of behind-the-lines operations became apparent. Individual divisions and corps began to activate LRP-style patrols and platoons. Official recognition of their value came in late 1967, when the US military authorities formally ordered the creation of LRPs. These were either of company strength, 118 men, when attached to a division or larger formation, or of reinforced platoon strength, around 61 men, if serving with a brigade. The new LRPs did not have a parent regiment or links with any previous force and so they were assigned to the 75th Infantry Regiment, which had a lineage associated with Merrill's Marauders, on February 1, 1969, and all LRPs were redesignated as 'Ranger'. The LRPs could not be given the honours or lineage of the Rangers of World War II as the traditions had been passed to the US Special Forces (Green Berets) in April 1960. The Ranger companies in Vietnam suffered the same fate as their predecessors – they were inactivated between 1969 and 1972.

PEACEKEEPING AND THE MIDDLE EAST

The completion of the withdrawal of US ground forces from Vietnam in 1973 was preceded by a reduction in Ranger strength, with just two companies, A and B, remaining in the United States. However, interest in the concept was renewed by the outbreak of the Yom Kippur War between Israel and Egypt, which threatened to destabilize the Middle East and involve the superpowers in direct confrontation. The US military acknowledged that it lacked lightly equipped forces mobile enough to be quickly sent to any trouble spot and the following year, General Creighton Abrams, the US Army's Chief of Staff, ordered the formation of the 1st and 2nd Battalions, 75th Infantry (Rangers) based around men from the surviving Ranger companies. the 1st Battalion was activated at Fort Benning, Georgia, on January 31, 1974, and the 2nd Battalion followed at Fort Lewis, Washington, on October 1.

The revitalized Rangers undertook their first combat assignment on April 28–29, 1980, during Operation Eagle Claw, the abortive attempt to rescue US hostages held in Teheran by the fundamentalist Islamic regime of Iran. The complex night-time operation involved a wide range of US special forces but only Company C of the Rangers' 1st Battalion was involved in the mission. Its role was to seize a desert airfield at Manzariyeh, some 35 miles (55 km) southwest of the Iranian capital, from where the hostages would be flown to safety in C-141 Starlifters after being rescued from the US embassy compound in the capital. Eagle Claw ended disastrously, when two of the helicopters detailed to move the hostage rescuers to their target failed to reach a rendezvous point known as Desert One due to mechanical problems and then one of the six that reached the position suffered similar difficulties. The lack of functioning helicopters made it impossible to move the rescue teams to Teheran and a withdrawal was ordered. During its execution a collision destroyed a C-130 and a Sea Stallion, forcing the remaining US forces present to abandon the surviving helicopters and withdraw in C-130 transports.

The failure of Eagle Claw was an international embarrassment, but the Rangers' next mission in October 1983 was much more successful. A palace coup ousted the populist, moderately left-wing leader of the Caribbean island of Grenada, Prime Minister Maurice Bishop, and his subsequent execution led the US authorities to use the unrest as a pretext to occupy Grenada. There were worries about the fate of US students attending various campuses on the island but, more importantly, its ongoing and strengthening ties with Cuba were of serious geopolitical concern. President Ronald Reagan, with support from other Caribbean leaders, ordered the deployment of troops to overthrow the new revolutionary regime and rescue the students.

Some 500 Rangers drawn from both battalions took part in the operation, which was code-named Urgent Fury and opened on the 25th. The Rangers' role was to secure the airfield nearing completion at Point Salinas on the island's southeast tip so that 750 men of the 82nd Airborne Division could land. The Rangers' parachute assault at around 0530 hours was met by heavy ground fire from local defence forces and hastily armed Cuban construction workers, but the area was quickly secured for the loss of five Rangers killed and six wounded. The assault teams next moved on the nearby True Blue Campus close to the eastern end of the airfield and within two hours had rescued 138 US medical students. The same feat was accomplished the next day, when 224 students were freed from Grand Anse campus, a few miles south of St. George, Grenada's capital. The Rangers' final operation on Grenada took place on the 27th, when an airmobile assault was launched against Calivigny Barracks outside St. George. Despite losing three men killed and five wounded when three of their four Black Hawk helicopters collided on landing, the surviving Rangers secured the objective.

Grenada and the possibility of similar operations in the future gave further impetus to the development of the Rangers. On October 3, 1984, the existing two units were strengthened by the activation of the 3rd Battalion and a regimental headquarters at Fort Benning, Georgia, with the whole force being named the 75th Infantry Regiment (Ranger). Two years later, on April 17, the three battalions were renamed the 75th Ranger Regiment, receiving all of the honours and the lineage of Ranger units that had served in World War II and Korea but sharing them with the Special Forces.

Above: The Rangers became airborne after World War II. This photograph is of trainees dropping at Fort Benning in 1950.

The Rangers' next major mission was Operation Just Cause on December 20, 1989, a multi-pronged US operation to overthrow the Panamanian dictator General Manuel Noriega, bring him to trial on charges of involvement in the illegal drugs trade, and maintain the free flow of shipping though the Panama Canal. They provided the bulk of Task Force Red, which was to seize various positions around Panama City at the Pacific entrance to the canal as a spearhead for the follow-on Task Force Pacific.

The 1st Battalion, along with the 3rd Battalion's Company C and headquarters detachment Team Gold, was code-named Task Force Red Tango and undertook a successful early-morning parachute assault against Omar Torrijos international airport and Tocumen military airfield to the east of Panama City, thereby permitting the landing of the 82nd Airborne Division, for the loss of one killed, five wounded and 19 jump injuries.

Known as Task Force Red Romeo, the 2nd Battalion and bulk of the 3rd, along with headquarters detachment Team Black, conducted a low-level jump on the airfield at Rio Hato 55 miles (88 km) west of Panama City at 0003 hours and had secured the target within two hours for the loss of four killed, 27 wounded, and 35 parachute injuries. The Rangers then moved out to capture Noriega's nearby beach house.

The various battalions remained in Panama for the next few weeks. They conducted various security missions, hunted down remnants of Panama's regular and paramilitary forces, and secured key positions. By the time of their withdrawal in the second week of January, they had captured over 1,000 enemy personnel and confiscated around 18,000 arms of all types.

The Rangers were next deployed on active service to the Middle East after Saddam Hussein launched Iraqi forces into neighbouring Kuwait in 1990. However, the Ranger presence was small, with only Company B and Company A's 1st Platoon of the 1st Battalion being involved in Operation Desert Storm. The Rangers were deployed in Saudi Arabia from February 12 to April 15, 1991, and undertook hit-and-run raids, reconnaissance patrols, and served as a rapid-reaction force. The liberation of Kuwait was swift and achieved with few casualties among the Coalition forces; the Rangers themselves recorded no losses.

If Desert Storm had been relatively bloodless, the Rangers' next mission was a much bloodier affair. Between August 26 and October 21, 1993, the 3rd Battalion's Company B and a command detachment was despatched to Somalia in the Horn of Africa as part of Operation Restore Hope, a US-led but multinational peace-keeping and humanitarian mission to bring order to a country torn apart by fighting between rival warlords. Task Force Ranger was ordered to capture the most powerful warlord, General Mohammed Farah Aidid, and conducted several sweeps through Mogadishu, the country's capital, in search of its quarry. On October 3 the Rangers raided Mogadishu's Olympic Hotel and then went to the assistance of a Black Hawk helicopter that had been brought down by the warlord's militia. The Rangers were quickly surrounded by thousands of Somalis and, as these were being kept at bay, some of the Rangers attempted to reach the crew of a second Black Hawk that had crashed. All of the Rangers that went to the aid of the second helicopter were killed and two, Master Sergeant Gary Gordon and Sergeant First Class Randall Shughart, were subsequently awarded the Congressional Medal of Honor. The surviving men were eventually evacuated the following day, thanks to the work of other Rangers and a battalion of the US 10th Mountain Division supported by Malayan and Pakistani forces. The intense fighting cost the Rangers 16 killed and 57 wounded.

Above: The training is as arduous as ever. Here SFC William S. Brown demonstrates the use of the M60 machine gune while executing the Australian rappel at Fort Benning.

THE WAR ON TERROR

The terrorist attack on New York's Twin Towers on September 11, 2001, led President George Bush Jr to authorize Operation Enduring Freedom – a worldwide campaign against Osama bin Laden and members of his Al-Qaeda network that had been identified as the perpetrators. Al-Qaeda's chief supporter was the fundamentalist Muslim Taliban regime in Afghanistan and the Rangers were deployed to the country to seek out the terrorists and, along with other Special Forces, aid the anti-government Northern Alliance in toppling the Taliban. The first Ranger action began late on October 19, when 100 Rangers air assaulted a suspected Al-Qaeda compound outside Kandahar and a small airfield in the south of the country. The Rangers successfully seized valuable documents and destroyed several weapons' caches, but two, Specialist Jonn Edmunds and Private First Class Kristofer Stonesifer, died when their helicopter crashed in neighbouring Pakistan.

Over the following months, as the Taliban regime collapsed, the Rangers began to sweep Afghanistan's extensive highlands in search of Bin Laden and Al-Qaeda suspects. Numerous caves were searched and weapons and intelligence on the organization uncovered but the terrorist leader remained at large. In one such operation during May 2002 the Rangers were called upon to respond to an Al-Qaeda group that had ambushed US Navy Seals being helicoptered to a mountain known as Takur Ghar. A 23-man Ranger quick-reaction force based at Gardez went to the Seals' aid but one of their two helicopters was shot down on the upper slopes. The men in the second landed lower down and then climbed the mountain to reach their comrades who were faced by a numerous enemy that was being held off by their fire and close-air support. The two groups were eventually reunited and evacuated under cover of darkness after killing several Al-Qaeda fighters.

The eventual removal of the Taliban and disruption of the terrorist network did not end the war on terror. Osama bin Laden escaped and the worldwide hunt for him continues at the time of writing as does the United States' intention to crush regimes that sponsor terrorism. It seems likely that the Rangers will again be called into action, thereby fulfilling their creed.

Below: In Iraq and Afghanistan, Rangers were involved in a variety of missions, the details of which are still sketchy. The modern Ranger unit is the 75th Regiment, whose shoulder flash mirrors that of the wartime battalions.

ASSESSMENT

The variety of roles undertaken by the Rangers during World War II in part reflected an age-old problem with special forces – what are they for? Most commanders of the time were trained to operate with conventionally organized and equipped brigades, divisions and corps-sized units, not with battalions of specialist infantry numbering a few hundred men. This problem led directly to the diverse multitude of front-line combat missions that the Rangers undertook between 1942 and 1945, and sometimes left them being deployed as nothing more than headquarters security details – a somewhat bizarre job for specialist infantry. This was temporarily the case in northwest Europe in late 1944 and on Luzon in 1945. Although the battalions underwent amphibious assault training and all took part in such operations, the Rangers were deployed on numerous other tasks, only a few of which involved the type of 'ranging' familiar to their eighteenth century counterparts. This very flexibility made the Rangers a prized asset for many senior commanders but for the Rangers themselves it sometimes meant learning on the job. Darby, for example, insisted that his 1st Battalion conduct night-time training during the North African campaign, a decision that was of immense and immediate value.

The Rangers' greatest successes in World War II were chiefly as spearhead assault troops during the opening phase of an amphibious landing. In North Africa, Sicily, at Salerno, Anzio, on D-Day and at Leyte Gulf they conducted operations, most involving neutralizing coastal defences, designed to ease the way for the main assault forces. Despite the dangers associated with such missions, most were quickly completed and, with the exception of the Pointe du Hoc assault on D-Day, achieved at little cost due to the speed of the Rangers' attacks and the often low-grade opposition they faced. Pointe du Hoc was an altogether tougher proposition as all of the other landings were conducted across nothing more than gently shelving beaches or low sea-walls and, by attacking under cover of darkness or at early dawn, the Rangers enjoyed an element of surprise. On D-Day, the Rangers had none of these factors in their favour yet they persevered and successfully stormed the cliff-top position. Despite their heavy losses the assault was undoubtedly one of the finest moments of June 6 and its inherent dangers were recognized by General Omar Bradley. In his autobiography, he remarked in reference to Lieutenant Colonel James Rudder, commander of the assault companies: 'No soldier in my command has ever been wished a more difficult task than that which befell the 34-year-old commander of this Provisional Ranger Force.'

Yet the Rangers were also called upon to conduct other missions and here the results were more mixed. There was mountain fighting in Tunisia, Sicily and Italy, attacks against fixed defences in northwest Europe after D-Day, and in an echo of the past, patrols and reconnaissance missions similar to those pioneered by the Ranger companies of colonial America. The results of the mountain fighting were generally favourable if occasionally costly. The Rangers were successful in Tunisia, Sicily, at Salerno and around Cassino,

BATTLE HONOURS FLAG

To celebrate the outstanding contribution of the Ranger battalions during World War II, the US Army Heraldic Branch designed a commemorative flag to reflect their history and combat record. It consists of a rectangular flag divided in two diagonally from top left to bottom right. The upper, darker half symbolizes the United States, while the lower scarlet portion represents Great Britain, where many of the units were trained and based. In the centre a white circle is used to represent Central Europe, chiefly Germany, while a superimposed black fleur-de-lys represents service in France and the Low Countries. Similarly red seed pods allude to service in Italy, while a double crescent indicates the campaigns in Algeria and Tunisia. Three sun rays indicate the role of the 6th Battalion in the Philippines, while crossed knives, based on the British Fairbairn-Sykes design for the Commandos, indicate the types of operation undertaken by the Rangers.

although the perils involved in fighting at altitude in winter were reflected in the high casualty suffered by the battalions in the last case. Attacking fixed defences is not usually considered the role of specialist light infantry, yet the Rangers were undoubtedly a valuable asset in capturing Brest during the late summer of 1944.

With regard to patrols, raids and larger operations involving movement through and behind enemy lines, during World War II the Rangers achieved some of their greatest successes – and one of their greatest defeats – in this way. Sened in Tunisia was an early indication of their capabilities and was followed by two highly regarded operations, at Irsch–Zerf in February 1945 and the Cabanatuan raid in January 1945. Both earned the units involved a Presidential Unit Citation, and the latter, which was the subject of a photo essay in *Life* by renowned war photographer Carl Mydans, brought the 6th Battalion immense fame in the United States. So intense was the media interest, the battalion's after-action report

Above: Rangers saw action in both European and Pacific theatres. This is Company F of 6th Rangers patrolling on Dinagat Island.

concluded that, 'If it lasted one more day, more buttons would have to be sewn on and larger hat sizes secured. The men were walking on air.' Yet Irsch–Zerf and Cabanatuan have to be balanced by the disaster at Anzio. Operation Shingle was badly managed for the most part but the the effective loss of three battalions outside Cisterna in January 1944 was one of its lowest points and an acute embarrassment to the Allies. Little blame can be attached to the battalions involved and the defeat did not end the Rangers' contribution to the Allied victory as a further three battalions took their place.

The Rangers chief weakness was that they were essentially light infantry trained for swift and short-lived operations, not prolonged fighting. For the most part the standard battalions were equipped with nothing more powerful than light/medium mortars and machine guns. Such weapons were suitable for fast-moving operations against light opposition that were expected to last only a few hours but proved inadequate against stronger opposition. Action reports also frequently speak of shortages of ammunition – a situation that reflected the Rangers' lack of integral logistical support. Indeed, it was not uncommon for Rangers to seek out other units for such supplies and they constantly had to rely on external mechanized transport. There were attempts to beef up their firepower by adding, for example, the Cannon Company, or seconding units with heavier weapons to them, but the battalions continued to rely on outside support, whether from warships or other independent ground units. During the final stages of the war in Europe, the situation was largely reversed. The Rangers were starved of opportunities to act independently and units were no longer being attached to them, rather it was the Rangers themselves that were being attached. Nevertheless the Rangers had an outstanding combat record and few units of a comparable size matched the range and number of hazardous mission they successfully completed before their temporary demise at the end of the conflict.

REFERENCE

INTERNET SITES

http://www.ranger.org
A site produced by the US Army Ranger Association containing pages on operations, honours, unit histories and related links. It also offers Ranger-related material for sale.

http://www.ranger.org/usara/s5/assoc/darby/darbys.htm
Home of the Darby Foundation, which is based at Fort Smith, Arizona, and is dedicated to preserving the memory of the founder of the World War II Rangers.

http://www.rangermemorial.org
The home page of the Ranger Memorial Foundation, an organization that created and maintains the Ranger memorial at Fort Benning, Georgia; the site also includes details of Ranger-related events.

http://www.ranger.org/usara/s3/Ops/wwii/wwii.htm
The site run by the Ranger Battalions Association of World War II recounts the history of the Rangers from colonial America to the present but concentrates on their exploits in World War II. It also provides information on the modern Ranger Training Brigade, unit honours and Congressional Medal of Honor winners.

http://www.ricakw.org
The Association of Ranger Infantry Companies of the Korean War, a body dedicated to recounting the story of those who served during the conflict.

http://www.75thrra.org/
An association for members of the 75th Ranger Regiment and associated units, mostly from the Vietnam War, with pages detailing forthcoming events.

http://www.grunts.net/army/rangers.html
The history of the Rangers from colonial America to the present, which also contains some Medal of Honor citations and links to other sites.

http://www2.gdi.net/agengreb
The Brotherhood of Rangers home page that includes pages on the Ranger Creed and links to additional sites.

http://www-cgsc.army.mil/carl/resources/csi/King/King.asp#B1
Part of the Command & General Staff College's Combined Arms Research Library

resources, this consists of Leavenworth Papers No. 11 by Dr. Michael J. King, which is an exhaustive account of several Ranger operations in World War II including those at Djebel el Ank, Porto Empedocle, Cisterna, Zerf and Cabanatuan. Also includes useful bibliography.

http://www.goarmy.com/job/branch/sorc/75th/Rangers.htm
A site from the US Army providing information for prospective Ranger candidates. It also has pages on their modern role, training and background history.

http://www.specialoperations.com/Army/Rangers/default2.html
Provides information on the Ranger School and training course as well as a profile of the modern unit and its antecedents.

http://suasponte.com/index/.html
Details of the Rangers' history, their creed and a quiz.

http:www.2ndRangers.org/
A St. Louis, Missouri, group of World War II re-enactors.

BIBLIOGRAPHY

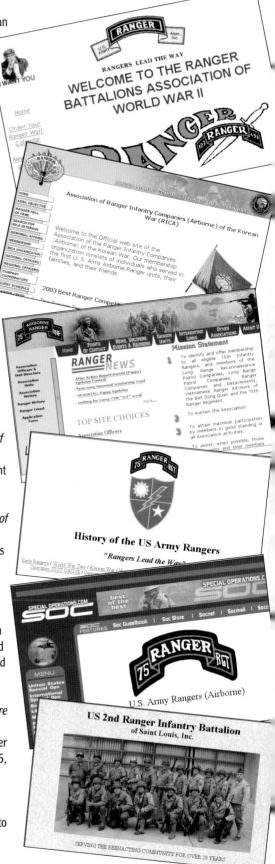

Altieri, James J.: *Darby's Rangers: An Illustrated Portrayal of the Original Rangers.* The Seeman Printery, 1945.
A history of the 1st, 3rd and 4th Rangers by one who served with them. The book is illustrated and written by a past president of the Ranger Association.

Bahmanyar, Mir, and Welply, Michael: *US Army Ranger, 1983–2001 – Sua Sponte: Of Their Own Accord.* Osprey, 2003
A highly illustrated account of the modern Rangers, their campaigns, battles, equipment and training.

Breuer, William B.: *The Great Raid on Cabanatuan – Rescuing the Doomed Ghosts of Bataan and Corregidor.* John Wiley and Sons, 1994.
A history of the famed rescue of US prisoners on Luzon during World War II and the basis for a forthcoming film.

Darby, William O., and Baumer, William H.: *Darby's Rangers – We Led the Way.* Presidio Press, 1990.
Based on conversations between Darby and Baumer in 1944, this recounts the formation of the Rangers, their training and operations from Dieppe to Italy involving the 1st, 3rd and 4th Battalions. It also includes brief summaries of missions conducted by the 2nd and 5th Battalions in northwest Europe and the 6th Battalion in the Philippines.

Drez, Ronald J.: *Voices of D-Day – The Story of the Allied Invasion Told by Those Who Were There.* Louisiana State University Press, 1994.
Contains a chapter that has first-hand accounts from survivors of the 2nd and 5th Ranger Battalions who assaulted the Pointe du Hoc cliffs and landed on Omaha Beach on June 6, 1944.

Eshel, David: *Daring to Win – Special Forces at War.* Arms and Armour Press, 1992.
Recounts action by various special forces on land, at sea and in the air from World War I to

50th Anniversary of D-day

Operation Desert Storm. One chapter deals with the Rangers' assault on the Pointe du Hoc on D-Day and another is on their role during the 1983 invasion of Grenada.

Field, Ron: *Ranger – Behind Enemy Lines in Vietnam*. Publishing News, 2000.
The core of the book concentrates on Ranger-style units of the Vietnam War, but also includes sections on the early history of such units from colonial America to the Indian Wars of the second half of the nineteenth century. A final section looks at modern Ranger campaigns from Operation Eagle Claw in 1980 to Operation Restore Hope in the early 1990s.

Garrett, Richard: *The Raiders*. David & Charles, 1980.
A study of special forces' operations through the ages that contains a chapter on the capture of the Pointe du Hoc on D-Day.

Johnson, Forrest Bryant: *Hour of Redemption: The Ranger Raid on Cabanatuan*. Manor Books, 1978.
The story of the daring behind-the-lines mission spearheaded by elements of the 6th Rangers to rescue US prisoners of war in 1945.

Krueger, Walter: *From Down Under to Nippon – The Story of the Sixth Army in World War II*. Combat Forces Press, 1953.
The commander of the US Sixth Army and the driving force behind the creation of the 6th Rangers recounts his part in the Pacific campaign.

King, Michael J.: *William Orlando Darby – A Military Biography*. Archon Books, 1981.
A review of the life and military career of the founder of the Rangers during World War II by an officer who attended the US Army Airborne and Ranger Schools.

Lane, Ronald L.: *Rudder's Rangers: The True Story of the 2nd Ranger Battalion D-Day Combat Action*. Ranger Association, 1995.
A history of the 2nd Ranger Battalion and its operation to storm the Pointe du Hoc on D-Day.

Lanning, Michael Lee, *Inside the LRRPs: Rangers in Vietnam*. Ivy Books, 1988.
The story of the revival of the Ranger concept and their role during the Southeast Asia conflict.

Lucas, James: *Commandos and Rangers of World War II*. Macdonald and Jane's, 1978.
A review of British and US Commando-type units that covers Ranger operations during the war and has useful information on weapons and equipment.

McDonald, Joanna M.: *The Liberation of the Pointe du Hoc: the 2d Rangers at Normandy, June 6–8, 1944*. Rank and File Publications, 2000.
An account of one of the epic actions of the Normandy landings, including the origins of the battalion and a facsimile of the Presidential Unit Citation it was awarded.

Macksey, Kenneth: *Commando Strike – The Story of Amphibious Raiding in World War II*. Leo Cooper and Secker & Warburg, 1985.
Although concentrating on British operations, this overview provides a useful introduction to the development of US special forces, including Rangers, during the conflict and covers some of their actions.

O'Donnell, Patrick K.: *Beyond Valor – World War II's Ranger and Airborne Veterans Reveal the Heat of Combat.* Touchstone Books, 2002.
Hundreds of first-hand accounts of Rangers and airborne personnel detailing their experiences from North Africa to the final battles in Europe.

Prince, Morris: *The Story of the Elite WWII 2nd Battalion Rangers.* Meadowlark Publishing, 2001.
A first-hand account by a private in the battalion's Company A following the unit's actions from D-Day to VE-Day.

Rottman, Gordon L., and Volstad, Ron: *US Army Rangers & LRRP Units, 1942–87.* Osprey, 1987
An outline history of the Rangers and associated units from World War II to the invasion of Grenada.

Rottman, Gordon, and Volstad, Ron: *Panama, 1989–90.* Osprey Publishing, 1991
An overview of the US invasion and occupation of the Central American dictatorship including details of the participation of the Rangers.

Sides, Hampton: *Ghost Soldiers – The Astonishing Story of One of Wartime's Greatest Escapes.* Time Warner, 2002.
An exhaustive but highly readable account of the mission by the 6th Ranger Battalion to release Japanese-held prisoners at Cabanatuan on Luzon during early 1945.

Truscott, Lucian K., Jr., *Command Missions: A Personal Story.* New York, 1954.
The excellent autobiographical account of one of the US Army's most skilled battlefield commanders and the officer most responsible for the formation of the Rangers in World War II.

MEMORIALS

The most evocative and moving memorial to the exploits of the Rangers in World War II is situated atop the Pointe du Hoc in Normandy. Lying some 8 miles (13 km) west of the US cemetery overlooking Omaha Beach, it consists of a single granite pylon positioned on the remains of a German concrete bunker and at its feet are tablets inscribed in English and French. Originally erected by the French to honour the operation, it was formally transferred to the care of the American Battle Monuments Commission in January 1979.

A second site associated with the Rangers is also cared for by the commission. This is the Cabanatuan American Memorial on Luzon, which lies on the site of the former prisoner of war camp and honours those Americans and Filipinos who died during their captivity. It was erected by survivors of the Bataan Death March and former prisoners of Cabanatuan.

In the United States, there is a monument at Fort Benning, Georgia, located in front of the Infantry School outside Building 4. It was erected by the Ranger Memorial Foundation in 1994 and was mostly funded by ex-Rangers and their families. Its chief features are the memorial stones that record the names and units of former Rangers, but not their ranks.

In Northern Ireland there is an exhibition based around the early history of the Rangers during World War II. Located in the grounds of the Andrew Jackson Centre at Boneybefore, Carrickfergus, is the US Rangers Centre. There is also a memorial stone at nearby Sunnylands Camp where the first recruits were billeted.

FILMS

The exploits of the Rangers have been a popular source of material for Hollywood over the years. One of the earliest movies to be released on the subject starred Spencer Tracy as Robert Rogers. Directed by King Vidor and released in 1940, *Northwest Passage* is based on a 1937 novel by Kenneth Roberts and recounts the 1759 raid on the Abenaki at St. Francis. The running time is 126 minutes and the supporting cast included Robert Young and Walter Brennan. William Wellman directed *Darby's Rangers* in 1958 and this 122-minute movie stars James Garner as Darby and covers the raising of the unit and its combat service. More recently Ridley Scott was inspired by the Ranger operation in Somalia to film *Blackhawk Down*, which was released in 2002. With a running time of 144 minutes, it was inspired by a book by Mark Bowden and stars Josh Hartnett and Ewan McGregor. Finally, there is a projected film of the 6th Battalion's Cabanatuan mission in the pipeline. Directed by John Dahl, *The Great Raid* stars Benjamin Bratt and Joseph Fiennes and filming began in Queensland, Australia, in early July 2002. A 2003 release date is expected.

Rangers training in Scotland in August 1942. The
log—as taught by the British Commandos with whom
they were training—forced groups of trainees to work
as a team, as well as building strength.

INDEX